JACO VAN GASS
UNEQUIVOCAL
MY STORY

Sophie
Dec 2022

'Having known Jaco since we shared a tent whilst on the 2011 Walking With The Wounded North Pole Expedition, his subsequent journey to three Paralympic gold medals is testament to the courage shown by our wounded servicemen and women. Jaco is one of life's most inspiring people.

'Jaco, you are kind, compassionate, highly amusing and incredibly down-to-earth, I enjoy our annual meeting at the Invictus Games and wish you the very best'

Prince Harry, Duke of Sussex

JACO VAN GASS
UNEQUIVOCAL
MY STORY

m
B

MIRROR BOOKS

MIRROR BOOKS

First published in Great Britain and Ireland in 2022 by Mirror Books, a Reach PLC business, 5 St. Paul's Square, Liverpool, L3 9SJ.

www.mirrorbooks.co.uk
@TheMirrorBooks

Hardback ISBN: 9781915306104
eBook ISBN: 9781915306111

Photographic acknowledgements:
Alamy, Jaco Van Gass personal collection

Written with Eleanor Updegraff.
Design and production: Michael McGuinness
Editor: Chris Brereton

Printed and bound by CPI Group (UK) Ltd, Croydon, CR0 4YY.

CONTENTS

Prologue...1

I. South Africa...15

II. The Recruiting Office..29

III. Becoming Joe..39

IV. Meeting Afghanistan.......................................50

V. The Fort at Kabul...61

VI. The Incident..75

VII. The Road to Recovery....................................88

VIII. Baby Steps 107

IX. An Extraordinary Expedition........................119

X. On Top of the World 133

XI. Escaping Everest...150

XII. Among the Mountains.................................174

XIII. Team GB...191

XIV. On the Road 207

XV. To Rio...224

XVI. Rainbows..240

Epilogue: Tokyo Gold 253

Acknowledgements 280

For the three women in my life:
Aloma, Lizanne and Kathryn

PROLOGUE

A crack in the dark. Louder than a gunshot, it was the sound of something being fired off. Francis and I looked at each other. The beams of our head torches lit up our faces and patches of the ice beyond. Outside the circle of light it was pitch black. We could see nothing.

'What was *that*?'

Nothing moved in the darkness, and yet we were aware of the whole world shifting. The ice below and around us was in constant motion, always changing, and it creaked and groaned and cracked as it did so. We knew this, and we also knew that the safest place for us to be was anywhere but there. We shrugged it off and hurried to keep moving ourselves.

'Something moved. Let's just go.'

We climbed on, following the guide rope. It was made up of a lot of short sections joined together, meaning that each time we came to a join we had to clip out and back in again. I was starting to struggle. The fingers on my one hand were growing colder and colder, and every time I had to touch the freezing metal through the thin protection of my contact glove it only made things worse. I concentrated hard on each clip and unclip, unwilling to let the Sherpa behind me take over. Just a little bit further. I was determined to do as much of this as I could on my own.

UNEQUIVOCAL

Just in front of me, the beam of my head torch caught the guide rope as it made a sharp turn to the right and vanished again into the darkness where Francis had gone. Two sections joined at the corner, so as I came up to the turn I clipped out. At that very instant, another shot rang out. Only this time it was bigger – far bigger. A deafening boom that echoed through the mountains, followed by a falling sound and then a rushing, the sound of something coming closer and closer. There was no need for questions. We knew what it was.

'Avalanche! Avalanche!' screamed my Sherpa from behind me. We could hear it so clearly now, the sound of snow and rocks and ice gathering speed and mass and hurtling down the mountain towards us. The noise got louder and louder, drowning out my Sherpa's cries. It was building momentum fast, and it was coming for us. The only problem was, we couldn't see it.

Without really considering what I was doing, I sprinted to the middle of the guide rope. I froze, thinking about what I was going to do, what was the best way to go, how I was going to get out of this. I knew that we were in the shadow of two enormous overhanging seracs, giant columns of ice that can tower as high as a house, with a sheer glacial wall that we had just climbed behind us. If the avalanche was coming directly towards us, it was going to come over the overhanging ledge and fall straight on top of us. I knew all this, but I didn't have a clue what to do about it. Standing there in the middle of the guide rope, for a split second I let myself be confused.

Then I saw it. To my right was a massive boulder, one of those huge ice rocks that had caused our guide, Harry Taylor, to nickname this part of the Khumbu Icefall 'Monster Popcorn'. I ran as fast as I could to the boulder and stooped down behind it. A couple of seconds later, Francis and my Sherpa joined me. And then, just behind them, was the avalanche. It just missed us. This big wave of ice and snow and everything it had picked up on the mountain passed by not two or three metres away from us, barely visible in the weak light we were able to shine towards it. The sound was deafening, an incredible roar that drowned out everything else. And then it was gone, further down the mountain, ripping away all that stood in its path. My heart was beating wildly; adrenaline levels were through the roof. The three of us just stood there for a few minutes, dazed and disorientated, a fog slowly coming in around us as the ice settled.

For as long as I live I will never forget the feeling of standing in the middle of that guide rope thinking, *shit, this could all go horribly wrong.* The decision I made to run to that boulder was done in a split second, but it could so easily have been the wrong one. Bruce, the guide who was just behind my Sherpa, actually went the other way, left instead of right, and he was even closer to the avalanche than we were. If any of us had gone much further to the left or the avalanche had been a metre further to the right, that would have been the end of us. We had been extraordinarily lucky.

It was a bad season on Everest for avalanches.

We lived in constant fear of them, not made any better by the fact that there was no pattern to it. They would fall all day and all night – in the middle of the day when you were reading outside your tent there would be a distant boom; at two o'clock in the morning you would wake up and hear one. In 2012 the weather was unusually mild, and so avalanches would fall without even being warmed by the midday sun. Russell Brice, manager of our expedition outfit and one of the most experienced men on the mountain, hadn't seen so many avalanches so constantly in all the twenty years he'd been coming here. Almost daily the Sherpas would have to go up to put in a new guide rope or replace any ladders that had been swept away. They were falling right in the path of where we needed to climb.

Francis was the first to move. 'Let's just get out of here,' he said. We did, scrambling up to the top of the ledge, and that was the first time it really felt like each for his own. We had agreed that we would all climb at our own pace, but you do usually still look out for one another. When you're on the hill, it's all about safety. But this area we were climbing in now was so dangerous – it was nicknamed the 'Death Zone' – that the rule here was 'every man for himself'. It still took me by surprise when Francis got to the top and was off. My Sherpa was next, and he reached the top of the climb and went for it too. When I arrived at the top of the ledge, I looked around and wondered where everyone was. I was confused, and the mist blurring my vision didn't make things any better. I realised I had no idea which way to go. It took me a few seconds standing there to get my orientation, and then I was off as fast as I could in the shadow of the seracs.

The end of the Death Zone was marked by a ladder, where a couple of weeks before a Sherpa had fallen. He had crossed this ladder a number of times and got a bit blasé about it all, so the last time he went across he hadn't clipped in. He had a big weight on his back, his crampon slipped, and he fell straight into the crevasse. The Sherpas with him had tried to rescue him, and when they went to retrieve his body they made a bit of a mess of things. The side of the crevasse was smeared with claret where his body had been slung against the wall. They could have got rid of the blood, but they didn't – it was a good reminder for people of why they had to be safe. Describing the route to us, Harry gave this section the name 'Blood and Guts Ladder'.

It was about half past five when we got to Blood and Guts, light just starting to filter in. It was an eerie sight. We could still smell the blood in the air and faintly make out the crevasse, which was just a black hole, really – endlessly deep. As I crossed the ladder the beam of my head torch caught the blood splattered on the wall opposite me and I shivered. I knew that I was clipped in, but I was still on a slippery ladder crossing a black abyss in which someone had lost his life just a couple of weeks before. As Bruce said when he got to us, it was all far too close for comfort.

For the rest of the day, that night, and all the nights that followed, the avalanche stayed with me. Every time I closed my eyes, there it was, coming for me. I would find myself standing in a dark place, my vision bound by what my torch could see. It was a dangerous area; I could feel it. And then it came – the crack, and the rumble of something coming towards me that was getting louder and louder and louder and was going to slam right into me... If you were having a nightmare, this would be the point where you would wake up, shaking and sweating, right before it hits you.

With me, though, that didn't happen. The whooshing noise rushed towards me, I braced for impact, and I always got hit. My body and brain were remembering the middle of another night three years previously. The avalanche on Everest might have gone past me, but it had swept me up and taken me back to a place I'd been before.

This wasn't a dream. It was a flashback.

*****

It was the middle of the night, the early hours of 20 August 2009. My twenty-third birthday had just begun. And as far as I was concerned, I'd been given the best birthday present ever: a surprise firefight in the Afghan desert.

Rounds were going off all around me. These guys were well dug in – there were quite a few locations on all sides of us and they were popping up all over the place. I was quite far down the back of the line, and we started aiming in the direction of the compounds nearest to us, where most of the fire was coming from.

Through my night-vision goggles I could see heads appearing and disappearing, and I kept on firing, changing through magazines and even shooting off a few rounds from my under-slung grenade launcher (UGL). They seemed to be quite accurate in suppressing the enemy, but after four or five I was already on my last one. That was when the radio crackled with the order to take cover and I dived automatically to the ground.

The whole earth shook. The sound of the rockets was unreal, the kind of sound you can feel inside you. The ghost ship, the support aircraft so stealthy that it could neither be heard nor seen above us, had been called in to fire on some of the dug-in locations, but we were too close for them to give as much as was needed for a really good effect. The radio chattered again – it was the ghost ship talking. Five or ten men were circling round us, trying to get into a position to attack us from behind.

We guys at the back swung round and in a couple of seconds saw shadowy figures moving through the dark. All of us started firing – Grant, Ryan, the Afghan next to me, and I. The Afghan had a big machine gun, a PKM, which was spitting a huge flame every time he fired. That was how they saw us. The first rocket-propelled grenade (RPG) came in from the compound on our left-hand side, far too high. It sailed over our heads and exploded somewhere in the distance. We kept on firing, to the left, towards the back of the line. All I could hear were the bullets whizzing around me, the crazy chatter on the radio and the occasional shout.

'Change magazine!' Grant yelled, and all of a sudden he was down on his belt buckle. I dropped to one knee, giving covering fire. And it was there, suddenly, in the corner of my night-vision goggles – a small red glow heading straight towards us. The sound of the rocket came a moment later, a roar that grew louder and louder as it came closer, the glow in my goggles getting brighter all the time. I twisted away from it, bracing for impact, and the blast of it hitting us blew me literally away.

Everything slowed down. My ears were ringing – physically stinging with the sound of the explosion – and I could still hear intense gunfire from the guys in the background. My mouth was full of dust and I was coughing and choking as I fought to sit up. I had no idea what had just happened, but the guys were firing and firing, and all I could think was, *why am I not firing back?* It was a struggle to sit up because of the weight on my back – I was carrying the telescopic ladders we had been using earlier that night. I heaved myself into a half-sitting position and noted briefly that I was on fire. I don't know why, but it didn't interest me at that point. All I could think about was that *I* needed to fire.

It was when I was trying to hold my rifle in the correct position that I realised something didn't feel right. There was nothing to support it on. I looked down again to see what was going on, and where my left arm should have been there was just empty space.

Although I understood at once that I had lost my arm, the only thing I wanted was to be able to return fire. I let off a few loose bullets, not really aiming anywhere apart from the general direction of the enemy, the rifle jammed against my hip. But as the realisation of what had happened to me slowly sank in, I knew I needed to start applying self-help. I dropped my weapon and lay back down.

All around me I could see a faint red glow – I was still on fire. The last thing I wanted was a burn wound, so I patted desperately at myself until the flames were gone. There was a tourniquet on my chest rig and I struggled with applying it, unable to get purchase on what was left of my arm. I was soaked with blood and shaking. Somewhere to the right of me, Grant was screaming. I lay back down on the dusty ground as the firefight around me went on and on.

It was Ryan who was nearest and got to me first. His face swam into view above me as he crawled up and assessed what was going on. He took one look at me before he started shouting.

'Fuck, Jaco, fuck! You've lost your arm!'

'I know!' I shot back at him, my fingers still fumbling around the bleeding stump. 'Just help me with this fucking tourniquet!'

'You've lost your arm, Jaco,' he kept saying. 'You've lost your arm!' He was saying it over and over; he seemed more shocked about it than I was.

'No shit, Sherlock!' I yelled at him. 'Now help me get this thing on!'

He did, cranking it up around the top of my arm as hard as he possibly could. That was when the pain really hit and I started to scream. He stopped, saying, 'I think that's enough,' but the blood was still pouring out and wouldn't stop.

'Medic!' Ryan turned around and yelled. 'Medic!' He turned back to me. 'I'll get a medic,' he said. 'But I'm going to give you morphine.'

Two of the things we always carried with us were morphine and money. The money – US$1,000 in cash – was blood money, to use if we got left behind or trapped somewhere and needed to buy clothes or transport or bribe our way out. While no amount of money could get my arm back now, the morphine was for moments like this. The money was in my left shoulder pocket, the morphine in my right. Ryan grabbed the pen and was just about to stab me in the left shoulder before he realised that wasn't the most effective thing to do given the blood pouring out of my wound. At the last moment he jammed it into my right arm and radioed in for the medic, who arrived on the scene pretty fast.

The medic took one look at me as well and got on his radio. 'We've got a C1 here,' he said. Injuries are always tiered in the army – a C3 is usually OK to carry on, a C2 is more severe but can probably still walk out of there.

C1 means immediate medical assistance.

As Ryan told him what he'd done, the medic got out his pen and started writing on my forehead. He scribbled down a rough time of the morphine shot, when I had been injured, and what he could see. The main thing was obvious: left arm amputee. But it was my left leg that was really bothering me, especially around my ankle. It was the worst pain I'd ever experienced, and I was sure that I must have lost my leg as well. I kept sitting up and trying to see, or asking the medic if he could check.

'Your leg's fine, Jaco!' he said. 'It's here, it's moving, we've got it.'

'But my ankle!' I knew I was complaining. 'My ankle, can you please just check my ankle?'

At the same time, the medic was directing Ryan to tighten the tourniquet on my arm, which was still pumping blood out all over the place. Ryan tightened it up and said he couldn't do it any more, but the medic insisted that he had to. Ryan was sitting next to me on the ground cranking the tourniquet round and round, and the pain was so bad that I started to scream my lungs out.

'I'm sorry,' Ryan was saying, 'I'm sorry,' and behind him I could hear the medic yelling, 'Get it on, just get it on!' Later on Ryan told me he was sure he had been going to snap my arm.

It got to a stage where there was too much pain for my nerves to cope with. My arm went almost numb, and I couldn't feel it any more. I was still complaining about my ankle, though, so to help with the pain and shut me up, the medic stuffed a morphine lolly under my tongue.

'Stay with me,' he was saying. 'Jaco, stay with me,' and in the background I could hear Grant screaming and the guys firing and the fighting getting more intense as the enemy closed in.

'Stay with me!' yelled the medic. I tried hard to focus. *You need to be with it,* I was telling myself. *Listen to every word he says, do everything he tells you to do.* I focused on obeying every order he gave, on staying awake, on reacting when he asked me if I could feel this or move this, but it was becoming a real struggle to even keep my eyes open.

The radio suddenly burst into life with the order to take cover. The enemy was gaining too much ground, getting too close to us, and with Grant and I wounded we needed desperately to get out. The JTAC had made the decision to call the ghost ship in again, which had been hovering above our heads all this time. Normally when a ghost ship fires there are rules about how close the friendly fire is allowed to be; the weapons on a C-130 Hercules have an incredible range. 'Close' is near enough to feel or be affected by it, 'danger close' is when soldiers are inside a firing area in which they shouldn't really be. That night, the JTAC put his career on the line to get us all out. He called in the ghost ship giving our position as 'danger, danger close', and immediately ordered everyone to get down as flat as he could.

I was lying on my back on the ground when the medic flung himself across me. He had to cover me several times as the C-130 Hercules opened fire, so close that I could feel the earth trembling through my spine. I could feel sand and stones and grit raining down on us despite the medic's body over mine, the dust filling my eyes and clogging my throat.

Someone radioed for an evacuation, but the remaining enemy

were too close. Despite the Hercules, we were still in a firefight, which meant our own helicopters couldn't land to pick us up. The medic got out a stretcher and kept working on me while the call was going out on the radio and the guys kept trying to keep the enemy down.

Luckily, there was an American call sign in the area that evening. They picked up our distress signal on the airwaves and sent in three Chinooks to get us out. Sound was coming and going and my vision was blurring, but I was still trying my hardest to stay awake. All of a sudden, there was the sound of a helicopter. It was the sound of salvation – a really good sound. I looked up to see they were landing almost on top of us, so close that we got covered with sand and grit blown up by the downdraught, and as they came down the door slid back and the gunner on the helicopter opened up. I could see a huge flame coming out of the side as everything that wasn't us was given the good news. The Chinooks landed ten or fifteen metres away from us, and the stretcher I was lying on was lifted and we ran.

*****

There was a point, when I was finally in the helicopter, at which I thought I might die. It wasn't that it hadn't occurred to me before, but more that I hadn't allowed myself to think about it. I had been concentrating so hard on what the medic had been telling me to do, on reacting to his instructions and trying to stay focused. It was so hard, because the morphine had slowed my heart down and all I wanted was to close my eyes. But I fought to stay awake; it was as though I didn't want to die down there on the desert ground. But as soon as we were in the helicopter, knowing that all the boys were on too, I felt like I could relax. I could feel myself starting to drift away, and I had this sense of simply letting go. I thought to myself, *if I die now, it's fine. It's OK. The boys are safe and I'm on the way home.*

And, in a way, I did die that night.

My heart stopped twice on the operating table while the doctors and nurses were working on me at the American base we were taken to. The only thing I saw of the hospital was the strip lighting flashing past above my head as I was wheeled into theatre, and the nurses starting to cut off my clothes and my beloved desert boots. I had bought those boots myself and no words can express how much I loved them. It was the only thing I could think about while I was lying there. I knew that they were going to cut my clothes off, but I kept on thinking, *not the boots, not the boots.* I wanted to scream at them not to cut them off, but it was already too late. And then, before I could start crying, I lost consciousness.

I am one of probably very few people to have been 'born' on the same day (in different years) three times. In the early hours of my twenty-third birthday the doctors and nurses brought me back to life twice. When they finally got me in, I had less than a pint of blood left in my body. Although I didn't notice all of them at the time, the injuries I sustained means that makes sense now. My arm was torn off and my chest ripped open, my leg was damaged from the bottom to the top with a third of my thigh muscle missing, there were shrapnel injuries to my side and my left lung had collapsed. At one point the doctors cut my stomach open and lifted my internal organs out to remove the shrapnel from them one by one. They performed a colostomy and stitched me back up, treated my wounds and pumped me full of blood. It's amazing how I'm here now, to be honest. It's those doctors and nurses to whom I owe this, my second – or, technically, third – life.

By the time I got to Camp Bastion I was in an induced coma, so I was simply flown in and straight out to the UK. But 90 per cent or even 95 per cent of all UK casualties went through Bastion, which is where the main British hospital was. Outside the operating theatre there was a big whiteboard, and every time a patient came in the staff on duty would write his or her details on it: rank, name, army number, date, time.

If the patient didn't survive theatre, they would put a big cross through the name. This procedure started quite near the beginning of the war, until eventually one of the nurses who worked in Bastion found herself coming in every day to face a huge board full of crosses. She started to think that there had to be another way. It was too hard to deal with, coming into work each time to be reminded of all those men and women who had died, and that today it would just be more of the same. It was she who came up with the idea of a board listing not everyone who had died, but everyone who had been saved.

Next to the name and number of each person who had left the operating theatre wounded, but alive, there was a date and a heart. And at the very top she wrote the heading 'Unequivocal Saves'.

In 2017 I became one of the founding members of the Casevac Club. It's an exclusive club to be in, and not necessarily one you would want to join. Every single member was 'casevaced' (casualty evacuated) from Iraq or Afghanistan, most of them in the bloody years of 2008 and 2009. We are single, double, even triple amputees, PTSD sufferers, blind and burned.

Every time we meet up I look around and think it's a miracle that we're all still alive. My name, lots of my friends' names, all the people in the club's names should have been or were written on that board in Camp Bastion. The motto of the Casevac Club is *haud dubium salvus* – Latin for 'unequivocal saves'.

On 20 August 2009 my life changed for ever. Not quite three

years later I would find myself having my very first flashbacks to that night, brought on by the roar of an avalanche in the dark as I huddled behind a boulder on the slopes of Everest.

That I should even find myself climbing the world's highest mountain was a miracle; that the avalanche didn't kill me, perhaps even more so. But the road to Everest had been a long and hard one, and I wasn't about to let it end now. From the South African plains to the desert of Afghanistan, the ice floes of the North Pole to the slopes of the world's highest mountains, I have never made it an option to give up. I have seen how one life and the events in it can have a ripple effect, reaching out far wider than you would ever guess.

My name is Jaco van Gass, and I am an unequivocal save.

This is my story.

I

SOUTH AFRICA

Soldiers patrolled the streets when I was growing up. Occasionally they would appear in our neighbourhood on foot, small groups of them who would stay for a week or two and then go. Nothing ever happened for them to deal with; it was more that they were there to show presence and keep the peace. I would wave at them as I rode my bike past, and think how cool they looked with their uniforms and weapons. Though I was too young at the time to understand why they were there, I did recognise that they were a force for good, protecting civilians, and thought maybe one day that could be me. Looking back on it, although our paths crossed so little, they had a profound impact on me.

South Africa in the 1990s was undergoing a great change. The apartheid era, whose laws had come into force in 1948, was finally over. Nelson Mandela was released from imprisonment on Robben Island in February 1990, three and a half years after I was born. I was six or seven when the soldiers appeared in our streets, keeping the peace in the weeks and months leading up to 9 May 1994, the date of South Africa's first democratic, all-race elections at which Mandela would become the country's first Black president. Tensions between his African National Congress (ANC) and other political factions were running high as the country tried to negotiate its way into a new, post-apartheid world.

UNEQUIVOCAL

My South Africa, though, was quite different from the country that appeared on the news. I was too young to understand or be concerned with politics. My South Africa was a place of great safety, in which my sister and I lived in the street as much as we did in the house. I loved the outdoors from a very young age and had an extremely active lifestyle, always out playing sport or doing something on my own. South Africa both gives you that love and enables you to pursue it. It was a great upbringing and a time in which I was very happy.

I was born into an Afrikaans-speaking family in a little town called Middleburg, in the north-eastern province of Mpumalanga. When I was still a toddler we moved one town over to Witbank (now eMalahleni), and it was there that I spent most of my life growing up. One of my earliest memories was of my first day at primary school. It was January, a beautiful summer's day, and I was nervous about the new faces and being at a strange, much bigger school. My nursery school had been right next door to the one at which my mum was a teacher; the two playgrounds had been separated by a wall, so if I jumped up and down high enough I could see her. My mum had kept an eye on me as well, monitoring me as much at breaktime as she did her own nursery kids. Now, all of a sudden, I was on my own.

Except not quite on my own. Walking into my new classroom, I saw a familiar face. My teacher for the year looked – and, it turned out, sounded – exactly like Carike Keuzenkamp, a famous South African singer at the time. She had short, blow-dried black hair and an open, welcoming face, and a husky voice that I knew well from the songs I used to hear. It made me feel at home. And then there was my best friend, Christiaan Leicester. We had met at nursery school and quickly become inseparable – it was Christiaan who had got me to put down the handkerchief, one of my dad's, which I had carried everywhere with me for the first years of my life. At nursery I had changed from a reserved and moody little boy, glowering from beneath my bowl haircut, into half of a constantly active duo. We were menaces, Christiaan and I. We ran everywhere, getting up to no good, flying as high as we could on the playground swings until we nearly went right over. We were full of energy and spent most of our time trying to burn it off.

Primary school was where I really fell in love with sport. Cricket, rugby, tennis, athletics – literally anything you could think of, we would do it. I had suddenly found an outlet for all my energy and, to make it even better, these were things I was naturally good at. When it came to sports equipment, I never had the nicest stuff. Before each cricket season began, all my friends would turn up with the newest Kookaburra bat, knotted and prepped and oiled by the manufacturer, whereas I would be using the school's equipment or have an old, lower standard bat. But it never bothered me somehow; I was lucky. In sport I became a Jack of all trades, master of none.

As time went on, though, my biggest love became rugby. I played throughout primary school, with the goal each year of making the A team and getting to go on that season's tour. The school would take us to another province, down to Pretoria or even Cape Town, and we would do skill development and play against other schools. I loved every minute of it; it was my real passion in life. By the time I reached my final year, at the age of thirteen, I had made provincial colours and was classed as one of the top players in the school.

During that year I was also facing the biggest decision of my life so far – which high school I wanted to go to. Rugby is a big thing in South Africa and several of the towns in our province were renowned as being among the top rugby schools in the nation. Quite a few Springboks – members of the national team – had come from here, but it was important to me to decide which school was best. There was the high school in Middleburg, the town where I had been born, or the one in Ermelo or – further away, but I could have stayed with some relatives in Kruger – the highly regarded Nelspruit boys' high school. Yet in the end it was new league rankings and the distance from home that helped to sway it. At the age of fourteen I would enter my first year at our local institution, Hoer Tegniese Skool Witbank (HTS Witbank, or Witbank Technical High School).

It was a whole new experience. Stepping into high school I went from being top of the school, a member of the First XV, to nothing but a spotty little fourteen-year-old. Most schools in South Africa at that time had initiation rites for their new pupils, and HTS Witbank was no exception. It was the prefects' job to welcome us new kids into the school, after which we spent two or three months being skivvied. We were given a collective name that we had to respond to, and we had to do a special salute, almost a dance, every time one of the prefects addressed us. On certain days we had to dress up, and for a while each of us had to look after a rock. We had to give these bits of stone names and personalities, carry them with us everywhere, and every day make some kind of change like adding a new smile or glitter or a little paper hat. It was like having homework just to fit in. Life went at a million miles an hour, but though it was hard work, it was fun and I soon settled in.

In South Africa at that time everything was about discipline and respect. Respect not just for your elders but for the people around you. My parents brought me up pretty strictly and we were still caned at school. People are horrified at the idea now, but I do feel that it teaches you to be a certain way and that's something you take with you for the rest of your life. It hurts and you remember; you don't want to get hit again. There were probably times when I felt like I didn't deserve it, but I did have a few good smackings in my time. I look back on it now and know that I had been nasty or offensive or crossed the line.

Our history teacher, Mr Broodryk, was a great one for the cane. He was also the school vice-principal and commanded a lot of respect. I remember sitting at the back of his history class revising desperately, because I knew the question was going to come to me soon and as I hadn't done my homework I didn't have a clue. If your answer was wrong, you would walk to the front of the classroom, bend over and hold on to his table, and be given two whacks on the bum with a cane. It burned like hell, but you wouldn't forget to do your homework again. At least not for a while.

I was in a very male-dominated school – HTS Witbank had only just been opened up to girls, so there were maybe two hundred of them out of 1,500 pupils. The female teachers had it particularly bad. It was obvious that they struggled to get the same respect as male teachers like Mr Broodryk, and one day I drove one of mine completely mad.

It started out with a minor offence like not having done my homework, but when I went to the front of the room to get my smack – she had a wooden spoon, which she used to bring down on your outstretched palm – she took too long swinging and I automatically flinched. The spoon missed my hand and came crashing down, almost on her knees. The rest of the class burst out laughing; they thought it was the funniest thing they had ever seen. I thought it was pretty funny too, and I was enjoying the attention and the furious look on my teacher's face. So I did it again. And again. And again. Four times she tried to hit me, and four times I flinched and she missed. By the fifth time she really was seeing red, and I was warned I'd have a visit to the principal if I did it again. That time I decided to keep my hand there. My teacher swung the wooden spoon back into yesterday, came all the way through and brought it down on my hand... where the spoon snapped. It was brilliant. I can still see the look of utter shock on her face as she thought, *now I've really overstepped the line, I've gone and broken a wooden spoon on a pupil's hand.* The class loved it; they thought I was such a cool, hard guy. I shrugged it off and never told anyone how much it hurt, but I know it was a time when I definitely deserved what I got.

In general, though, I was pretty good about doing my homework – I didn't get punished often. Most of us had Afrikaans as our first language, so everything at school was taught in Afrikaans, and that was what I spoke at home. I struggled hugely with English classes, and I would never have thought that I would one day find myself living in the UK, speaking and writing English 95 per cent of the time.

In English I was always just scraping through, getting the lowest grade possible to allow me to continue. It was always my biggest fear that I would be that one kid out of a hundred to fail the school year, so I set myself very high standards and worked extremely hard to make sure that didn't happen. I was always fairly confident in subjects like maths and technical drawing – a couple of times I did so well that I didn't even have to sit the final, end-of-year exam and had more time to devote to things like English and Afrikaans. Most of the time, though, it was my competitive nature that helped me to keep up.

While I can't say I was the brightest in the class, I did love high school. We had a couple of good groups, I made loads of new friends, and it was very sport-driven, which was the most important thing for me. As with primary school, my sights were always set on being in the rugby First XV, which I did eventually achieve in my final year. I also had the honour of being both a school prefect and Head of Sport, along with my good friend Jarques Le Sueur – we would oversee various events and took charge of our annual Sports Day.

Some of my greatest friendships came from the rugby team, friendships that have lasted my whole life long. Right back in primary school my best friend besides Christiaan was Michael Laubscher. Michael played rugby along with me – he was number 9 and I was number 10. We had an incredible relationship where we each instinctively knew what the other was going to do when he picked up the ball. We didn't have to say anything; we would just do a trick or a move to score a try or gain some ground. And the bond between us extended far beyond the rugby pitch – he became like a brother to me.

Michael and I would always be at his house or my house after school, doing our homework or out playing in the street together. His family would invite me to go on fishing trips and holidays with them, and they also became like adopted parents to me. I felt like they loved me as much as they did their own son.

The relationship I had with Michael and his family, which would repeat at high school with my good friend Ian du Plessis, who eventually moved with me to the UK, was born largely from my need to find a father figure. While my parents were always very supportive of whatever my sister and I wanted to do, they were never involved to any degree in what our lives actually looked like.

Whatever Lizanne and I achieved we did entirely on our own merits, which I am proud of, but there were times, especially early on, when I wanted them there.

To give her due credit, my mum *was* always there. She would help out with things I needed for school, sometimes cooking stuff that I had been asked to take in the next day, and even when I had left school and was working she would wait up at night until she knew I had come home safe. It was sometimes frustrating having a curfew at the age of twenty, but I knew it was only because she cared. Mum did come and watch some of my rugby games and Lizanne's netball games when we were younger, but it was out of love for her children and certainly not for the game. My mum's knowledge of sport is so horrendous that she would shout for the other team when they scored. The parents would look at her and ask, 'What are you doing?' She might not have even known what colour we were, but the fact that she was there was always nice.

I can count on one hand the number of rugby games my dad came and watched: I remember four games from my entire career. Initially I would have loved him to be there, but there came a time when I didn't worry any more – he was actually more of a distraction. All the other parents would be on the sidelines, screaming and cheering and passing out oranges or water, but when I looked for my dad, I wouldn't be able to find him. I wanted to play the best game of rugby I possibly could for him, but I could feel myself getting distracted, desperately scanning the sidelines to locate him instead of concentrating on the game.

Eventually I *would* spot him, sitting in the very highest corner of the pavilion on his own, and this would bother me even more because I couldn't understand why he wasn't mingling with the other parents or cheering us on. It got to a stage where I almost didn't want him there, because then I could just focus on what I needed to do. And by that time I had found other father figures – Michael's dad, or Ian's – who supported me and who I could look up to.

Looking back on it, I don't really know where my sister and I got our sporty natures. Our dad did enjoy tennis, but that was it, and

Mum couldn't swim or even catch a ball. But our lives revolved around sport. In her younger years, Lizanne was mistaken for a boy much of the time – she had very short hair and she was always with us guys, and she played cricket as well as I could. She could bat and bowl and field, so it was natural that at high school she became women's cricket captain. We were constantly playing cricket and hockey in the street; as children we moved house quite a lot within the town and this was our way of making neighbourhood friends.

Wherever we lived we would establish little street communities with all the other kids around, using spray paint to mark out a tennis court in the road or the height of cricket bails on a lamppost. When I was very young I had a little red BMX bike, and I would spend hours exploring the neighbourhood on it or making little ramps and jumps for myself in front of our house. My mum always says that I could ride a bike before I could walk.

She also says that I could drive before I could walk, but it's my grandfather she has to thank for that. And while it's not quite true that I grew up with pedals for legs, I was behind the wheel by the age of about ten. Driving was just a part of spending summer on my grandparents' farm, the most magical place in my childhood.

*****

My grandparents' farm was in Hendrina, a small farming community in Mpumalanga, and we had been spending time there since before I could remember. Every summer we would be there – along with my aunt, uncle and cousins – from the day after school ended until the day before we went back, and it was the same for many of the other holidays as well.

My dad had partly grown up on the farm, which was mainly dairy and chickens with some fields of sunflower and corn, and my grandparents had worked it for many years. It was a paradise of freedom for us children and some of my best childhood memories come from then.

Hendrina was about seventy kilometres away from Witbank, an hour's drive through a relatively flat landscape that was lush and green with young crops in the summer months. My grandparents' farm, Grasfontyn, was a little way out of town, down a gravel road that became a total mudbath in the rainy winter season, sending the car or pickup (what in South Africa is called a *bakkie*) skidding all over the place. In good conditions, that road was one of my favourite places to ride my BMX or mountain bike, especially because there was a natural speed bump in the middle where I could get a bit of air.

We had acres of space on the farm and spent hours playing football, rugby, cricket and volleyball, climbing trees and swimming. My sister and I would have competitions as well, using my granddad's ancient bicycle. When I say ancient, I mean ancient – it had a heavy black frame and a seat with springs in it, and to brake you had to pedal backwards. We would cycle laboriously all the way back up to the gravel road, turn around and then get up as much speed as our little legs could manage. Not far down the sloping track was a gate on to the lawn, so from there we would push back on the pedals as hard as we could, locking the back wheel and leaving a satisfying skid mark on the grass. The winner was the person who left the longest mark. Of course our parents or granddad would see us out with that bike and come and ask us what we were doing.

'Nothing,' we always said, innocently.

'Are you skidding again?' they asked.

'No,' we said, but the twenty-five or thirty skid marks on the lawn would already have given us away.

Once we were coming to the end of a skidding session and, as usual, I was determined to win. I pedalled as hard as I could on the road, coming into the garden at high speed and pushing back on the pedals as soon as I passed the gate. The skid went on and on, and I leaned forward as far as I could to get all the weight off the crucial back wheel. The bike kept going, all the way down the garden... I was already utterly triumphant: I was definitely going to win! And then, before I knew it, the garden was at an end, the bike was crashing through my grandma's flowerbeds and the front wheel was wrapping around a tree. And because I was so far forward, I hit my privates really hard on the frame of the bike. So hard that they swelled up – I was in agony for weeks. Even when we went back to school I was walking funny, and I ended up having to get my bits out a lot as my friends all wanted to see. Lizanne would probably disagree, but I maintain that I won that skid fair and square – even though I ended up in tears for a while and left my grandma's flowers a bit the worse for wear.

My grandparents, but especially my grandmother, absolutely adored gardening. She was so keen on it that for a number of years they had had their own gardening service in the local area, and you just needed to take one look at the house and grounds to see it. The variety of shrubs and flowers was absolutely amazing, running all the way down to the bottom of the garden in a blaze of colour.

Right in the middle of it was the house, a single-storey, flat-roofed building, which I truly loved. Because my grandparents appreciated the outdoors so much they had brought it inside as well – the first thing you found when you walked through the front door was an indoor garden, filled with small plants and flowers and fountains, with the room almost built around a small tree.

For kids this was a perfect place to play in and I would spend hours there with my tractors and farm equipment, cars and plastic soldiers, finding hiding places and creating worlds amid the green.

My favourite rooms in the house were probably the kitchen and dining room, although it was only ever the weather that could drive us in from playing outdoors. The kitchen was warm and spacious, centred on an old, coal-fired stove. It had to be kept alive all the time, and as we grew older we were allowed to help with the stoking. Everything from boiling a kettle for tea to making food was done on that stove, and it radiated heat that we appreciated in winter. Every morning we would wake to the smell of bubbling *pap* – maize porridge that we would eat with finely chopped *biltong* and sugar sprinkled on top of it. It was delicious.

My granny was a fantastic cook; at Grasfontyn, no one ever went hungry. The arched windows in the dining room were stacked with jars of things she had made: rusks, biscuits, cakes of baked oatmeal. She made a lot for practical reasons, too – the area was fairly isolated and prone to power cuts, so we would sometimes go without electricity for four or five days. But with the coal-fired stove and candles and plenty of board games, we weren't actually reliant on any modern technology. If something went wrong – which it sometimes did – we could crack on with life exactly as it was.

Hendrina had very pronounced seasons, unlike some other parts of South Africa. Until I came to the UK it was the only place I had ever seen snow, and sometimes it rained heavily for days without stopping. In high summer it could get extremely hot, but the *dam* (a large pond) behind the house was the perfect place for cooling down. It was the main water source for the farm, but as there were a few filtering systems between us and the kitchen we were always allowed to swim in it.

One year we built a raft by collecting old pallets and oil drums from my granddad's store and lashing them together with rope.

Our oar was a long, thin plank with the lid of an ice cream tub nailed to it. By the time we had got the thing down to the *dam* it was extremely unstable and tipping all over the place, but my granddad was impressed with our efforts all the same. He told us that he would help us build a proper one tomorrow, and he did – sawing and drilling and tying knots until we had a floating raft two or three times the size of the first one.

My granddad knew how to do everything. He was busy but he always had time for us, and I really looked up to him. It was he who first taught me how to drive, sitting on his lap in the cab of the *bakkie* while he controlled the gears and pedals and I did the steering. When I got older I was allowed to do the clutch and the gearstick as well, and by the time I was ten or eleven I was pretty confident driving around on the farm by myself. I would put the driver's seat forward as far as it would go and get a couple of pillows to sit on so I could see over the wheel.

As well as driving, my granddad taught me how to shoot. I must have been about seven when I held my first air rifle, although I wasn't strong enough at that stage to crack it open and put the pellet in, or even to hold it without the help of a tree stump or an arm across my knees. Still, I learned very early on how to aim and compensate for elements like wind, and I quickly found that I was becoming quite good. By the time I was ten I was shooting with a rifle – one of those small, pump-action .22s like you see in John Wayne films. My granddad would often send me out to the chicken coops to keep the pigeons down.

As the years went on I became more of a help on the farm. I spent a lot of time with my granddad, riding around with him on the back of the *bakkie*, jumping off to open gates or chase livestock out of the way, repairing wires and fences, managing the crops.

I particularly loved the end of summer when it was time to *stroop*, or bring the crops in. When the combine harvesters arrived we would jump in the trailer and hold on to the sides as they dumped the grain in. It was like swimming.

No matter what time of year it was, life at Grasfontyn was amazing, and I started to develop a desire to have my own farm. But then there was my rifle and my skill at shooting. A lot of it was about the weapons at first – I always thought they looked really cool, especially on the soldiers I had seen in our neighbourhood – but as I grew older the stories I heard from my granddad and friends' dads about their time in the army began to have an increasing appeal.

Somewhere between Hendrina and Witbank a seed was planted. I was going to be a soldier.

II

THE RECRUITING OFFICE

'So, you chaps are looking to join the RAF?' The man behind the desk sounded keen.

Ian and I glanced at each other.

'Well...' I said, the cogs in my brain starting to turn. *Maybe I could be a pilot*, I was thinking. *It might not be so bad. After all...* But no, I hadn't come all this way to give up on my dream at the last moment.

The man behind the desk said something else. His smile was broad but his accent was unfamiliar. Ian and I looked at each other again. It was our first Monday morning in London. How could it possibly have gone wrong already?

*****

There's that pivotal moment that comes in your life: your final year at school. Everyone is thinking about where they're going to go, what they're going to do, where they're going to study. I knew my family didn't have the finances for me to go to university and, to be honest, I was a bit unsure about what I would study even if I could go. South Africa was in a state where people would spend five years working for a degree and still not be able to get a job, because they had the wrong skin colour or not enough connections. I've

29

got friends who studied to be architects and went on to become PE teachers.

Because of my upbringing I had always loved the idea of being a farmer, and so I played with this thought for a while. My plan was to go to America and spend a year or eighteen months on a massive farm, getting the experience that would enable me one day to take over Grasfontyn from my grandparents. It was a popular thing to do at that time, but just before I was about to hand over a deposit for flights and visas the company I was arranging things with went bust. Luckily we didn't lose any money, but it did send me back to the drawing board.

I had had my mind made up: I was ready to go away and do something. But what now? Directly after school I started doing a part-time course in computer science and programming, thinking that it might be useful for the world we live in today. It wasn't my thing at all, though – I can't remember a bit of it. At the same time I was working with my dad, learning the ropes of the family distribution business and being a driver for him. But deep down I was desperate to do my own thing and get out of the house. In my mind, I had already opened the door to leaving South Africa.

As a child learning to shoot on my granddad's farm, I had dreamed of being a soldier. It was a dream that never left me. My granddad had been in the army, although he never really talked about it. My dad, too: he was a driver, and he also did a stint on the Angolan border.

There had still been national service back then, so nearly all my friends' dads had been in the army as well. I used to love standing around a *braai* (barbecue) with them at the age of sixteen or seventeen, having a beer or a brandy and listening to their stories. They'd tell me about missions out in the bush, tracking terrorists trying to get in over the border from Angola or Mozambique; how they had to sleep and cook in the field, look after themselves and protect the border. They told me terrible stories about running out of fresh water for days, but also about the mischief they'd got up to – how they'd cover themselves with brake fluid to get a better tan. I'd seen photos of them all bronzing up, or standing on parade in the middle of the bush, their kit and equipment gleaming despite the dust. They'd seen proper action and it fascinated me.

The South African defence force once had an extremely good reputation: the job they did, their fitness levels, their durability and versatility were well known. The Parabats were one of the most elite forces in the world. They were trained very highly; it comes naturally to a South African to do things like that. But standards were starting to slip and there was a lot of corruption. I thought that if I joined now it wouldn't be anything like the stories I'd fallen in love with.

By the time I turned twenty, the question of what to do was eating away at my insides. Then I heard from friends of my mum that their daughter had joined the British Army and loved it. Someone else's son had done the same. Lizanne had got married and she and her husband, Hans, had been living in London for a couple of years by then, so I asked her to help me find out more about it. Because South Africa was a member of the Commonwealth, it would be possible for me to join the British Army as well. I would need to apply online, get a criminal record check, have a minimum reserve of six months' income in my bank account, and fly to London on a two-year work-and-travel visa to complete the application process in person.

There was no certainty that I would even get in. But as soon as I heard it was possible, I knew this was what I was going to do.

People thought I was crazy. It seemed so far-fetched that no one thought I would do it. It wasn't that I seemed unlikely to make the commitment, but people thought I wasn't the type of guy to join the army. They simply thought I was quite soft-hearted and caring, always wanting to do the right thing. And I *am* that guy – out in my civilian clothes, watching the rugby in the pub, I've always been the same Jaco. But that's what Basic Training does to you: it teaches you to have two lives. I think that even back then I knew that.

I was quite far along in the application process when my friend Ian called me up. He wanted to know if I was still planning on joining the British Army and if he could come with me. It was a mad rush trying to get his visa sorted and all the paperwork done, but somehow we managed it. I sold most of my belongings – my hi-fi, all my CDs, and eventually even my beloved *bakkie* – to be able to buy my ticket, and in June 2006 Ian and I got on a plane to the UK.

My first-ever international flight, and I was leaving the whole world behind. It was exciting, it was heart-wrenching, it was nerve-wracking... it was everything at the same time. It was also pretty stressful. That morning we had gone to see some family in Johannesburg and my dad had left it too late. It was rush-hour traffic by the time we were on the way to the airport, and I sat in the back thinking, *I'm going to miss this flight, I'm going to miss this flight*. I felt like screaming or crying; I didn't know what to do.

Eventually we got there and I ran past everyone – all the friends who had turned out to wave Ian and me off – checked my bag in and rushed through the gates. I barely had time to say goodbye to anyone. It wasn't the best way to leave, and I had plenty of time to think about that on the flight afterwards.

But still, it was exciting. I'd never been on such a long plane journey before, and then there was the fact that we were starting a whole new life. When we landed at Heathrow my sister and her husband were there to pick us up, squeezing us and our enormous suitcases into their tiny Mercedes A Class. It's hard to fit a whole new life into twenty-three kilos, especially when all you know about England is that it's cold and rainy.

Actually, that summer is probably one of the best I've ever experienced. It was absolutely gorgeous. The sun was shining on the drive into London from the airport and Ian and I were so excited. Almost every building we passed – every flyover, even – we would ask if it was famous. Lizanne and Hans kept saying no, there wasn't anything to see until we were actually in London. We asked constantly anyway. Eventually they said that we were there, and for the first time in my life I saw a black taxi and a red double-decker bus.

We drove past Big Ben and the Houses of Parliament, over London Bridge and then along to Canada Water. There was quite a large South African community there back then, and Lizanne and Hans had arranged a big *braai* with lots of their friends to welcome us. We instantly felt at home.

That weekend we stayed on my sister's sofa. She showed us around London, introduced us to lots of people, and we started to settle in. It was new and different but I loved it immediately. On the Saturday night I had my first (and last) experience of Snakebite – I'd never drunk it before, but it turns out you can have too much of a new and exciting thing. And on the Monday morning, once we'd recovered, Ian and I went to the army recruiting office on the Strand.

Except, at first, we didn't. Somehow we had managed to end up in the RAF recruitment centre. Even though the man was very keen to sign us up, I eventually managed to pull Ian out of there and, just around the corner, we found the right building. At that stage I wasn't at all sure exactly what I wanted to join – just the army, really. I wasn't even very sure what being in the army actually meant. To me, it was just being a soldier with a rifle, but in fact there's a lot more to it than that. You have engineers, chefs, mechanics, drivers, medics, clerks... it takes a big machine to help that soldier with a rifle do his job.

But all I wanted to be was that soldier, and so I was quite happy when the recruitment officer on duty started trying to sign us up for the Royal Green Jackets (which would later become part of The Rifles regiment). Ian and I were nodding and agreeing to everything, concentrating hard on understanding the English we had barely spoken up till then, when another recruitment officer came down the stairs.

He was very neatly dressed, with a maroon beret, and as soon as he heard our accent he looked at us. He let the other recruitment officer continue talking, but just as we were about to leave he called us over.

'You boys are South African, aren't you?' he said.

'Yes, sir.'

'You come from a farm, don't you?'

'Yes, sir.'

'And you can both shoot very well, can't you?' he continued. 'You like the field craft, you like travelling...'

He went on mentioning all these things, and Ian and I were nodding and saying 'yes' to everything.

'I know you guys,' he said. 'I know South Africans, and you don't want to join the Green Jackets. What you want to join is the Parachute Regiment.'

It was the first time I'd ever heard of the Paras, but at that moment my course was set. The recruitment officer gave us a leaflet and we went straight home and on to the internet.

We saw what they do and how difficult it is – the website said it's one of the hardest regiments to join, with a pass rate of something like 20 per cent. It was quality they were after, it said, not quantity. I always wanted a challenge, and I knew that this was the one.

One thing I had really liked about the recruitment officer was that he hadn't just been recruiting for the Paras. He gave us other options as well – maybe do a couple of years with the Parachute Regiment and then transfer to the Army Air Corps to be an engineer or a small-helicopter pilot. But, he'd said, if you want to lay the foundations, join the Regiment and be an infantryman. I liked the sound of that. On the British Army Recruitment Battery (BARB) test Ian and I took – which was the next stage of the application process – I actually scored highly enough to go straight into the Air Corps, but I stuck to my position. I wanted to join the military; I didn't want to do anything else. I wanted to become an infantryman.

In the meantime, I needed to pay my rent. Because our visas allowed us to work for a year, we signed up to a company called Showforce. They set up events all over the UK, and our job was basically to do the manual labour – building seating and stages for big events and then breaking it all down again.

We went on tour with the Rolling Stones, to the Goodwood Festival of Speed and the Queen's Club tennis tournament. If there wasn't anything big on we would be doing little jobs around theatres in London, and we got to know the city well.

The work was physically hard, but it certainly helped with my fitness. The Parachute Regiment has stricter entry requirements than the other army regiments – whereas you have to run 1.2 miles in eleven minutes and fifteen seconds to get into the army, to get into the Paras you have to run the same distance three minutes faster. You also had to be able to do more sit-ups and press-ups in the space of two minutes.

Eventually we got invited down to Aldershot for a recruitment weekend, turning up with around two hundred other guys. We did the fitness tests and had a medical, and all through the weekend they gave us little insights and bits of information: things like how to use a grenade or ways of obtaining intelligence. Later on they would come back to it to see how much we'd remembered. There was a lot to take in but I loved every bit of it.

At the end of the weekend I was told that I'd passed, but the medical examination had picked up on an old knee injury from when I was at school. I couldn't go straight into Basic Training, they said – first I would need to get clearance from my doctor back in South Africa, explaining what he'd done and that the knee was now fine. Once that came through, I'd have to go through all the tests again just to make sure. I got in touch with my doctor, gritted my teeth, and sat down for a long wait.

*****

We were well into autumn by the time my medical clearance finally arrived. I passed the assessment centre at Aldershot again and came home from a Showforce job one day to find a letter waiting for me. I had been accepted into the army, and I could choose from a series of start dates for Basic Training in late November and December 2006. I went for the earliest one.

I was so excited to be getting started at last, but a few days later another letter came. The South African government was in the process of passing what was known as the Mercenary Act, which was aimed at preventing any South African citizen from serving in foreign military organisations.

In part it was spurred on by the failed coups d'état in Equatorial Guinea and Zimbabwe, in 2004 and 2007, in which South African mercenaries had been said to play a significant role. Although the final ruling was unclear, what it effectively meant at that stage was that any South African citizen serving in a foreign military would have two choices: to leave that military and go home, or to stay and risk being arrested as a mercenary if they ever tried to go back to South Africa. Faced with that prospect, the British Army had put a stop on recruiting South African soldiers.

I was shocked by the news, and as the year ended it looked like it was never going to get resolved. In my head I had already decided to stay in the UK as long as I could, but then I would have to go home again and continue working for my dad. Before I'd even really had time to process this, in early January another letter from the army arrived.

After extensive talks with the South African government, the British Army had decided to continue recruiting. I would be able to start my Basic Training, but I did need to be aware that I might end up facing a difficult decision.

At the time, I didn't think much of it – it was only later on that it would become an issue again. I was so keen to get started that I just thought I'd worry about it later. To be honest, I was so led by the idea of being in the army that I probably would have stayed on anyway, even if the law had affected me.

My parents had always been very supportive of everything I did, even though I'm sure that my mum in particular worried loads. But at that moment all that mattered was starting Basic Training, and the first date available to me was 2 February 2007.

I started doing lots of running and fitness, getting ready to leave London for Catterick. The letter they'd sent had given me two options: either I could arrive as I was and have my hair cut there, or I could come with a Number Two. On my last weekend in London I sat at the table in my sister's kitchen as she shaved my hair, practising my salutes on her. It was fun and exciting – the beginning of a whole new life again.

A few days later, at the start of a bitterly cold February, my newly shaved head was on a train to North Yorkshire.

III

BECOMING JOE

At the start of Basic Training, they give you fourteen days. You have a two-week period, from Day One to Day Fourteen, when you're allowed to leave at any point. Because everyone's Basic Training is the same, whether you want to be in the Parachute Regiment or the Welsh Guards, an infantryman or a clerk or a chef, leaving during those fourteen days is you leaving the army as an institution.

Beyond that, it's still possible to go down the transfer route, but leaving the army becomes a lot harder from then. Day Fifteen is what all the corporals look forward to, because after that point they can make it as hard as they like.

Once you've passed Day Fourteen, you're theirs.

Arriving on the train at Darlington, I felt nervous and excited. It was funny – looking around the carriage, I could see exactly who the other new recruits were. We all had the same shit-what-am-I-doing look on our faces, and most of us had weird new haircuts. Those who didn't were given one almost as soon as we'd got off the coaches at the barracks and been issued our new kit. I was so glad Lizanne had cut my hair for me, because it did *not* end up looking good when the corporals took a pair of clippers to you.

That first evening we were split up into platoons, assigned bunks in our section rooms, shown the scoff house for dinner and told how things work. We were issued a locker and kit to keep in it – at first there was just a maroon tracksuit top and tight blue jogging bottoms, tiny little PE shorts and a couple of green army T-shirts with a big white patch on the front which we had to stencil our names on to. There was a pair of trainers and a few socks, and that was it for the next couple of weeks. As soon as our own clothes were off, the process of leaving behind our civilian identities began.

Although I was full of adrenaline and hugely excited finally to be starting Basic Training, I was also very aware that I was on my own. Right back when we had gone down to Aldershot for the first physical assessment centre, Ian had decided that the army wasn't for him after all. I was quite sad and disappointed, because it would have been nice to continue on that journey together, but I understood his reasoning – and, as I would see at Catterick, joining the military really isn't for everyone.

During those first two weeks, though, I never thought about leaving. Not even once. It was mainly preparation and I enjoyed every bit of it. We went through a number of medicals and more physical tests, had various lectures and were taught all the basics of life in the barracks, like how to iron our kit and the standards expected of us. Over the two weeks we were gradually given more bits of our proper uniform: army boots and trousers, smocks, helmets, a tie... The last thing we got given was a beret, although we wouldn't be able to shape and wear it until we'd completed the next six weeks.

And then it got hard. Really hard.

*****

Catterick was cold. Actually, it was bloody freezing – and that's putting it mildly. As a South African experiencing my first British winter – only the second time I'd ever seen snow; the other occasion was on my grandparents' farm when I was eight or nine years old – the temperature of the North Yorkshire moors in February came as a real shock. Every morning would start with a fitness session in just a T-shirt and shorts, and we would stand outside the barracks waiting until the corporal came to join us. There was no jumping up and down on the spot allowed – we weren't even supposed to shiver.

If that was unpleasant, there were also some times that the cold had a bad effect on my performance. One night we were out doing a field exercise and I was on 'stag' (sentry duty). It was cold and wet and I was already miserable after being woken up in the middle of the night to get out of my sleeping bag and back into my damp, cold and dirty kit from the day before. Lying there on the muddy ground I slowly started freezing. I knew that the corporal was watching me – but the cold was getting to my brain and all I wanted was to sleep.

All of a sudden, we were under attack. I was one of the only people between the enemy and my platoon, but my fingers were frozen so stiff that I couldn't even move them. I couldn't get the safety catch off my rifle, let alone fire a few blank rounds.

'What the fuck is wrong with you?' the corporal screamed in my face. 'Can you not see the enemy? He's right there! You need to fire at him! Fire at the enemy!' As he yelled at me he aimed a few kicks at my helmet. I was lying there in agony, in a cold and muddy trench, frozen to the bone and unable to do what I was supposed to, and all the while I was getting kicked in the head. Not exactly the high point of my career.

There were a few instances like that, but eventually in one debrief the cold was spoken about as a serious issue. It was true that the South Africans and Fijians did feel the cold much more than the

British guys, so we got given an extra pair of thicker gloves. It didn't make our morning fitness sessions any more pleasant, but at least I was able to work the safety catch after that.

The temperature wasn't the only thing where being South African put me at a disadvantage. My first corporal in Basic Training was a Scotsman, Corporal McDiarmid. I had only recently come from South Africa, where I had grown up speaking nothing but Afrikaans, and then lived in London, where at least they spoke decent English.

Now, scared shitless and not knowing what was coming, I had stepped into the army and found myself with a corporal who was supposedly speaking English... but certainly not a language I could understand.

He also couldn't understand a lot of what I was saying in my terrible South African accent. Often he would shout instructions and I would either stay where I was or run off blindly and end up doing the wrong thing. That always ended in a 'beasting' (physical punishment) like running an extra mile or doing press-ups. But Corporal McDiarmid was a good guy, a really good guy – he recognised where the problem lay and over time things did get better. Adjustment was a crucial element of Basic Training. Things did get explained to us, but there was so much to take in that a lot of the time we just learned by doing.

Carrying a notepad and pen in the right-hand pocket of our trousers became law – we were constantly making notes. Every regiment prides itself on its past, so military history was a big element of what we were taught. There were also daily lessons in things like navigation, field craft, weapons and tactics, and every evening we would be up until midnight writing up the things we'd learned. There was late-night ironing to do as well, or boots to be polished, so tiredness quickly became a big part of our lives.

We were woken up at five o'clock every morning, and by five minutes to six had to be lined up outside in the corridor. We had to be correctly dressed, kit pressed and boots shined, but most importantly we needed to be holding a large, black, standard-issue mug. The mug held a litre of water exactly, and it had to be full to the brim. If the water level was even a millimetre below the top, the corporal on duty would pour it over your head. Once we'd all been inspected and the corporal was happy, he'd walk down the line and shout, 'Drink!' We had a minute to down the water in the mug, thirty seconds to put it away, and then we would parade over to the scoff house.

Funnily enough, it's something I still do to this day – I don't down a litre of water, but first thing in the morning I do take a big gulp from the bottle beside my bed. Little things like that become part of you.

The army teaches you to do stuff fast: ten minutes here, two minutes there. We even had to run everywhere as soon as we'd stepped out of our section room – there was absolutely no walking in the corridor. It also teaches you to be exact, and to manage your time better. Like with the bed block: every morning we had to make the bed precisely, folding each sheet and blanket in a certain way to make a block that looked like it had been cut with a knife.

Of course, we hated it, so a few of us started making the bed blocks perfectly and then at night we'd just place them gently on the floor and sleep on the bare mattress in our field-exercise sleeping bags. It worked really well for a while, but the corporals weren't stupid – they'd been privates themselves once. If we were ever caught doing it again, they said, we'd be made to sleep outside.

That was how life was, day in, day out, for the next six weeks. Although there were a lot of things we didn't understand at the time, now I see why we were given certain lessons or had to do things a particular way. It was all about forgetting what the world was like before and building up a new identity as a soldier.

When you go into your Basic Training, you're nothing. You don't even have a name; it means nothing any more. Collectively, everyone is known as Joe, and individually you're a Joe with a number. An officer would shout 'Joe!' and everyone had to run into the corridor.

In the first couple of weeks we would be too slow, looking around for the person called Joe before we realised it was all of us. They'd make us get down and do fifty press-ups for being too slow and thinking we were better than them. That's what it was about: you're no better than the guy to the left or in front of you, and no one's better than you. You're all the same; you're all Joe. It didn't matter whether you came from the richest family or the poorest, from a broken background or a close one – we were all brothers and they were going to treat us all exactly the same.

This can be quite difficult to explain to other people, but it's a necessary part of the military system and it works extremely well in battlefield situations. We learned to respond to a lot of things automatically that only later started to seem significant. Relaying messages was one of them – if a corporal shouted 'Joe!', we all shouted 'Joe!', and it was the same with instructions given out in the field, like 'Change magazine!' If we didn't pass the message on, we'd get thrashed.

They did explain why, but it's only really when you're on the battlefield, you're under fire and your ears are ringing, that you see the importance of this small, fundamental stuff. Out there, you relay messages like 'Move to the left!' or 'Medic!', shouting it so that the guy fifteen metres to the right will hear it and pass it on too. It's things like that that can help save a life – just like they did mine.

A lot of the time, though, because you don't understand it yet, you just think you're going through hell. There were many, many times when I found myself wondering if that was all the army was and what the rest of my career was going to look like: not being able to walk anywhere, shouting all the time, constant beastings... everything just moved at a hundred miles an hour. If that was what life in battalion looked like, I wasn't all that keen on it after all.

In fact, it's the total opposite. Once you become a paratrooper – once you take out that little green backing behind your cap badge, pass your jumps course and get to battalion – you're a soldier and you get to look after yourself. There are still things you need to do, still battalion runs and exercises, but you can customise your own kit and be in charge of your own fitness. You can walk from place to place and no one's shouting at you all the time. But back in Basic Training, all of that seemed like a long way off. And even to get close to that stage, I first needed to pass the dreaded P Company.

*****

P Company is the end of the second phase of training, following Phase One which is exactly the same for all new army recruits. P Company is specific to the Parachute Regiment – and if I'd thought that Basic Training was hard, this was horrendous.

To pass P Company, we had to complete a week of physical tests, each of them harder than the last. If you failed even one you'd be 'back-squadded', which meant having to redo that entire phase of training, so everyone was under a lot of pressure. And because no one knew exactly what was coming at us, it made the whole thing even more terrifying.

The P Company tests are a series of simulations that also turn out to have a purpose when you find yourself on the battlefield. We started off with a ten-mile TAB (tactical advance into battle), which we had to complete in an hour and a half with sixty pounds of kit on our backs. Later on in the week there was a thirty-miler as well, both of them simulating real advances into combat zones when the battalion has parachuted or been helicoptered in to a designated landing site.

There was also a steeplechase, which was basically an obstacle course to test our stamina – it involved climbing frames, mud, water and rough terrain. At one point we had to climb a pole and stand on the plank on top of it, about thirty metres up in the air, spread our arms wide and shout out our rank, name and number. Some guys can't do it because they're so afraid of falling off, but the aim of it is to control that fear and show that you can cope under pressure. If you're about to jump out of a helicopter into a battle zone, you're going to need to remember what you've been told to do.

Controlling fear is important, but so is controlling aggression. We did this through a test called 'milling'. In that one, two individuals have to box each other, but it's not like the boxing you see on TV. In milling, you aren't allowed to duck or throw any uppercuts. All you're allowed to do is punch straight out in front of you, and you have to keep going for a full minute. It teaches you to keep your head up under enemy fire at the right moment, to get down but have the courage to come back up and return fire.

Through a twist of fate, I actually ended up milling twice – first against a guy who was around the same size as me, and then against Private Davies, the biggest guy in our platoon who absolutely no one wanted to fight.

It was the first time I ever realised how long sixty seconds can be – it seems like forever when you're constantly being hit in the face – but somehow I managed to keep my head up and landed enough punches that they called it a draw. From something I had been dreading, milling turned into a real highlight of mine.

Other bits of P Company came back to me later in my career in an even more obvious way. One of them, the log race, in which we had to run a five-mile obstacle course in teams of eight with an old telegraph pole between us, was designed to replicate carrying ammunition up to the front line. Later on, in Afghanistan, we needed to get ammunition to a gunner in a vital position, and it came back to me then, that log race. Knowing instinctively what to do, you go through so many pain barriers. You know that this is what you've been trained for and that it's going to save many lives.

I launched myself into P Company, but by Day Three there was a problem. During the very first test, the ten-mile TAB, I had been right at the front of the pack but in doing so had torn my groin. I carried on regardless for two days and did myself a lot of damage. Eventually, I was in so much pain that one of the medics pulled me off the course. I didn't want to go – I *had* to pass P Company – but there was no arguing with him. I was going to do permanent damage if I didn't stop.

I was devastated. The injury meant that I would be back-squadded – I had to spend several weeks in a rehab unit before joining a new platoon and going through Phase Two and P Company again. I was in such a bad place, both physically and mentally. Physically because I was in a general training rehab unit – away from the regiment, I was mainly among 'crap hats', which is what we paratroopers call all the other regiments. I had formed such a strong bond with the guys in my platoon as we had watched the initial 120 recruits shrink down to the group of thirty who went on to P Company.

I'd done the hardest things I'd ever done in my life with them, shared so many experiences and emotions, and suddenly I was cut off, stuck in a rehab unit on my own. When you start Basic

Training you're a nobody, but when you find yourself in a rehab unit you're even less than a nobody.

All this started putting doubt in my mind, and suddenly the world seemed a very dark place. All I had ever wanted to do was to be in the army and now I was faced with a massive setback. I knew the fitness levels that were required for P Company and how hard I'd worked to reach them, and I had no idea how long it was going to take to build that back up again. Self-doubt is a terrible thing, but it's something I still face today as a professional athlete. One minute you can feel on top of the world, and the next minute you've fallen off the bike and don't know how you're going to get that result back again. It's enough to make you want to give up.

I knew I needed to get my injury fixed, but the road ahead seemed so long. The South African Mercenary Act was still rumbling on in the background, and I started thinking that maybe I should look into it more. I thought it might be an easy way out – if I wasn't *allowed* to carry on being in the British Army, I would be able to go home and tell my friends and family that, rather than just the flimsy excuse of being injured. I also considered transferring, looking at tank and artillery regiments or the Army Air Corps. All these stupid thoughts were going through my head because of a few moments of self-doubt.

My mum likes to say that everything happens for a reason. I hate it when she says that, but it is actually true. Often you can't see why at the time, but looking back you realise that certain things happen to get you where you're going to end up. I approached my second P Company in a much better frame of mind. Knowing what was coming, I felt a lot more relaxed about it. And then there was my new platoon. Although I had to re-establish all those relationships, I was lucky – there were three other South Africans in my new group, so I was no longer the only one. We all quickly became very close friends and ended up going off to battalion together. If I had decided to transfer or pack it all in after my injury, I wouldn't have made those lifelong friends. I might never even have become a paratrooper, and that would have been something I'd always have regretted.

Towards the end of our training we were allowed to submit our battalion choices. Within the Parachute Regiment there are three battalions that need men: 1 Para, 2 Para and 3 Para. Each of them is different – 2 and 3 Para have more of a green-army role, but 1 Para is a Special Forces Support Group, and that was the battalion I wanted to join. In the end it doesn't really matter what you choose – the training staff will assess you and place you where they think you're most suited. I was very lucky to get my first choice, along with my South African friends, Stef, Koos and Brendan (also known as Tony), and Dan and Joel who were British. The six of us went on to 1 Para like a little clan.

The only thing left to do was our jumps course, and within a week of joining 1 Para we'd been sent to RAF Brize Norton. Over four weeks we had to complete parachute jumps from different heights, with kit and without kit, some of them at night, and at the end of it all we were given our 'wings'. Although they weren't 'wet' yet (we hadn't jumped through cloud or done any operational jumps), I was so proud to be able to wear the badge on my shoulder.

Training had taken longer for me than it should have – including rehab, I was there for about eight months – but by the end of 2007 I was a fully qualified paratrooper. It was time for the good life to start.

IV

MEETING AFGHANISTAN

The start of battalion life was a bit of an anti-climax for me. The six of us who had been sent to 1 Para had been allocated to B Company, which was in Afghanistan at the time. We were raring to go out there too – every soldier dreams of seeing action – but our initial excitement was quickly shattered. The message came through that it was nearly the end of their tour so they couldn't see the point in us joining them. Afghanistan would have to wait.

In the meantime, though, there was plenty to do. Because of 1 Para's role with Special Forces there were a number of weapons systems and bits of radio equipment that we needed to learn how to use – the battalion didn't always work with the standard-issue British Army rifle and radio systems. While we were waiting we completed weapons-handling drills and qualifications for pistols, rifles and heavy weapons, plus several pieces of radio equipment. We also ticked off various vehicle qualifications, learning to drive everything from Land Rovers to heavy armoured vehicles like the Jackal. By the time B Company returned to start their next rotation, they had six new soldiers who were fully qualified and up to scratch. We were able just to fall into our new platoon and crack on.

Of course, it wasn't quite that simple – during the first two weeks we still got treated like shit just for being the new guys. It's always like that. But once they realised we were all badged up and ready to go, we started getting a bit more respect. Obviously we had a huge amount of respect for the men who had just come back from Afghanistan, but because we'd already learned so much we did get treated differently than we might otherwise have done. It made easing into battalion life that little bit smoother.

Our main base was in St Athan, in south Wales, and with all the guys back in camp we started to settle into the flow of things fast. 1 Para runs on the basis of rotations, so each company will spend six months in Afghanistan, followed by six months on a standby rotation and then six on a UK-based counter-terrorism rotation. The standby rotation was usually the most relaxed of the three, but the one downside was that it meant we could never go very far from camp. The company was on standby in case anything were to happen (whether in the UK or somewhere else in the world), so we were always on a certain number of hours' notice. 'Three hours' notice to move' meant that you would have to be ready within three hours of getting instructions to deploy, so you could never be more than about an hour away from camp and weren't allowed to drink. If you weren't on three hours' notice you could go further afield, but there were still limits. And everyone always had to have a bag packed and ready under their bed. It was essentially a lot of 'hurry up and wait'.

In early April 2008 we were down in Portsmouth for a training session when the sergeant came to see me. His words were a fastball that came out of nowhere.

'Hey, van Gass, you need to pack your kit. You're going to Afghanistan.'

It was the last thing I'd expected him to say.

Before I knew it, I was back at the base in St Athan signing out a box of desert kit. A small group of guys were heading out to

Afghanistan on an operation to train the Afghan National Army (ANA) and I had been given the one spot remaining. It was pure luck for me, really – during B Company's last tour of Afghanistan, just as the six of us had arrived at battalion, their captain, Martin Hewitt, had been shot and badly wounded. I didn't know it at the time, but he would later end up becoming a great friend when we walked to the North Pole together. My captain from training, Paul, had been called back to B Company to replace Martin and, because he knew me, he had given me the place on the team.

My friends were very jealous. We were all still finding our feet in B Company, and suddenly I was off to Afghanistan. As a soldier, that's all I wanted – it was what I had trained for, to a certain degree even what I had signed up for. All of us wanted nothing more than to get out to Afghanistan as soon as possible. We weren't scared; we just wanted to go.

Even though this wasn't going to be an actual fighting role, I was still extremely excited. I can clearly remember packing my kit and the nerves that came along with that. Although I was the new private, I was desperate to hold my own and show the rest of the company that I was the right man for the job. We had been given a list of packing essentials, but even with that as a starting point working out what to take and what to leave was a massive learning curve for me. I went through my kit over and over again, hoping I wouldn't seem like an amateur.

Getting on a bus to drive to RAF Brize Norton, going through all the operational briefings and then climbing on to the flight – all this stuff was normal to most of the other guys on the team, but to me some of it seemed quite extreme. On the aircraft we had to have our helmets with us, and as soon as we breached Afghan airspace all the lights were turned off so we were flying in the dark. That didn't seem quite right to me. Then we were ordered to put on our helmets. *What the hell?* I thought. Was it over before it had even begun? Looking around me, I was amazed to see the other guys looking relaxed – they knew it was just a safety protocol in case the plane was shot at during landing. I wasn't able to feel that calm about it, but at the same time it was fascinating to be learning all these new things.

The plane landed on Afghan soil and slowly, slowly, the back door came down to reveal a different world. The heat hit me like a wall and the air was thick with the dust swirled up by the engines. Even though it was the middle of the night there was plenty of action going on, men and vehicles moving all around. We had landed in Camp Bastion: a place that until then had only been a legendary name for me.

Everyone talked about Bastion. It was the main British military base in Afghanistan during the conflict, shared with US forces and troops from a number of other countries like Denmark and Estonia. What started out as a desert landing strip in 2006 had become an enormous strategic hub that could house over thirty thousand people by the time I arrived in 2008. Bastion was like a city – there were camps within the camp, a huge airport, hospitals, a water-bottling plant, sewers, streets, an electricity network... It was infrastructure on a scale I could never have imagined, all of it in the middle of the desert in Afghanistan's southern Helmand Province. Arriving, I felt dazed.

But there wasn't much time to be overwhelmed or even get used to Bastion, because after one night we were on the move again. The morning after we flew in we collected our kit from the colourman in an enormous tent filled with equipment, and then the Snatch Land Rovers were there to pick us up. We were moving to Camp Rego, around nine miles from Camp Bastion, which was to be our home and training centre for the next four to six months.

Sitting there in the open back of the Snatch as we drove through the desert, I couldn't keep the smile off my face. I was already in my element: dressed in my combats with my weapon at my side, feeling the heat, sweat and dust of the desert on my skin. This was something I loved, a journey I had always dreamed of.

But even though I was an inexperienced young private, war had already made its mark on me. IEDs (improvised explosive devices) were having such an impact on our forces that not even twelve hours into my tour I was praying we wouldn't drive over one. I'd never seen anyone injured by an IED, but I'd heard plenty of horror stories. And although this was a well-driven road, that only made it more dangerous. In Afghanistan it was common to vary routes and routines as much as possible for safety, but there were established roads that just couldn't be avoided. Those roads were always most at risk of IEDs, because the enemy knew that their chances of getting an effective hit were higher. All the way to Rego, I couldn't stop hoping that the route had been recently cleared.

The camp was situated on the lower slopes of a mountain and made almost entirely from HESCO. Essentially a heavy-duty sandbag, HESCO blocks are large wire-mesh containers lined with tough fabric and filled with soil, gravel or sand. I'd see a lot of them in Afghanistan, but almost nowhere as much as at Rego. Security there was extremely tight.

It needed to be – the job we were there to do was dangerous. Although we could provide operational support to the rest of our unit if necessary (they were there in a fighting capacity), our main focus was on training the ANA. We were taking on new recruits from across Afghanistan, people who had walked in off the street and signed up to join the army just like I had. In Afghanistan, though, there were no background checks. Before I had been allowed to join the British Army I had needed to provide police clearance and all the usual details like passport and national insurance numbers that could be used to prove my identity. In Afghanistan there was nothing like that, which meant we had no idea who our new recruits really were. There had been incidents before in which the Taliban had infiltrated the ANA by simply signing up and waiting for the right moment to turn on their trainers with a weapon. Sometimes they even put a guy in a suicide vest in the queue waiting to come through the gate. We might not have been on active operations, but what we were doing was equally dangerous.

Safety was a big issue for us and so we made sure to spend enough time getting it right. Over the next ten days we set up open-sided tents as a classroom and built shooting ranges outside the camp, facing up the mountain behind it. We went over our training plans with the ANA staff working with us and got to know the interpreters, who would be essential for communication. It was a lot of build-up, but we had to be very clear about what we were going to do. We might never know who we were taking on, but we could do everything possible to reduce the risks involved.

Finally the day came on which we had to open the gates. The tension was almost unbearable, but we knew we had created an effective screening system. The new recruits had to line up outside and then pass one by one through a little funnel of HESCO blocks where Afghan soldiers would search them. Then they provided their details – name, place of birth and so on – and were moved to a holding area before being assigned accommodation. We positioned ourselves in strategic locations to oversee what was going on at the gate and alternated stag (patrol) duties every couple of hours. It was a hugely stressful couple of days, but eventually we had a pool of new and seemingly willing recruits.

Although not all of them were that willing, it turned out. We modelled the training plan on our own Basic Training, giving them a mixture of classroom lessons and fitness sessions and every day issuing a little bit of kit. Immediately we had guys not liking this or that part of their kit, not wanting to get up in the mornings, not wanting to go for a run... It was hard, especially because we were trying to build a rapport with them through interpreters. We also had to stay vigilant all the time; we always had a sidearm on us, if not a rifle.

I had been given the acting rank of lance corporal, because if the Afghans had realised they were being taught by a private they would never have given me any respect. Even though I was only a couple of months into my army career, I was already acquiring new responsibilities and I absolutely thrived on them. Unfortunately everyone else knew that I was still really just a private, so as the youngest member of the team I was always made to be the demonstrator. I spent most of my time dressed up and crawling through the sand, demonstrating various firing positions or showing how to take cover or change a magazine. I was back to the Basic Training I'd so recently gone through, only this time there was less being shouted at or kicked in the head.

We were training the ANA to a very high standard, which meant incorporating lots of the drills we ourselves had done. At six o'clock every morning we'd take them for a run or fitness session, and in the afternoon we'd do exercises to simulate bringing ammunition up to the front line or carrying someone off the battlefield on a stretcher. We filled boxes with sand and ran races up and down the side of the mountain in full kit. Lots of the recruits just didn't get it, even with the help of our interpreters, and we went up and down the side of that hill many, many times. That wasn't without its dangers either – the camp was built on the site of an old Soviet military base and there were lots of landmines left over from the

Soviet–Afghan War of the 1980s. A route had been cleared and marked with white stones; so as long as you stayed within them you were safe. Anything else and you were on your own. Engineers occasionally came in to fix the radio mast at the top of the hill and their vehicles would sometimes veer off the marked route and cause an explosion. At times it all seemed quite surreal.

It could be funny, too. When it came to weapons, we started out with dry fire drills – we would give the new recruits a stick or half a broomstick to use as a rifle and they would run round a little obstacle course in patrol formation, making shooting noises as they pretended to fire. Eventually, though, we moved on to real weapons, and there came a point where the only thing left to do was to go on operations and test the men out as soldiers. We were lucky in the few missions that we did – they were easy and nothing ever really went wrong – but, again, we always had to be two or three steps ahead. Training was all very well, but how would the new ANA soldiers react under live fire? Would they turn on us? What if they were part of a plan to ambush us? Those few months changed me from a new private into a soldier who really thought beyond his role.

It was a lot of fun as well, despite the stresses of the job, and six months flew by in no time. Before we knew it we were due to go back home – and for me that meant all the way home.

*****

It was the first time I'd been back to South Africa in a long while and things seemed different. *I* wasn't any different – I was sure of that – but people treated me as if I was. It was as though they expected me to have PTSD or be traumatised by stuff I had seen in Afghanistan. Of course I'd seen distressing things out there – it was war, after all, not an everyday environment – but I didn't feel that it had changed me as a person. It bothered me that people assumed it had.

But maybe I *had* changed in some ways after all, because back home in South Africa and later in the UK I started picking up on things I might not have noticed before. The main thing I felt was that people were so oblivious to what was going on in the world. They might pick up a newspaper or watch the evening news and think they knew what was happening in a country like Afghanistan, but the reality was something else entirely. I also really struggled with the way people took their lives for granted and moaned a lot about the small stuff: their coffee not being warm enough or their train being delayed. What they didn't see was that they were lucky to be able to wake up every morning and go to work without fearing for their lives. They were able to walk around in freedom when so many people in the world couldn't.

It was sometimes hard to deal with the way people fixated on the simplest things in life, when I had so recently been in an environment that was the complete opposite of all that. Settling back into a normal routine after a tour can be very hard, which is why army guys tend to stick together. We understand each other and cling on to each other for support, but we can alienate ourselves from civilians even more as a result.

I felt a kind of relief to get back to St Athan and fall in with B Company on their counter-terrorism (CT) rotation. It was a whole new range of skills and drills to learn – while Basic Training had been all about warfare out in the field, CT was to do with close-quarter combat. We travelled all over the UK doing really cool exercises, like learning how to enter and secure a house full of potential terrorists, training to fight on oil rigs and container ships, and even taking part in a large-scale hostage simulation with Special Forces and the emergency services. We had to learn how to use new weapons systems for fighting at close range, and even had some experts come over from America to teach us pistol drills. By the end of a week I was so slick on a pistol that it felt like being in the movies.

At times, it was repetitive – we did the drills over and over and over again – but it was laying down an incredible foundation of knowledge and giving me confidence that I would automatically know what to do in any situation. And because we were all getting the same training, I could be sure that one of the boys would be there on my shoulder to cover me, too, no matter what happened.

Our CT exercises were going to have relevance in real life very soon – at the end of the rotation, B Company would be going back to Afghanistan. The kind of job we were going to be doing out there would involve a lot of close-quarter combat during enemy house clearances, so it was amazing to be getting all the practice in beforehand. Following our training sessions we did several little operations around the UK, and just before the tour began we headed to Oman for a full-scale practice operation.

Oman was fantastic – imagine a lads' holiday on steroids, with some guns and bullets and grenades thrown in for good measure. We spent six weeks out in the desert going through absolutely everything we could come across on active operations, and when we weren't playing around with weapons, respirators and night-vision goggles we would have our shirts off to see who could get the best tan. That was an unwritten rule in the regiment: any opportunity you got to take your shirt off, you did.

I was having the time of my life out there in the desert. Better still, I was about to go to Afghanistan again. My first tour had been a huge learning curve for me, and in the course of just one year I'd gained so much confidence and experience in being a soldier. I understood the job I had been trained to do and I was determined to do it as well as I possibly could. More than that – and most importantly – I absolutely loved it.

V

THE FORT AT KABUL

It felt good going back to Afghanistan.

Getting on the plane at Brize Norton, the lights going out when we flew into Afghan airspace, the heat that rushed in to meet us when the doors were lowered at Camp Bastion: I'd seen it all before. Even though I was back to being a private I came with a lot of experience, and with the training from our counter-terrorism rotation fresh in my mind I knew I was well equipped to do my job. As my boots touched Afghan soil again, I felt strong, capable and ready for the challenges that lay ahead.

I had been in Afghanistan the previous year, but this tour was different from the off. For a start, I was with all my best mates from B Company, and we were there to take part in active operations rather than training ANA forces. We were also at a different base – although we flew into Camp Bastion again, we quickly transferred to a largely American base just outside Kandahar.

If I'd been impressed by the infrastructure at Bastion, this was something else. There were shops and markets, hairdressers and gyms, actual courts for playing tennis and volleyball, and, best of all, American scoff houses. The way the US Army catered for its soldiers was unreal and we took full advantage of being able to sign in for a meal. Salad bars, dessert counters, Mexican buffets, barbecues, Pizza Hut, Tim Hortons... the list just went on. The choice was probably better than in lots of towns back home.

By far the biggest thing at Kandahar was the airfield, which we called The Pan. The scale was absolutely indescribable. Half of it was reserved for the US Marine Corps, which is only part of the US Army but still bigger than all the British services combined. The number of aircraft they had was staggering, and all day and all night long the camp throbbed with the sound of helicopters taking off and landing.

The British Army had its own camp within a camp and we settled in quickly to our new accommodation, sharing four or five blokes to a room. There was a huge warehouse of kit and equipment and our own much smaller version of The Pan, including a hangar that housed two Special Forces Chinook helicopters. They weren't your standard Chinook, but had been fitted with a bigger engine and stripped down to make them much lighter and faster. Another important feature was that there was no glass in the windows, apart from in the cockpit, which meant that we could fire our weapons from inside the helicopter if needs be. As a Special Forces Support Group (SFSG), it was these helicopters we flew with most.

The days were hot, but nights in the desert were cold. Or, to be more exact, bloody freezing. Most of our missions involved going after high-value (HV) targets within the Taliban network – either a leader or a major influencer – who we often targeted directly at their house or logistics centre, and for this reason we almost always operated at night. In the afternoon we'd be given a briefing covering everything from background information on the target to how we were getting in and out, and in the early evening we'd have time to prep our kit, go to the gym, take a shower and eat. At a certain time we'd be driven to The Pan for a bit of 'hurry up and wait' while the pilots were making their final checks. If there was a dog coming with us on the mission – which there often was – it was really important to spend as much time with it as possible and make sure it got your scent. It was bad enough having to contend with monster Afghan dogs, a huge fighting breed that was on guard in nearly every compound. You didn't want your own dogs turning on you as well.

The experience I'd already gained worked in my favour and I was selected to take part in our very first mission. I still remember how surreal it all felt as we drove to The Pan and got our final instructions. Sometimes things could change at the last minute – if the wind speed or direction suddenly altered, the helicopters might have to drop us at another location. This time everything was going to plan, and as the pilots made their final checks we were issued thick, full-length puffer jackets to wear in the Chinook.

As soon as the engines started up it all became real. We got into formation in reverse order and ran from the hangar on to the waiting helicopters. I was excited and nervous in equal measure as I jogged through the hot downdraught coming off the Chinook. There were soldiers ahead of and behind me, all of us kitted out in really cool gear – night-vision goggles, Diemaco rifles, sidearms, radios – that made us look like we were in a movie. I'd watched this scene a hundred times already, only now I was a part of it. For a little boy who had once played at being a soldier, this was the moment a dream came true.

Up in that beautiful helicopter with no windows, I wasn't sure for a while whether I was extremely nervous or just freezing to death. We left the lights of the camp behind and headed for the pitch black of the desert. My radio was constantly chattering in my ear, giving live updates on the target which was being monitored by drones, until suddenly the call came through that we were five minutes off target. I nudged my neighbour, showed him five with my hand and shouted 'Five minutes!' so that he could pass it on to the next guy. We all stood up and took our jackets off, pulled down our night-vision goggles and switched them on to let our eyes adjust. Even when you've had them on for a while it can be hard to walk in a straight line, so I was always deeply impressed by the pilots who flew enormous helicopters while wearing them.

'Two minutes!'

It was time for action. The pilot swooped down fast and low and we all clung on to the grab ropes running down the middle of the ceiling. Our target was an isolated compound in the middle of a sea of poppy fields, one of which we were landing in. We had pre-planned our formation, the positions we would take to storm the compound, but as the ramp came down we had no idea what was waiting for us out there. For a few seconds I could feel my heart beating wildly, but then I was running and there was no more time to think.

I ran down the ramp into a field of flattened poppies... and sank straight up to my knees in mud. It had rained earlier that day and the ground we were supposed to be running over rapidly had turned into something the consistency of treacle. After ten metres I was out of breath, desperately trying to keep my gasps quiet and listen to the radio, which had gone crazy with shouts. All around me guys were having the same problem – it was chaos. And then the first bullet flew.

I don't know why or how, but as soon as that first bullet flew everything slowed down. My ears were ringing and the radio was still screaming, but somehow the world around me seemed to be in slow motion. Looking back on it, that was the first moment I really appreciated my training. I'd spent months and months going through the same drills, changing a magazine on my rifle over and over again, and at the time I had often wondered what the point was. Why were we doing this yet again? But out there, Taliban running and bullets flying everywhere, I fired my rifle correctly and changed through magazines automatically, following a set of procedures that had become reflex. It was the simplest thing, but right then it was the only thing that mattered.

Afterwards, everything seemed like a blur – it was hard to remember exactly what we'd done. I'll never forget the buzz of landing back at The Pan with the sun just coming up over the desert. I'd completed my first mission and come back with a good feeling. It had been a very successful operation; we'd captured the guy we were after and found loads of evidence in the compound to bring back to base. After a quick debrief we ate breakfast, cleaned our rifles, showered and went to bed for four or five hours' sleep, ready to get up around midday and start all over again.

Each mission was different and I absolutely fell in love with the variety involved in my job. Sometimes we'd land close to the target like we did on the first night, other nights we'd abseil down on to the roof of a compound, and still other times we'd do a ten- or fifteen-mile TAB to keep the element of surprise. We worked closely with Special Forces, setting up cordons around targets and helping to blast through compound walls to announce our arrival loudly. From three or four a week at the beginning, the number of missions started to pick up.

I didn't go out on a mission every night – sometimes there wasn't one, or I just wouldn't get picked. I always wanted to be selected, but during the early ones I did often feel scared. I think we all did. We'd been training for this for a long time, but we'd always been sending bullets one way down a range – there had never been real ones coming back. Hearing the whip and crack of them in the air was something quite different. There was also a lot to think about: each mission was different, but the one constant was the fact that we weren't there to kill people, but to try to capture information instead. There was always a split-second decision to be made in the instant before you pulled the trigger, which is not something you come across in everyday life. But sooner or later we got used to it. Life in the desert had become the new normal.

*****

Just over a month into my tour and things were about to change again. A request had come through from another Special Forces operation, based up at Camp Emperor in the mountains near Kabul. Just at the time when their anti-narcotics operations were starting to heat up, involving more and more high-value Taliban targets who were linked to local opium smuggling rings, they had found themselves chronically understaffed. Unable to get more support from SF, they called on 1 Para to provide a few men.

Of course everyone put their hands up, so I was extremely fortunate to get chosen to go along with my best mates Stef and Ryan. We were still under the command of Wayne and Cas, our sergeants from 1 Para, but from now on we would be working for the Special Boat Service (SBS). Those of us who were still privates were again given acting ranks of corporal or lance corporal and each of us usually oversaw a team of four or five ANA soldiers. It was a big responsibility and gave our operations quite a different feeling – now, instead of being part of a cordon along with all the other 1 Para guys, I was the most experienced soldier in my little team and the only one responsible for getting them all in and out safely.

Because our new operations were more focused on anti-narcotics, our jobs took on even more variety. My role changed with each mission: one day I would be a cordon commander, the next day attached to a sniper, other times a purple call sign, providing security for our 'head shed' (bosses) out in the field. Sometimes I found myself clearing a compound right alongside the SBS boys. Whatever they needed us to do, we did it. We dropped off and covered Special Reconnaissance Regiment (SRR) guys disguised as Afghans, who would bug shops and houses suspected of harbouring high-value targets. We also took charge of VIP transfers for big generals or ministers of state, collecting them from Kabul and bringing them out to the base in an armed convoy of jeeps. It might just have been chauffeur duty, but I loved driving those big armour-plated vehicles through the streets at top speed.

It was a good life at Camp Emperor and we settled in quickly. I thrived on the new atmosphere, which was a lot more self-sufficient; we didn't have the infrastructure of somewhere like Bastion and even had to cook for ourselves. The camp was situated within an old mountain fort, with a landing strip off to the side and wide views over the desert. The area was heavily strewn with old Soviet landmines – even more than at Camp Rego – and a Zimbabwean contractor was working to try to clear it.

There were guys in blue suits bouncing all over the place, detecting mines and then detonating them, so every day was punctuated by regular explosions. Red and white stones marked the areas that were still mined or safe to move through, which we had to pay close attention to any time we left the camp.

Every morning, no matter how tired I was from operations the night before, I'd get up and go for a run. I did circuits of a two-mile loop around the perimeter of the camp with my pistol strapped on over my running kit in case anything happened. Later on we'd usually fit in a gym session as well – while we were out in Afghanistan we were all on what we called 'Op Massive' – so after a few weeks I was fitter and stronger than I'd ever been. I didn't know it at the time, but the work I put in during those weeks helped save my life in the end. My body was in the best shape it could have been to survive and recover from the injuries I sustained.

Early one morning I had just come back through the gates when an almighty explosion rocked the air. I'd never heard anything like it before. The earth shook and several windows shattered with the force of the blast. Without even thinking, I ran to my room and threw on my body armour. Lots of the others had still been asleep and ran back into the compound with me, their body armour and weapons pulled on hurriedly over their pants and flip-flops. From the wall of the compound we could see an enormous dust cloud rising from a point about four hundred metres beyond the main camp gates. We'd just been paid a visit by our local Taliban insurgents.

Our local Taliban leader was a troublesome guy. His main hobby was to make our lives difficult in any way he could, and most days he'd send a few men down the road in a pickup truck with added mortar plate to have a few pot shots at the camp. There was never an incident so major that the ANA couldn't deal with it, and those small-scale assaults soon became a part of everyday life. This attack, however, had crossed a new line.

Later on we found out exactly what had happened: our local Taliban had got hold of a Bedford truck and packed it out with explosives. The guy driving the truck on the suicide mission was supposed to simply ram it through our camp gates and detonate where it would have made a huge impact on us, but in his hurry to maintain the element of early-morning surprise he'd taken a corner too fast.

The truck had rolled and, panicking, he'd pressed the detonator anyway. It was a spectacular failure. Three civilians by the roadside had also died, and the only inconvenience he'd caused us was a few blown-out windows. The intention behind the failed attack had been malicious, though, and this time we needed to react.

We took a little bit of time gathering the right intelligence, and about ten days later went after the Taliban leader at his compound. I had a cordon commander role that day, so I was looking after a number of Afghan soldiers and making sure we secured the perimeter effectively. The compound was a perfect square with a house in the middle, but the walls were so high we couldn't be too close to them – if someone decided to jump over or even just ambush us from around the corner we'd have absolutely no warning. Assessing the situation, I realised we needed to move.

About ten metres away from the wall I spotted an irrigation ditch: one of the most perfect hiding places you could hope to find. Deep enough to offer protection, it also allowed me to position a couple of guys facing outwards to cover our backs and the rest facing in towards the compound, giving us 360-degree arcs of vision. There wasn't much time to explain my plan to my team. I simply started running towards the ditch and yelled, 'Move! Follow me!'

The moment I jumped into the ditch I knew it had been the wrong decision. I sank up to my knees in what I thought was mud – and then the stench hit me. What I hadn't seen, not too far away, was a common feature of many Afghan compounds: the outdoor toilet. What I'd jumped into wasn't an irrigation ditch but a shit pit.

As I jumped, all my Afghan soldiers followed; some of them even fell over as they landed. I could see their looks of horror, but I couldn't lose face in front of them now. It was the perfect position and we were going to wait it out.

I lasted about half an hour before the smell became completely unbearable. Scouting around, I found another secure location on the corner of the road and we all moved up there. When the operation was over and we were picked up, the first thing everyone said was, 'What's that smell?' I was gutted, especially because of my boots – they were a relatively new pair I'd bought myself and I absolutely loved them. My trousers got thrown away that night but I washed my boots about four times. For a long time afterwards, the elation of having finally got our local Taliban leader was tainted by a lingering smell of shit.

*****

Although there were plenty of instances like that when an operation didn't go quite according to plan, there were just as many amazing times. It was a hard environment to be in and almost impossible to prepare for all the things that could happen, but the best thing to do was just embrace the situation and get on with it. We tried to have fun as well, or at least to see the funny side of things where we could. Otherwise it could all get to be a bit too much.

On one operation we had just cleared a compound belonging to an IED facilitator, which was packed to the rafters with opium, explosives and a lab's worth of chemicals. We couldn't just leave it lying around, and as luck would have it one of the SBS boys was keen to get rid of some C4 he'd been carrying for the whole tour. He scattered it around the compound while we packed an old car full of all the IED parts we could find – explosives, wires, vests, everything. Then we walked out of the compound and took cover behind a wall. The guy in charge of the demolition was last out.

'Hmmm,' he said when he saw where we'd taken cover. 'Lads, I think we need to move a little bit further away.'

We all got up again and moved about two compounds away. There were now multiple walls and fifty metres between us and the car – surely this would be fine? The demolition guy agreed and started the countdown. We covered our ears as he pressed the button and an almighty shockwave ran through us. I could feel everything inside my body move with the force of it. Within seconds the wall we were sheltering behind had collapsed on top of us, and as we dragged ourselves out from under the barrage of rocks we looked up to see a flaming car bonnet hurtling down out of the sky towards us. Fortunately no one was seriously hurt, and that ended up being one of those near-miss moments we had to laugh about.

Working on anti-narcotics operations involved quite a lot of explosions. It was the best way to get rid of the charges of opium we'd intercept in the desert, many of them being smuggled in the backs of lorries across the border to Iran. The vehicles would go one way with drugs and come back filled with money, weapons or explosives for the Taliban, so it was very important for us to cut those supply routes off.

We even spent three weeks out in the desert on a big operation, driving around following intel and sleeping on the ground under our vehicles. It was like being in the movies again – someone would come and wake you up to go on stag duty for an hour or so, and once your shift was over you'd go and nudge the next person awake. At first light we'd all be back on the vehicles to move on. It really was the stuff of adventures.

Helicopter chases in particular were pure Hollywood. During our three desert weeks we stopped at a US Air Force base for a couple of days and casually borrowed three of their Black Hawk helicopters. One would fly higher as the command helicopter, while the others were sniper and assault craft. A US drone flying around the area provided intel on the locations of smugglers' lorries, and as soon as we received the information we'd start up the engines and set off in pursuit.

There were various methods for getting the lorries to stop:

sometimes we'd create what's known as a 'brown out', flying low enough to whip up a dust storm that prevented them from seeing the road ahead, and other times we'd simply fire a volley of warning shots. As soon as the lorries stopped, the assault helicopter would touch down and we'd jump out on to one knee, shouting at the drivers to step out of the vehicles. I was always on the assault helicopter and absolutely loved it. Each time was different so there was always a thrill.

Some of the smugglers were incredibly brave – they would even fire back at the helicopter. One of them was determined not to stop no matter what kind of manoeuvres we tried, so in the end there was nothing for it but to bring the sniper helicopter in. Benny, who is one of the best snipers I've ever seen, could fire a .50-calibre bullet straight through the engine block every single time.

The split-second calculations he needed to make to do it so exactly blew my mind, but each time it was perfect. The lorry would stop dead and we could touch down and clear up the scene. The drivers were taken back to the American base. The opium, we burned.

*****

In the middle of this strange new life I was sent on R&R. After three months on tour we were each entitled to fourteen days' leave, which we started taking in shifts. I was one of the first and, in a dilemma about where to go, I took the plunge and booked a flight back to South Africa via London. My sister had young kids by then and I didn't want to interrupt her for longer than a couple of days, and anyway, there was now an extra incentive to go to South Africa. Jeandri.

I'd met Jeandri just before heading out to Afghanistan on this second tour – or, I should say, re-met. She and my sister had been at school together and our parents were good friends; in fact, my parents were renting a house from her family at the time. While I was there on that stint of leave she and her mum came over to visit my mum, and Jeandri and I got chatting. We had plenty in common – we both loved sports and the outdoors – and we went out for coffee a few times during my stay.

Afterwards, in Afghanistan, we kept in touch by email. It wasn't always easy, because very often I was out on operations for days or external camp communications would get shut down because a major incident had happened. News travels very quickly, so if something happened like a fatality or an assault on the base we were barred from communicating with the outside world so that nothing could be leaked.

Despite the challenges, it was nice to have someone to keep in touch with. Back in South Africa I caught up with various friends and Jeandri and I spent a lot of time together. It re-established the relationship we'd been trying to keep up via email but at the same time it left me feeling confused. In theory we were just friends, but especially when I got back to Afghanistan it felt like it could be more than that.

Even though I wasn't allowed to tell her anything about what we were doing out in the desert, I did try to keep up the exchange of emails with general conversation. It was a small link to the normality of the outside world. Eventually it got to a stage where I really looked forward to reading her emails and would feel disappointed or even hurt when I got back from a few days on operations to find my inbox empty.

After a few weeks of soul-searching, I made a decision. At least for as long as I was in Afghanistan, it was unfair on both of us to keep things going. We weren't actually a couple – our relationship was totally undefined – but I didn't want her holding back from meeting someone else when it was highly unlikely I'd ever go back to South Africa for good. Part of me also didn't want to hear her tell me she had met someone; I think it would have upset me. The whole thing was more drama and confusion than I needed in what was already a high-stress environment, so one day I sat down to write her an email cutting things off.

I remember that morning clearly. The camp was strangely quiet; there was nothing much going on. We didn't have any operations planned for that day, so after a morning run and breakfast I sent my email and headed off for a weapons session on the ranges. Later on there would be a gym session, camp admin, cleaning my boots and rifle, and whatever kind of dinner that day's head chef managed to rustle up.

It was a scorching-hot day at the height of summer, 19 August 2009, the day before my twenty-third birthday.

Life was about to change beyond all recognition.

VI

THE INCIDENT

As a soldier, it doesn't get much more exciting than seeing real action. Or at least that's how I felt that day in August 2009, coming towards the end of a tour I'd loved every minute of. There had been plenty of high-stress situations, plenty of difficult things to see, but I was doing a job I loved and was good at, surrounded by all my best mates – men I would die for and who would lay down their lives for me.

It wasn't an exaggeration to say that. Being in the army – the training we went through, but especially the situations we faced together in Afghanistan – gives you a bond with your fellow soldiers that's hard to explain to anyone who hasn't experienced it.

Although I was closer to some than others, I loved all those men in a way that went beyond friendship or even family. Maybe it was the utter trust we had in each other, the knowledge that we were all there for each other no matter what. I knew that I could rely on them completely; my life was in their hands. Later that night, it very literally would be.

As I've mentioned, the morning started very quietly, but around lunchtime an unexpected mission came in. We were called into the briefing room to be given our orders and detailed information about the target. It was a good mission – I could feel it in the air in the room. Every single man was alert and motivated, visibly kicking into gear and doing what he did best. I'd been on plenty of operations by that time, but still I felt a buzz of excitement.

Our objective was an IED facilitator we'd been after for a while, a high-value target who had so far always managed to escape our net. He was like a ghost, a man we'd always heard of but never found. By that stage of the conflict, IED facilitators had become almost more important to capture than high-ranking Taliban officials – although the leaders had the ultimate decision-making power, it was the IED facilitators who wreaked havoc on the ground. Many soldiers from all the nations present in Afghanistan had been horrifically injured or killed by IEDs by that time, not to mention the civilian casualties. Some facilitators had got so good that they started incorporating little trademarks into the bombs they built – always using certain equipment or constructing their devices in a particular way. They were like artists. We'd come across this one particular guy's handiwork many times, and now it was vital that we catch him.

The intel was solid and we felt good about the mission. I was going to be attached to a sniper, Grant. Together we'd be dropped off a short distance away from the village where the IED facilitator lived and would make our way in on foot, securing the perimeter and keeping an eye out for what we called 'diggers', hidden Taliban scouts who would be watching out for us. Stef and Benny would come in from the other side.

We were essentially security, while the rest of the team would abseil in and land on the guy's roof. Maintaining the element of surprise was crucial. First of all, we didn't want to let the target get away yet again. Secondly, it was fighting season and the general atmosphere was tense.

'Fighting season' came round every year in Afghanistan and was in effect the summer months. For farming communities it was a quiet period, the time in between planting and harvesting when there was little to be done in the fields, and traditionally these months had always been used to settle disputes or claim territory. It was the same in this conflict. Things always heated up in the summer, and as it turned out 2008 and 2009 would go on to be the bloodiest years of the war from a British military perspective.

In 2009, there was an extra reason for things being heated: for the first time in a long time, Afghanistan would be holding a general election. The vote was scheduled for 20 August and it was vital for the government that it be free, fair and safe. Our intel suggested that the IED facilitator we were targeting was planning to disrupt activity at the polling stations the next day. How exactly, we didn't know, but if we managed to get to him we would most likely be saving a good number of civilian lives.

Fully briefed and happy with the plan, we spent the rest of the day getting ready. Kit needed to be prepped, weapons cleaned, rigs adjusted – what we chose to carry where in the many pockets and pouches on our uniforms was personal preference – and then there was a gym session and dinner. We were picked up by the helicopters at around 11.30 p.m., so by the time Grant and I were dropped in a farmer's field it had just turned 20 August.

My twenty-third birthday.

I barely even registered that fact as we went about the mission, taking the very steps we'd been walked through in such detail that afternoon in the briefing room. Grant and I made our way slowly towards the target compound, observing anything and anyone that came in or out of the village. We ran from compound to compound, using a set of telescopic ladders to scale walls and climb on to the flat roofs of the buildings, from which we had a great view. We'd looked at the map beforehand to know exactly which compounds we wanted to access, and one by one we ticked them off. Everything went according to plan; there were hardly even any dogs to bark at us.

By the time we reached the target compound, the mission was wrapping up. The SBS boys had abseiled on to the roof, stormed the house and caught not only the IED facilitator but also ten other men who were planning to go out later that day as suicide bombers. We'd had no idea that they would be in the house as well, but there they were – suicide vests and all. The disruption they could have caused at the polling stations would have been massive, and the civilian casualty count enormous. We'd been incredibly fortunate to find them and didn't waste any time getting them roped together to move off the target.

The SBS boys were fantastic; it couldn't have been a more successful mission. It actually made the local news the next day because of the high-value target we'd succeeded in capturing. We were already elated on the way out of the village, Grant, Stef, Benny and I bringing up the rear to make sure the others could get out safely. Out in the desert we caught up with the back of the line, all of us moving as fast as we could towards the helicopter landing site (HLS).

The radio crackled into life. Despite the fact that it had been carefully checked and cleared, the pilots weren't happy with the designated HLS. It seemed that there was a compound too close to it, and they were worried that someone might try to fire a rocket-propelled grenade (RPG) or another weapon from it. Even small-arms fire could do severe damage to a helicopter if it was at close range. New coordinates came in over the network. We had no choice but to move away from an extraction route we knew was safe and into unknown desert territory.

By the time we were about half an hour into the walk, we were making slower progress than usual because of the eleven detainees we had with us. They were blindfolded and roped together, which made moving along difficult. Suddenly another call came in over the radio: movement had been spotted on the high ground to our right. We all cleared off the road and took cover in irrigation ditches, trying to make sense of the rapid chatter in our ears. Shouts came from the distance. We sent a couple of the Afghan soldiers with us forward to meet the shadowy figures approaching and find out who they were. A handful of compounds were located nearby, which would need to be searched as well. All of a sudden we'd found ourselves in a poor position, and I think more than one of us wished we could just have used the original HLS.

It was impossible to see which one of the men fired first, but AK47s crackled into the night. Before we knew it, we were in the middle of an intense firefight. Although we had the advantage of night-vision goggles and the element of surprise, what we didn't know was that we'd walked pretty much straight into the middle of a Taliban training camp. The compounds around us lit up with muzzle flashes and the C-130 Hercules circling silently overhead radioed in sighting after sighting of dug-in fighters. They were on all sides. We were trapped.

When a firefight like that breaks out, you switch on to autopilot. I've said it before and I'll say it again: I deeply admire the training we were given for the way it made so many actions into reflexes. I was capable of changing a magazine in six seconds without even realising I was doing it. We all could. And when Grant yelled, 'Change magazine!' and dropped flat on the ground to switch cartridges, I automatically fell to one knee to give him covering fire.

Rooting myself in a solid position, I concentrated on my sights. Because we didn't know exactly where the enemy was, there was little we could do but aim towards the flashes of incoming fire.

UNEQUIVOCAL

I was going through the motions, and although there was barely time to think of anything I did feel a brief flare of elation. I was young and invincible, just turned twenty-three and enjoying the best birthday surprise ever: an adrenaline-filled firefight alongside all my friends.

The next thing I knew, I'd been given a candle I couldn't blow out.

*****

Grant was probably down on the ground for less than ten seconds, but they were ten seconds that would change my life for ever. I saw the RPG before I heard it, its red glow filling up the corner of my night-vision goggles as it approached. The sound was delayed, a roar that got louder and louder until I could hear nothing else.

At the last second I twisted, bracing for impact, and it was this slight movement that probably saved me. The rocket clipped the telescopic ladders strapped to my back – heavy and unwieldy, they'd been hampering my movements and I would never have imagined feeling grateful for them – and exploded on impact, tearing off my arm and part of my leg with the force of its blast. If it hadn't been for the ladders, though, it would have exploded on contact with my back, and I wouldn't be here to write this book. The RPG also narrowly missed my sergeant Cas, whose daughter had been born just a few weeks before. He hadn't even met her yet.

In a story like this, there are so many 'what ifs'. The biggest one of all is probably 'what if the RPG hadn't hit me?' I've seen enough of war to know that it would have hit someone else – Cas or Grant or Ryan, perhaps, all of whom were near me. It's one of the many reasons why I don't for a second regret what happened to me or feel it was unfair. I would far rather have taken a hit – even died

– myself than see it happen to any one of those guys. A world in which Cas never got to meet his baby girl, now my goddaughter, is a world unthinkable to me.

The force of the impact knocked me out, and when I came to again I was lying on the ground several metres away. My eyes were stinging, my ears ringing, my mouth full of dust and grit. Although I dimly registered that I was on fire, my first thought was to keep shooting – I could still hear the firefight going on around me. Screams cut through the chaos; Grant was rolling on the ground somewhere nearby, yelling in agony. He'd been caught in the hail of shrapnel raining down from the exploded rocket and the backs of his legs were studded with molten-hot metal.

It was only when I realised I couldn't actually fire my weapon that I noticed my left arm was missing. Even then I took it surprisingly calmly. Because the nerves had been shredded I couldn't even really feel it, until Ryan started tightening the tourniquet on my arm under the medic's instructions, clamping it down to the bone in an effort to stop the bleeding. That was when the pain kicked in and I started screaming.

People used to talk about the 'Golden Thirty': the first thirty minutes after an accident being the most decisive in whether the casualty will live or die. Out there in Afghanistan it was more like 'Golden Ten'. The decisions that were made and the first aid that was given in those first ten minutes were what saved lives on the battlefield. We were all trained for it, and it could be something as simple as applying a tourniquet that would make the crucial difference – it certainly was in my case. If it hadn't been for what Ryan and the medic, Phil, did, working with frantic concentration in the middle of what was still a very intense firefight, I would have bled out on the desert floor.

As it was, I was still alive – but barely – when the helicopters came in. They were American Chinooks, part of a TF Brown call sign known as 'Flippers', and they were willing to come in where our own British helicopters weren't. I remember clearly the sound of the engines approaching, the whir of the blades and the clouds of sand and dust that enveloped us as they landed. Days later, in hospital, that sand would still be in my hair, but at that point I couldn't have cared less. I heard those helicopters and it was the sound of my salvation.

It was also a chance for me to finally let go.

On the ground I had been concentrating hard on the medic's face hovering above me, which occasionally disappeared from view as he threw his body across me to protect me from the storm of bullets unleashed by our own support aircraft. The C-130 Hercules above us was firing in a desperate attempt to subdue the enemy enough to get us out, and the incoming fire was so close it could easily have taken us out too.

Phil would use his own body as a shield for me, then pop back up and continue working. He was writing down as much information as he could on my forehead, assessing my injuries and keeping an eye on Ryan, who was still cranking the tourniquet round on my arm.

'Stay with me, Jaco, stay with me!' Phil kept yelling. I did my best. Although I knew that blood was still gushing out of my arm, I had no idea about the extent of the other injuries I'd sustained. The outer part of my left leg had been blasted away and shrapnel had ripped through my chest and abdomen, collapsing a lung and tearing my intestines. I was bleeding from just about every possible location, but strangely enough, the only thing I could think about was my ankle.

'My ankle, my ankle!' I kept moaning. 'Can you please just check it? Make sure it's there?'

'Your leg is fine, Jaco!' The medic was exasperated. 'We've got to take care of this arm here.'

I tried obediently to follow his instructions, but I was secretly convinced that no one was paying proper attention to my ankle. It was the worst pain I'd ever been in. As it turned out, I was right, but no one would find that out for a long time.

By this time my sergeant Wayne had made his way down the line to be with me. He had always been fiercely protective of me and now he refused to leave my side. It was Wayne who supervised me being loaded on to a stretcher – really just a big tarpaulin with various straps and buckles to hold the casualty in. Because of my injuries I couldn't be strapped in very tightly, but as the helicopters came down four Afghan soldiers hoisted the stretcher, ready to run.

I hit the ground almost instantly. The soldiers had started to run with no coordination whatsoever and I was jolted off the stretcher. I screamed as my body slammed into the ground. Wayne was there instantly, yelling profanities at the soldiers and physically pushing them away with the butt of his rifle. Wayne, Ryan, Phil and Dave, an SRR soldier, grabbed the handles instead, lifting me and running head-on into the powerful downdraught of the Chinooks. Stef and Cas were running beside them, my kit in their hands.

Inside the helicopter was chaos. Enemy fire was still coming in from all directions, bullets ricocheting off the Chinooks, and the helicopter guns were blazing loudly. Because it was an emergency extraction everyone had scrambled on to the three helicopters in no particular formation. The radios were going crazy and people were shouting as they tried to make sure no one had been left behind. To make matters worse, we still had eleven blindfolded detainees with us, who were scared shitless and unable to see what was going on. One of them was thrashing wildly as he was pushed into the helicopter and stepped hard on my injured leg. The pain was so intense I nearly passed out.

Wayne was livid. He seized the man by his shirt and threw him bodily to the other side of the helicopter. 'If anyone so much as touches Jaco again, I'll kill him!' he screamed. After that he sat down next to me and held my hand. I think he was talking to me, but I was slipping in and out of consciousness by then. Occasionally I did manage to squeeze his hand back.

Faces loomed above me. Phil's was still there, but now there was a new one as well – an American doctor was on board the Chinook. He was wearing an enormous helmet that made him look like something out of a sci-fi film, and he was constantly talking into his radio, communicating with the pilots and the field hospital. I could feel my clothes being cut away and Wayne pressing my hand, but for some reason I was fascinated by the TF Brown medic. He seemed so cool and collected.

Seeing that my arm was still pouring with blood, he stepped deliberately on to my shoulder, boot and all, and pressed down with his full weight. It was more effective than even the most tightly wound tourniquet, clamping off the blood supply at my shoulder so that I wouldn't bleed out through the artery in my arm. I cried out in agony, and it was shortly after that that I passed out for good. The last thing I remember was looking up at the medic standing on my shoulder and seeing him still talking away into his helmet as though it was the most normal thing in the world.

As the helicopters finally took off, I think I realised that we were safe.

The pain and the morphine were having their effect, of course, but at that moment I had a real sense of letting go. In the desert I had been focused so hard on the medic, on following his instructions, on not dying, but as the Chinooks lifted off I finally relaxed. Even if I did die, I thought, it would be OK. The boys were all safe and we were heading home.

*****

We were flown to an American forward operating base, FOB Sharona, in the mountains of northern Afghanistan. It was the closest field hospital, but when we arrived the US Special Forces weren't happy with us. They didn't want the Afghan forces and especially not the detainees knowing about the base, so almost as soon as Grant and I were unloaded the Chinooks took off again with the rest of the team. We were rushed to two waiting ambulances and once again I was half-dropped – this time by an American soldier who stumbled over a detainee.

I was so out of it by this point that I didn't even feel it. Scenes flickered past my eyes. I remember the strip lighting in the hospital corridors as I was wheeled along on a gurney, and then I was mumbling at the doctors and nurses around me to try to stop them from cutting my clothes. My desert boots were one of the most precious things to me in those days – the same ones I'd jumped into the sewage canal in – and I was desperately upset at the idea that they might cut them. It was the same with my rigger's belt.

'Don't cut it, don't cut it,' I was murmuring, but of course they ignored me. As I felt the boots go, I wanted to cry. Although I can't say I thought it at the time, I think I equated them with being a soldier – a life that I had chosen and which I loved above all things. As I was put on to that operating table, it was more than just a pair of boots that was being cut away. It was part of my identity.

Colin, my captain, Stef, Wayne and Phil stayed behind at FOB Sharona with me and Grant. I was taken away from them pretty quickly, but Stef and Colin were able to look through a little window in the operating room door to see me in surgery. Stef remembers seeing the doctors cut open my stomach and remove my internal organs one by one to clean them of shrapnel. He turned and walked away from the window, thinking, *how could anyone survive that?*

Colin saw what Stef saw and went outside for a cigarette, unable to watch either. As he was standing there, a nurse came out for a break herself.

'He's gone, isn't he?' Colin asked. 'He's brown bread.' (Cockney rhyming slang that was also the army term for dead.) He was thinking of all the paperwork he'd have to do, of breaking the news to my family. Of telling the rest of the guys, who had fought so hard to save me.

'Oh no,' said the nurse cheerfully, lighting up too. 'No, we've seen worse than that.'

'*Worse?*' Colin said afterwards that what really shook him was the calmness with which she uttered that statement. It was as if she had become completely numb to the horror.

She nodded. 'He's a fighter, that one, you can see it. He'll pull through. Don't worry.'

She was right. Even though my heart stopped twice on the operating table, the doctors and nurses worked tirelessly to bring me back to life. There were many things that conspired to save me that night, not least their incredible skill and dedication. The work that Ryan and Phil did out in the field, the TF Brown doctor bodily clamping my wound, even Wayne sitting there holding my hand – all of it kept me clinging on to life. And I was – am – a fighter. Even though part of me was ready to die if that was what was to be, my body and mind unconsciously fought back. Something in me knew it wasn't over yet. Not then. Not there.

Still under anaesthetic, I was flown back to Camp Bastion and from there to RAF Brize Norton. Although there wasn't a scheduled medical flight to the UK for another two days, the Special Forces we'd been working with managed to pull some strings and I was taken back almost immediately on a different plane. I was put into an induced coma for the flight, but just before I went under I remember being pushed on to the aircraft. My mouth was full of tubes and I couldn't talk, but I desperately wanted to get a message to Stef. I think I wanted him to speak to my mum, to tell her I was OK. Whatever it was, it was vitally important to me. Paul, B Company captain, and Taff, a sergeant, were with me and one of them produced a notepad to let me scrawl a message. I could barely even lift my hand and what came out was illegible, but they promised to pass it on to Stef.

That's my final memory of Afghanistan: my consciousness receding as I was rolled on to a waiting aircraft. I would spend the next few days in an induced coma, hooked up to machines in the Intensive Care Unit at Selly Oak Hospital in Birmingham. Although I had no sense of time passing, I was plagued by vivid dreams, in most of which I was about to die. I would wake up screaming and shouting before slipping back into an artificial sleep. And always, each time I came to, I was convinced I was still in Afghanistan.

VII

THE ROAD TO RECOVERY

The knock on the door is the thing feared most of all by anyone with a loved one in the army. Because my sister was living in London at the time, I'd designated her my 'next of kin' contact, so it was she who received the knock early one morning in late August. Two men dressed in black told her I'd been in an accident in Afghanistan and that she should drive to Birmingham as soon as possible. Lizanne took the news with as much composure as she could and when the men had gone, she picked up the phone to make the hardest call of her life.

'Why are you phoning at this time of the morning?' my mum asked, still in her pyjamas in her flat in Pretoria.

'It's Jaco,' Lizanne managed to say. 'He's been in an accident.'

'Where?'

'In Afghanistan.'

'Is he dead?' my mum wanted to know.

'I don't know.'

'Well, is he alive?'

'I don't know that either.'

Although it might sound incredible not to tell a relative whether their loved one is still alive or not, like many seemingly inexplicable things in the army there is a logic to it. At that point I was in an induced coma somewhere over Europe; although I was alive I was in a very fragile state and anything could have happened to me by the time I arrived in Birmingham. It would have been deeply cruel to tell Lizanne I was alive only for her to get to the hospital and find me dead. So the army went for the next best thing: wait and see.

My mum broke down on the phone, screaming and crying. Lizanne calmed her as best she could and a few minutes later a cousin arrived – my sister had already phoned her to tell her to go and be with my mum. She also gave my mum a telephone number for the British Embassy, which arranged a visa and booked her a flight. Less than twelve hours later, she was on a plane to London.

When my mum talks about that journey, during which she felt like she was in a dream, she always tells the story of Annette, the lady who sat next to her on the plane. A complete stranger, she started talking to my mum and asked why she was flying to London. When Mum explained, Annette took her hand and said simply, 'He will be OK.'

'How can you say that?' my mum asked her.

'I know, because I see you're a strong believer. Your son will be OK. I'm praying Jaco will be OK.'

They prayed together for the rest of the flight. My mum's faith is something that has always seen her through.

Meanwhile, Lizanne and Hans were on their way to Selly Oak, the main military hospital in the UK, which was later relocated to the Queen Elizabeth Hospital, also in Birmingham. They were already there by the time I arrived at the Intensive Care Unit (ICU) and were shown to my bedside as soon as I'd been settled. Finally Lizanne knew that I was still alive.

Except the bed she was being shown didn't appear to contain her brother.

The soldier lying in it had a puffy face and unkempt hair, shaven on one side and long on the other. A moustache drooped over the oxygen mask covering his mouth.

'No,' said Lizanne. 'There's been a mistake. That's not my brother.'

It was mainly the moustache that threw her, a new addition since the last time I'd been on leave. Lots of the guys grew beards or moustaches in Afghanistan and, as with many things, Stef and I had turned the moustache into a bit of a competition. The piss got taken out of us all the time, but I'd grown quite fond of mine. When I eventually woke up to discover that Lizanne had asked the nurses to shave it off, I wasn't best pleased to find my hard work ruined.

It would be several more days until I woke up. Mum and Lizanne sat by my bed during all the visiting hours. Mum cried the first time she saw me, and when Lizanne tried to comfort her the nurse said, 'Let her cry.' They reassured her that I already knew about the loss of my arm, but what really bothered my mum was the state of my hair, which had been partly shaved off and still had half the Afghan desert in it. They couldn't wash it in case I had an undetected spinal injury, so eventually they just shaved it all off. Knowing the care I usually took with my appearance, my mum was devastated to see me like that. I think part of her felt I no longer looked like her son.

The first time I woke up properly was during the night. I asked for my mum and they phoned her in the hospital flat she and Lizanne were staying in. Mum came running in her pyjamas and flung herself into my room.

'Are you OK?' was the first thing I said to her. Her answer was to burst into tears.

The coming days and weeks passed in a blur. I was moved from the ICU on to Ward S5, which was still a very high level of care, only this time there were other wounded servicemen around me. Most of the time I was out of it on medication, so I barely remember the stream of visitors that passed by my bed. At one point a group of officers came to see me and asked me questions about the night of my incident; other times there were friends from the army or London. Mum and Lizanne were there all the time. I worried about Mum a lot, especially when the vivid nightmares I was having spilled over into real life. In one of them, I dreamed that the hospital was under attack – all the doctors had been shot, the nurses were being lined up against the wall, and I was trying to overpower an attacker to get his weapon away from him. It all seemed so real that when I woke up I was horrified to see a strange man looming over my mum where she sat beside my bed.

'Who's that man?' I kept asking.

'He's a nurse, Jaco,' they reassured me, but I wasn't having any of it. I ordered the other nursing staff to take my mum away to safety.

In another dream, I was put through a big machine, a bit like an MRI scanner. It scanned my entire body and, using my right arm as a template, made me a new left arm that appeared as I slid out. I was wheeled into an operating theatre to have the arm attached, and all of a sudden I was complete again. When I woke up I was desperately confused.

'Where's my arm gone?' I asked the nurses. When they tried to explain I waved them away. 'No, you don't understand. I just had a new one made.'

Even when I was fully conscious, I spent a lot of the time convinced that I was in a hospital in Afghanistan. I could hear the sound of helicopters all day long, like I did on the base; I could even smell the sand and sweat of the desert. Probably I could just smell myself.

As I slowly regained awareness of the world around me, I started to sit up and pay attention to my surroundings. One of the first things I did was give Lizanne my bank cards and ask her to go and buy me some clothes. I'd been given a little kit in hospital – a grey Help for Heroes tracksuit and T-shirt, a razor, toothpaste, shaving foam and so on – but I didn't have any clothes of my own. The kit I'd been wearing in Afghanistan had been cut off me and everything else had been handed over to the army as part of the investigation into what happened on the night of my incident. Eventually I got some of my kit and personal items back, including the webbing I'd been wearing when I got hit, which turned up about eighteen months later. It was bloodied and burned and torn to pieces by shrapnel. I kept one pouch and gave the rest of it back.

Ward S5 wasn't a regular hospital ward. Because we were in a military hospital, we were paraded (given a roll call and inspected) every morning and still had to make sure we looked presentable, neatly shaved and with our hair cut. Anyone who couldn't shave himself would be helped by a nurse. There were lots of rules, but it helped – this was the world I was used to, after all. Suddenly being cast back into civilian life would have been far too much of a shock on top of my injury.

The ward worked on a kind of tier system, in which the newest and most badly injured arrivals were placed furthest away from the door. When I arrived from the ICU that was where I was, in the furthest row of beds, and over time I was gradually moved up towards the door. It gave me hope each time I was moved, because beyond the door was Headley Court – an almost legendary name among us soldiers there on the ward. From a very early stage, the aim was always to get to Headley Court as quickly as possible. Headley Court meant serious rehab, interspersed with stints of living in the real world. Headley Court meant getting better and re-joining my unit.

It would be many days until I got there, though, and during

that time I got to know plenty of new faces. That year, 2009, was one of the worst years of the conflicts in Afghanistan and Iraq, and the ward was always full. Everyone was at a different stage of injury, from the very weak, bed-bound guys in the furthest row to the ones who were progressing through rehab and would zoom around the ward in their wheelchairs. I found it inspiring to watch them; it gave me something to work towards. There was also always someone worse off than me, which meant I never had a chance to feel sorry for myself. Like Jack, who was in the bed opposite me for a while. He was eighteen years old and a triple amputee.

I saw Jack struggle with the idea that he would always need someone there to do things for him – for the rest of his life. He's actually made an amazing recovery and even drives these days, but back then in the hospital things looked very different, as they did to all of us. It's a very hard prospect to have to face when you're eighteen or twenty-three – or any age, really – especially when you've been as active and independent as we were. In the space of seconds I had gone from invincible to incapacitated, and I was terrified of being physically dependent on someone for the rest of my life.

I had accepted the loss of my arm pretty well, but it was my leg that was causing concern. My knee was fractured, some of the wounds had become infected, the skin graft I'd been given wasn't taking properly and there was talk of having to amputate. If that had been the case, it would have been above the knee. Whether it's a knee or an elbow, losing a joint always dramatically restricts what you can or can't do in the future and I was horrified by the thought of eventually losing both left limbs. Every time I made a little bit of progress – when a wound finally healed or I managed to get into a wheelchair for the first time – I was elated.

Mum had gone back to South Africa by this time, but Lizanne

still came regularly at weekends and I had lots of other visitors. They distracted me from my own thoughts, gave me a reason to be cheerful and strong and encouraged me to keep pushing down the road to Headley Court. One day I even got a surprise phone call, for which I was summoned to the nurses' station. I was so confused that the person wasn't just calling my phone, but then I lifted the receiver and heard Jeandri's voice.

News of my injury had made it back to my friends in South Africa pretty quickly, but it had taken Jeandri a couple of weeks to figure out how to contact me – and whether she even wanted to. After all, the day before my incident I'd sent her an email calling things off. In the end she decided not to respect my decision and my heart leaped when I heard her voice on the other end of the line. It was so nice to talk to someone outside the situation I was in and especially to feel that a girl might still be interested in me. Looking down at myself, I felt incredibly insecure. At the very least I would be wheelchair-bound for who knew how long, I was missing an arm and I had a colostomy bag. That was something I'd only ever associated with the elderly. I wasn't sure what the future would bring, but chatting to Jeandri brought with it a rush of hope and I clung on to the feeling she gave me.

Being injured opened up a whole new world, one I hadn't known existed before. Much like the army or the world of professional cycling, it's a place you don't understand or even have much awareness of until you're in it. Suddenly I was learning just what is possible with an injury, hearing stories of men and women who had recovered and gone on to do amazing things, even going back to serve in Afghanistan with a hand or a leg missing. There were opportunities I'd never even known existed and I held on to the idea of them as hard as I could.

Although there was definitely an element of not knowing what lay ahead – I knew I would get better, but I didn't know what 'better' meant – I was utterly determined to work hard and make my recovery as good as it could be. I exercised every day in my hospital bed, using resistance bands to build up muscle strength, and eventually I progressed to wheelchair-based rehab. Headley Court was always my goal and, beyond that, Afghanistan. I didn't know quite what the future would look like, but there was never any doubt in my mind that I would re-join the regiment. Being a soldier wasn't just my job. It was who I was.

*****

After a few weeks, the day finally came for me to transfer to Headley Court. Set in the Surrey countryside, Headley Court Defence Medical Rehabilitation Centre was then the leading rehab unit for wounded service personnel and a major base for the charity Help for Heroes. Before leaving Selly Oak I'd been given a brochure detailing all the facilities, like hydrotherapy pools, prosthetics workshops and a special lower-limb programme. I'd be moving into a series of rotations: four weeks of intensive rehab at the centre followed by four weeks back at my unit in St Athan, where the Parachute Regiment's occupational therapists would work with me. With all the wounded returning from Afghanistan and Iraq, Headley Court was too full for us all to be there all the time. We also needed to start getting used to life in a more 'normal' setting, away from the care of nurses and therapists.

A big personal step in my recovery was getting off pain medication, which was something I was determined to do as quickly as possible. I've always hated taking painkillers, but for obvious reasons I was on incredibly high doses. It would take many months, but I gradually started leaving them out, forcing myself through six hours between doses instead of the usual three, and eventually through entire nights. Sometimes I did have to give in and take them, but I always tried only to medicate myself when I really felt I needed to. These days I don't take any routine pain medication at all, something I'm very proud of.

My arm bothered me with phantom pains – because of the nerve damage I could still feel it, as I do to this day – so I was often kept awake at night by my missing limb throbbing and the feeling of my fingers being crushed. Not being able to scratch or massage them was agony. Phantom limb pain is a common problem for amputees and at Headley Court I started doing daily mirror therapy to help. I had a small box with a mirror on the interior side wall, which I would place so that my stump was on the outside, hidden behind the mirror, and my right arm was reflected. Looking at the mirror, the brain is tricked into thinking that the reflection of the right arm is actually the left arm, so whenever I moved my right hand it felt as though my missing left hand was moving. Making a fist and opening my fingers very slowly released the discomfort of my left hand feeling crushed.

My leg was still the main issue and the cause of most of my pain. My ankle in particular was incredibly tender; even the weight of a bed sheet on it would cause me to cry out. I had to do a lot of gritting my teeth and bearing it. Although I knew I wouldn't be able to put weight on my left leg for a long time – the muscles were either missing or wasted and my flesh wounds and skin graft were still healing – I was determined not to spend the rest of my life in a wheelchair. One day I would walk again, and getting to Headley Court was the first step in that process.

I had only been there for a matter of days when disaster struck. I picked up a virus from somewhere, which rapidly turned into an infection. With my body already weakened, I was unable to fight back. Before I knew it I'd been sent back to Selly Oak, urgently in need of hospital care.

Going back to Birmingham was a huge setback for me. I had been pushing so hard to get better, concentrating on every little improvement I made, and now all of a sudden I had taken several steps backwards. I was back in a hospital environment, where the guys around me were more recently injured and completely unsure about what the future held – there wasn't such a positive attitude to recovery as I'd briefly encountered at Headley Court. Not that they weren't determined as well, but they were just at the beginning of the road.

More than that, though, I was on my own. When I'd been in hospital the first time I'd had my mum, Lizanne and Hans, and a constant flood of visitors. Now I was alone with my thoughts and for the first time was able to reflect properly on what had happened to me. Until then I had always put on a brave face, smiling for and joking with my visitors, trying to prove to them that I was going to be OK. I'd been trying to prove it to myself as well. I don't think I'd realised just how tough the journey was going to be and now I was getting my first glimpse of it.

My attitude had always been that I would be fine, that in a couple of months I would be walking again, probably back with my regiment before the end of the year, learning to fire a gun with a prosthetic. Deep down, I simply hadn't accepted the fact that I'd lost my arm, was still in danger of losing a leg and had a colostomy bag attached. I'd only been living in the moment, using a bravado attitude to push away the truth. There in my hospital bed on my own, it all suddenly sank in. That was when the demons in my head started.

Many nights I lay in my bed crying, overwhelmed by loneliness and my fear of the future. I missed my friends, I missed Afghanistan,

I missed the job that I did and the person I'd been. I was coming to the realisation that life would never be the same again, and at the thought of having to create a new life for myself – for the person I was now – I often wished I'd never survived. I would rather have died on the battlefield than have to face up to my future. I didn't see how I was going to have any kind of quality of life with the injuries I'd sustained.

I might never be able to run or even walk again, and I just wasn't sure I could cope. I questioned the future and my ability to deal with it and, at the same time, I felt a wave of anger and bitterness. Why had it happened to *me*? And why had I survived? Should I even still be here? The nights were long and dark and full of doubts, and they spilled over into the days as well. Soon I had nothing but grief, loneliness and despair.

In the midst of all this darkness were occasional flashes of light, when my belief in myself would flare up again. Then I was more determined than ever to get back to the army, back to battalion, back to Afghanistan, and I bitterly resented the fact that I was stuck in a hospital bed. Sitting there, I started figuring things out for myself – what kind of prosthetic I'd need to be able to hold a rifle, for example.

That one was quite easy, but then my mind would move on to changing a magazine. I had no doubt that I'd be able to do it, but I also knew it would take me far longer than the six seconds I'd needed before. And that was a problem, because for the length of time it took me to change a magazine, my partner was exposed to more danger by giving me covering fire. It didn't matter whether it took me thirty seconds, a minute or five minutes – anything over ten seconds was putting his life at risk for longer than necessary.

It slowly dawned on me that going back to Afghanistan wouldn't just involve satisfying myself and showing the world what I could do. It would involve being the guy that others relied on and placing more lives than just my own at risk if I wasn't able to do the job I was there for properly. The knowledge that it was about more than just me really sank in and I started questioning why I was so determined to return. What did I have to prove by going back? And to whom? Yes, I had loved Afghanistan – loved the army lifestyle, loved the career I had chosen, loved the work I did and the men I lived among. But to satisfy my own deluded needs, I'd have to be willing to put other men at risk of also getting injured or, even worse, killed. I knew in my heart that was something I couldn't do.

There was one particular night when all these realisations caught up with me and I reached the bottom of the well. I broke down completely in my hospital bed, sobbing uncontrollably for hours as a tide of emotions rose up inside me and flowed out. I'd spent so much time being brave, putting on a face in front of my family, friends and even myself, when really I wasn't OK and didn't know if I ever would be again.

That night forced me to accept the fact that things were different now. I most likely wouldn't go back to Afghanistan; my career in the army was probably over. The road ahead was going to be long and hard, with absolutely no guarantees and many, many frustrations. I was not invincible, and that was all right.

It was a tough night, probably the toughest of my life. And yet it was a night I needed to finally accept what had happened to me, for my mind to make peace with my body. I woke up the next morning feeling somehow lighter and refreshed, more complete than I had done for a while.

My mind – which had constantly been pushing at my body, willing it to get better and frustrated by what it couldn't do – had accepted my physical condition. From that moment on, my mind and body worked together. I was aware of how hard the road ahead was, but I was finally willing to take it.

*****

Even after that night there were many more difficult days to come. My recuperation from the infection was slow and I was still on my own a lot. Lizanne tried to come as often as she could, but she and Hans both worked in London and I felt strongly that they needed to get on with their lives. I spent many days just sitting on my bed, unable and unwilling to do anything.

On one of those afternoons of nothingness the warden came up and told me I had a visitor. 'It's another lad from the Paras,' he said. 'He got injured a couple of years back and came in for a check-up, and when he heard about you he asked if he could come and say hello.'

'OK,' I shrugged. 'He can come in.'

I wasn't quite sure what to expect – 'injured' could mean many things, as I'd learned – but when Tom whizzed in in his hi-tech wheelchair, a massive grin plastered on his face, I couldn't believe my eyes. I'd never seen a triple amputee out of bed before, let alone one who genuinely seemed to be enjoying life.

Tom chatted to me for a long time about Headley Court, explaining the rehab process in great detail and singing the centre's praises. I'd only been there briefly so I was keen to learn as much as I could, and also to know about life after rehab. We got on to cars somehow – I've always loved them and driving was one of the things I was worried about – so I asked him straight out if he drove.

'Yeah, and *do* I drive!' he said brightly. 'You should see my adaption systems. And by the way,' he grinned. 'It's a Porsche 911.'

THE ROAD TO RECOVERY

I was stunned. Tom had arrived like a ray of positivity in my life at a time that I needed it most. He opened my eyes to the world beyond injury and gave me reason to hope. I'll forever be grateful to him for that.

Aside from being a setback that I needed mentally in order to be able to move forward, my second stay in hospital gave me my ankle back. It was still intensely painful and so I asked the doctors to give me another scan. It turned out to be pretty badly broken – an injury they'd somehow overlooked in dealing with all the others.

As I was due for another operation on my leg anyway, they opened it up and put in some metal plates to pin the bones back in place. I came round from the anaesthetic and for the first time in weeks my ankle was pain-free. It felt so good I could have leaped out of bed that minute and run around the ward.

Having that nagging pain lifted from me proved to be a big motivator. I came out of Selly Oak a different person: my eyes wider open, my mind more settled and content to take things one day at a time. I was going to get better – I always knew that – but this time it would be without any pressure. One step at a time.

*****

Back at Headley Court at the end of October I made rapid progress. I loved the positive mindset of the place, being surrounded by guys who were often far worse off than me but always carried on despite their pain and frustration. We spurred each other on, often simply by taking the piss. I started feeling better in myself and saw every day as a tiny step towards independence.

Learning to focus on the small things was a great way of measuring and feeling good about my recovery. After weeks of physiotherapy on my arm I was able to move on to remedial instruction (RI) and finally a fitting for a prosthetic arm. The RI sessions taught me how to do things for myself again – basic tasks like cutting up food or opening a bottle. It involved a lot of thinking outside the box, as well as aids like sticky mats that helped me to hold things in place.

A bread board, for example: I would place it on a sticky mat to keep it still, while a spike on the board held the loaf. Then I could cut a slice with a normal bread knife. Just doing something like that gave me an intense feeling of satisfaction. I'll also always remember the day I finally peeled and chopped a banana for myself. It was a big moment.

As well as learning how to cope with daily life again, I worked hard on my physical wellbeing. I'd do exercises in the gym to keep the muscles I did have strong and active – I wouldn't be able to bear weight on my left leg for a while, but my right leg didn't have to suffer because of it. I also needed to work on my left shoulder muscles and spent hours doing scar-tissue treatment.

In early November my mum flew over from South Africa again, this time accompanied by Jeandri. We'd stayed in touch over the intervening weeks and she'd suggested coming to visit. I was extremely nervous before she arrived, aware of how different I looked and afraid that she wouldn't like what she saw. I needn't have worried – she was great. She was so caring and willing to help, which meant a great deal to me.

At that stage I couldn't see how any other woman would be willing to step into my world, so the fact that she was in it already and seemed willing to stay was a huge thing for me.

She and Mum stayed in London at first and then in an army welfare house closer to Headley Court. I was on a rehabilitation admission, but there were visiting hours every day and at weekends I was able to go to London with them. Eventually my admission came to an end – the next one would be starting in a couple of weeks – so we all went back to stay with Lizanne and Hans for a while. They had to have their flat checked out by Headley Court staff to make sure it was wheelchair-friendly.

Being in London had a huge impact on me. Even though the city is comparatively easy to get around in a wheelchair, especially with people to help you, everything we did seemed to be a struggle.

One day we went to a restaurant on the South Bank. My leg was sticking straight out in front of me and people were constantly walking into it, and then we got to the steps by the Hungerford Bridge. Lizanne helped me to hop up them while Jeandri carried the wheelchair, and even though neither of them said anything I was intensely frustrated on their behalf. In the restaurant things weren't any better – the staff were flustered by moving tables around to fit us in and I kept needing to be wheeled to the toilets to change my colostomy bag. I felt utterly helpless all day; it seemed that the more I tried to do things, the more restricted I became. I was depressed and angry and hated the thought that the rest of my life would look like this.

That day a subtle shift took place. I enjoyed the rest of the time I had with Mum and Jeandri, but when they went home and I returned to Headley Court for my next session of rehab it was with new determination. I'd made my decision: life was not going to be something I didn't want it to be. I was going to learn to walk again.

My goal was Christmas, just a matter of weeks away. I wanted to be able to fly home to South Africa and not be in a wheelchair – I didn't care whether I still needed a walking frame or a stick, but I was determined to be standing on my own two feet.

The doctors were a bit nervous about me flying that distance, but eventually they agreed to sign me off if I was able to pass various tests before I left. From that moment on, all my focus was on them.

The first stage was to get out of my wheelchair. I'll never forget standing up again for the first time – I'd actually forgotten how tall I was. I'm not a very tall man, but after months spent sitting down, in a wheelchair or hospital bed or on the sofa, I'd grown used to looking up at people all the time.

Standing up straight made me feel a bit dizzy and looking someone in the eye felt utterly amazing. It was a big breakthrough for me and boosted my self-confidence no end. I couldn't apply any weight to my left leg at all, but I was able to let it hang down straight and slowly start to move it back and forth.

Eventually I progressed to using the treadmill. There was a special one at Headley Court for exactly this purpose, fitted with an enormous air bag that had a pair of what looked like cycling shorts in the middle. I'd be lifted into the shorts and the air bag was inflated so it could take my weight, holding me up in the centre of the treadmill.

At first it took 100 per cent of my weight, my feet barely touching the moving band so my muscles could learn how to make a walking motion again. Then I took two or three per cent of my own weight back, four, five, ten, twenty. Slowly, slowly I built up my muscles and taught my body how to take steps.

I worked incredibly hard on my recovery, often to the point of physical exhaustion. The deadline I had set myself was fast approaching and even though no one else was putting pressure on me I knew that this was something I had to achieve for myself. A few days before Christmas I was at Heathrow Airport, where Lizanne had booked wheelchair assistance to take me to the departure gate. That was going to be the last time I sat in a wheelchair. When I got off the plane in Johannesburg, I was going to walk.

And walk I did.

I hadn't told Jeandri or anyone in my family, so when I came through the door in Arrivals – unsteady and leaning heavily on crutches but on my own two feet – they couldn't believe their eyes. My mum absolutely loved the surprise; she'd been worried about manoeuvring my wheelchair around her tiny flat and was just overwhelmed to see my progress. Strangely, though, Jeandri didn't seem quite so happy about it.

After Christmas I left Mum's in Pretoria and went to stay with Jeandri and her family in Witbank for a few days. Most of my friends were still there and I was looking forward to catching up with them all again. It was great to see them but I also found it very exhausting – I couldn't spend much time on my feet, I was still in a lot of pain and taking medication that made me need to sleep for long hours, and going out anywhere was made more difficult by my colostomy bag.

The diet in South Africa is different – spicier and more meat-heavy – and I found myself constantly having to change my bag with my intestines working overtime. I found that very embarrassing so I preferred not to go out for long stretches of time if possible. It was also something I worried about a lot when it came to thinking about a potential relationship with Jeandri.

Although Jeandri still seemed caring, things were different. My surprise had backfired and she was very upset that I hadn't told her I was walking again – she'd spent a lot of time worrying about how to get me around in a wheelchair for nothing. I could also see her realising my limitations, which maybe hadn't been that clear to her in the UK with lots of other people around to help. Although I was unwilling to admit it at the time – I was still just glad that a girl was willing to talk to or even look at me – I think she believed that I'd be that way for the rest of my life.

I found it hard leaving South Africa again. A big part of me wanted to stay there, but the army was never going to let me go until I'd completed my rehab and could live fully independent of its care. I had no idea how long that was going to take or whether I would even end up leaving the army altogether, so I returned to the UK with a heavy heart and the feeling that there was still a long road ahead of me.

At the same time, I clung on to the hope that my relationship with Jeandri could become something more. We lived on two different continents, but I was sure we would be able to figure something out.

It wasn't to be. Not long after I got back to the UK she told me she wanted to leave things as they were: just friends. I think she thought I'd reached the point where I was as good as I was ever going to be and that wasn't something she wanted to be tied to for the rest of her life.

She was entitled to her feelings, of course, but they devastated me. I felt heartbroken and my already low self-esteem took a further dive. *Who is going to want to be with someone like me: a guy with only one arm, half a leg missing and a colostomy bag?* I asked myself. I found it very hard that someone else couldn't see a future in me, had effectively given up on me, and it brought back all my doubts.

January 2010 saw me return to Headley Court with my body stronger but my mind and spirits at a low ebb. Despite the amazing progress I'd made in the past few months and the fact that I was beginning to be able to walk again, I still felt like my identity was missing.

I was living from one day to the next with a strong sense of who I had been but no idea of who I was now.

It was time to find my self again.

VIII

BABY STEPS

Recovering from a life-changing injury is a long process, one that goes on for many years beneath the surface even after the wounds have healed. When I returned to the UK in January 2010 to resume rehab after a couple of weeks in South Africa, I was physically far more able than I had been in the autumn, but recovery was still a long way off. Even though I never had a major period of depression again, there were plenty of ups and downs.

Some days I was simply too tired and had to force myself through whatever rehab or gym session was on the cards. Other days it was a mental battle to get through the plateau I seemed to have reached in my recovery. After weeks of seeing almost daily progress, I found myself at a stage where I wasn't getting any worse – but nor was I getting better.

Jeandri's decision to break off all ties had also hit me hard. Back at Headley Court and focusing on lower-leg rehabilitation, I found myself surrounded by new faces who were at very different stages of their recovery from me. Some hadn't even been injured in action, but had been in accidents during training exercises held in the UK. They had a very different mindset to both injury and recovery, and with my contact to Jeandri gone as well I often felt very lonely.

The one thing that saved me during this time was my relationship with the McDonald family. John McDonald had come into my life in the autumn of 2009 when he had donated a few front-row tickets for a Matchroom Boxing 'Prizefighter' event to Headley Court. Various trips were always being organised by the centre staff – we might have the chance to go to a football match, the cinema or a West End musical – and this was one I was lucky enough to get a place on.

That evening around ten of us loaded up into a van and were driven to the ExCel Centre in London, where we had a close-up view of all the action and were bought several rounds of drinks by the people sitting near us. It was one of my first times out in public with a group of wounded servicemen and I was impressed by how many people wanted to talk to us and hear our stories.

John also came to talk to us after the event, making his way down the line and speaking to every man in turn. A former Paratrooper himself, he had gone on to work as a sports commentator and ring announcer for Matchroom Boxing after an accident during a training jump had broken his neck and ended his army career. I didn't know any of this at the time – to me he was just a generous supporter of Help for Heroes and Headley Court – so when he stopped to speak to me we were amazed to discover that we'd both served in 1 Para, B Company.

John seemed especially excited to have met me and started reeling off a list of names of people he'd served with. I only knew one or two of them – he's old enough to be my dad and had served well before my time – but he gave me his card and told me we should keep in touch. The next day I dropped him a line to say thank you for a great evening, and out of this grew an email conversation that culminated in a phone call a couple of Fridays later.

'So, what are you doing this weekend?' John asked once we'd finished discussing mutual acquaintances in the Paras.

'Oh, nothing,' I said. 'Everyone's going home for the weekend, so I'll probably just sit here and watch films with a couple of the other lads. We might get to go to the cinema.'

This was quite a standard weekend for me during an admission to Headley Court – most people went home for the weekend, but because the regiment in St Athan was so far away and I didn't want to disturb Lizanne's family plans all the time, I usually stayed in the centre along with one or two other guys. It was quite lonely, but I was used to it. John, however, was appalled.

'No, no,' he said, 'that will never do. You're coming to have dinner with us. I'll come and collect you; I'm getting in the car right now.'

It was the beginning of what would become an incredibly close relationship with John and his entire family. That Friday evening I met his wife, Sharon, and his four boys, Darren, Johnny, Anthony and Christian, whom I fitted exactly into the middle of in terms of age.

From the first moment we all got along incredibly well – we shared a love of sports and a similar sense of humour – and I was overwhelmed by their closeness as a family and generosity in opening their home to me. For the rest of the year, until I flew to South Africa for Christmas, I spent almost every weekend there, and John was there to pick me up at Heathrow when I came back in early January.

As well as all the practical care he gave me in welcoming me into his family, John was a wonderful emotional support. Over time he's become like a father to me and I've found myself able to open up to him about things I could never have told my own dad. During those first couple of weeks back, when I missed South Africa and Jeandri and felt frightened and confused about what the future would bring, John stepped up to be the father I needed.

He spoke to me a lot about similar feelings he had had when

a terrible accident had ended the career he loved, sharing stories from his experience of injury and recovery and reassuring me that in the end everything would be OK. I will forever be grateful to him for guiding and mentoring me every step of the way, even when I felt that next step was just too hard to take.

We had a lot of deep conversations over the months, but there were plenty of laughs as well. The boys became like brothers to me and we spent hours at the weekend playing *Call of Duty* or *Fifa*, taking the piss out of each other and sitting around in the hot tub. To start with I couldn't get in the water at all, so I would sit on the edge in a parka and beanie, my injured left leg stretched out to the side and my right leg in the water. Gradually easing my limbs into that hot tub was also a way of marking progress in my recovery, and when several months down the line the moment finally arrived when I was fully in the water, all five of us started cheering crazily in celebration.

I also vividly remember the Friday evening I arrived at the house with a new prosthetic to show off. It was an electrical arm that weighed a tonne and was operated through sensors at the top. If I squeezed my biceps the hand would open; if I squeezed my triceps the hand would close; if I squeezed both together it would switch into a different mode in which I could operate the fingers individually.

There were almost no limits to what I could do by invisibly squeezing my muscles – as we found out when I made an accidental series of flexes and ended up with only the middle finger pointing up and the hand rotating round and round. The five of us nearly died laughing.

John and his family were also there for me just a few weeks later when I went through a colostomy reversal. It was something I had started pushing for almost as soon as I came back from

BABY STEPS

Christmas in South Africa: of all the things to happen to me, it was the colostomy procedure I had found the most debilitating. Constantly having to think about the practicalities of where and when I could change my bag was stopping me from doing things I wanted to, like going out with friends or spending time with the regiment in St Athan.

It could be incredibly degrading as well – many times during a hard workout in the gym it would start leaking, spilling its contents all over my shirt. I blamed the colostomy bag in part for Jeandri's unwillingness to take our relationship any further, and I knew that until I'd got rid of it I'd never feel completely better in myself.

When the operation date came through for mid-February I was elated, but coming round from the anaesthetic in Birmingham's Queen Elizabeth Hospital I felt nothing but fear that I'd made the wrong decision.

The pain was like nothing I'd ever felt before – especially when I had to put the procedure to the test by going to the loo again for the first time. My abdomen had been sliced right through – all the scar tissue, all the muscles I'd spent months of rehabilitation working on – and the wound I'd been left with was big and ugly. When John saw it for the first time his face said it all. He was horrified.

The McDonalds looked after me for about a week before I transferred back to Headley Court, where there were nurses on hand to help me clean the operation site and gradually remove the staples. With my newly severed muscles I had to go back several steps in my rehab programme, but as soon as the wound had healed and I realised that the reversal procedure had been successful I started making incredible leaps forward.

The amount of confidence I had regained was unbelievable and it was around that time that I stopped doubting whether I would make a full recovery. I still didn't have a clear picture of how the future would look, but I was about to have the opportunity to try out different versions.

*****

Before coming to the UK I had seen snow once in my life. Basic Training in Catterick had acquainted me with it more closely, but my experience was still limited to running around and playing army rather than doing any kind of winter sport. That didn't stop me from signing up for Exercise Snow Warrior, a trip run by Headley Court in March 2010 that took a group of us out to Bavaria for a week of skiing.

I had never strapped on a pair of skis, but for this trip that didn't matter in the slightest. All of us were beginners to some extent – even the people who had skied before were having to relearn how to do it with their injuries.

Those who had lost legs were taught how to use mono-skis, in which you sit down in a frame and use your arms to steer, but despite the continuing weakness of my left leg I was going to learn to ski on my own two feet. On our first day we were divided into groups and we absolute novices headed out to the baby slope.

My first instructor for the week was Rick, an army interpreter and experienced skier who has since become a good friend. He started us off doing snowploughs on a slope so shallow it was almost flat, but still it didn't take much for me to fall over. My right leg was strong and capable of controlling my ski, but none of the signals in my left leg seemed to be firing straight.

That ski would be all over the place, governed by the snow, and as we moved higher up the slopes I was constantly getting tangled up and collapsing to my left. It was funny in part – and also embarrassing, especially when groups of five-year-olds would whizz past me without a care in the world – but my competitive nature meant that I often felt frustrated. Even when I'm trying a completely new sport I want to be able to do it as best as I can.

Midway through the week we switched instructors and I found myself in the care of Sally. Also a good friend now, she is without doubt one of the most caring and compassionate people I have ever met. Her commitment to the wounded is boundless and she genuinely puts others before herself. She also has a bit of a wild side to her – her approach was far more about enjoyment than technique and I soon found myself pushing off down a mountain with little fear. After six days, my confidence was soaring.

On the final day of the trip I went out just with Sally. Before I knew it she was bundling me on to the highest lift, saying something about the views from the peak and how there were plenty of safe routes down. When we got to the top, though, I could only see two choices: a red run and a black run.

In the café Sally bought me a shot of Disaronno liqueur 'for the cold and the nerves' – my first taste of a drink I'll now always associate with skiing – and then she asked me to make my choice.

She didn't ask in a way that gave me any option. 'Well,' she said. 'Are you going to reg it out?' In the Paras, that's the kind of thing we say as a challenge, and any real paratrooper will instantly rise to the occasion no matter what the demand. Although I couldn't believe she'd pulled that one on me, I had no choice but to point at the black run.

Sally smiled. 'Remember, you have the whole slope. It's very steep but it's big and you have all that space just for you. Use it.'

I don't know how I managed to keep her advice in my head, especially when I dropped over the edge and found myself going from nought to sixty in about half a second on what looked like a near-vertical slope, but somehow I managed to get myself to the edge and execute a pretty wobbly right-hand turn. The next turn, to the left, I did with more confidence and soon I was riding from edge to edge. We did have to stop for the occasional break to let my aching left leg recover, but I got to the bottom all in one piece. Looking back up at the steep incline, I couldn't believe that a week ago I'd never even touched a ski and now I had just skied – or, more accurately, survived – a black run. If I could achieve that in six days, I thought, what might be possible with some time and training?

As well as introducing me to a beautiful new part of the world, that skiing trip really opened the door for me in terms of showing me that it *was* possible to get out there and learn new skills, to be active and do the sports I had always loved. I was still learning on a daily basis what I could and couldn't do with my altered body, and it turned out that skiing was one of the 'cans'. In part because I genuinely loved the adrenaline and in part because it was the first activity that came my way, from Bavaria onwards I was hooked.

A few weeks later I headed to Manchester, where the Combined Services Disabled Ski Team (CSDST) was holding an open day. After an introduction to the programme and the main instructor, Scorgie, I had the chance to chat to some other members of the team, including Martin Hewitt (with whom I would later walk to the North Pole), Mick Brennan and Pete Dunning. Both Mick and Pete were incredible para-skiers, almost at world-circuit standard, and skiing with them for even a day was a huge inspiration. I applied to join the team instantly and was accepted.

Over the next year or so I became a competitive skier, representing the army and my regiment in inter-services competitions. I had never realised before how every regiment in the army, navy and RAF has its own sports teams, and I was amazed to discover how many men and women represented their regiments at an almost professional level. During the rest of the 2010 season and the 2010–11 season I skied slopes in France, Austria, Germany, Italy and Switzerland, thrilled to be back in an army environment and giving my competitive streak the chance to flourish again.

I even got to go to a Skiing World Cup as an observer, where I was blown away by the standard and skill of the competitors. The blind categories in particular amazed me. I still can't fully fathom how someone can follow another person down a steep mountain at such high speeds, listening to what they say and acting on their advice to ski a course so gracefully.

That to me is one of the true beauties of para-sports: seeing that someone else is always worse off than you in terms of physical impairment, yet thriving just as well as, if not better. Watching those competitions inspired me to push myself to do things I didn't think were possible, whether that was becoming a professional para-skier or something else.

At the same time I saw how incredibly hard the sport could be, especially for someone like me who carried multiple injuries. Sometimes my leg would be taken into account when I was classified; other times it was only my arm. I often found myself at a disadvantage, pitted against one-armed skiers who still had two perfectly functioning legs. Despite setbacks like that, I started seeing an improvement in my times and was happy with the results I was pulling in by spring 2011.

My confidence and strength on the slopes were greatly aided by two other challenges I took on in 2010: the Safaricom Half-Marathon in Lewa Wildlife Conservancy in Kenya – considered one of the toughest races in the world because of the heat, rough terrain and relatively high chances of encountering a leopard, as we nearly did – and the US Marine Corps Marathon held in Washington, DC, which I completed in full battle kit as part of a Parachute Regiment team. It certainly wasn't one of the easiest races I've ever run, but I loved getting back into that army attitude and completing a challenge like a true Para. I might not have been on operations any more, but I was still a part of my regiment – for now.

*****

When I was finally discharged from Headley Court around eight months after beginning my rehabilitation there, I moved back to my regimental base at St Athan in Wales. Before I had been discharged I had had to pass a series of tests, one of which included spending a couple of nights alone in a self-contained flat on the premises.

In the flat I had to do various tasks like ironing, taking a shower, washing the dishes and even baking a carrot cake, which proved that I was capable of looking after myself. In actual fact, going back to life on the base wouldn't give me much chance to utilise these newfound skills, but getting officially discharged from Headley Court was still a moment of immense pride for me.

In between four-week admissions at Headley Court I had been gradually spending longer periods in St Athan, doing rehab work with instructors like Phil Dodds and taking a part-time job in the intelligence cell. At first this mainly consisted of drinking tea and eating biscuits while I waited for my security clearance to come through, but eventually I was charged with various tasks like writing briefings and updates on missions.

I was also responsible for checking the information that was leaked to the outside world, which involved spending a lot of time on Facebook making sure that no one was posting photos or statuses that revealed too much about their activity with the regiment. Whenever I found something sensitive I tried not to report the soldier in question, but instead took them aside to ask them to take the photo or post down. The job was hardly thrilling – it was a reason to put on my beret in the morning, to polish my boots and iron my shirt, but there was little else to it.

The day came when I had to sit down with my commanding officer, Ed Sandry, to discuss my options. Although it had been a painful realisation, it was clear to me that I would never be any more than a private soldier. Having lost my left arm, I wouldn't be capable of passing any promotional courses that would see me progress up the infantry ladder, not to mention the challenges I would face in completing tasks that were essential to my job, like firing a weapon.

Speaking with Ed, it seemed that I had two options: to try to join the Intelligence Corps – which after various stages of training might see me end up back in the Parachute Regiment, albeit in a different capacity to the one I'd been in before – or to settle for life as a storeman.

Neither option was particularly appealing. Staying in the army would give me stability and security in almost every aspect of life, from a pension plan to daily accommodation and food, but my heart just wasn't in either of the two roles open to me. I had loved being an infantryman, loved being what I had always imagined a soldier to be, and deep down I knew I couldn't settle for any less.

All my life I had been striving to be better, striving to become more, and to let injury change that mentality so early on wasn't something I was prepared to do.

That left me with the third and final option, which was to accept a medical discharge and leave the army. Sooner or later, I knew, leaving was something I was going to have to do anyway, so it seemed sensible to do it right away while I was still very much in the process of adapting to a new life. It wouldn't be quick – I would have to go through a medical board and an eighteen-month phase of resettlement, which would involve living at the Royal Artillery Barracks in Woolwich Arsenal – but by the middle of 2012 I would be officially returned to civilian status and free to live a life of my choosing.

It was the right decision, but even as I told Ed I could feel my heart breaking. The next eighteen months would be tinged with sadness, but they would also prove to be some of the most exhilarating of my entire life.

IX

AN EXTRAORDINARY EXPEDITION

In November 2010 I was in the gym on base in St Athan when a familiar figure walked into the room.

It was Martin Hewitt, a B Company captain I knew well from the CSDST and rehab sessions in the gym. Martin had been shot in Afghanistan a few months before I had – I didn't know it at the time, but his injury was actually the reason I ended up doing my first tour there – and although he still had his left arm, it was completely paralysed. Perhaps because of our similar injuries and interests Martin and I had become good friends, and he had seen me go from strength to strength during my recovery.

I knew that Martin was training to go on an expedition to the North Pole, but what I didn't expect was the conversation we had that morning. Things were not going well for the team. Not one, but two members had dropped out recently, and they were desperately looking for replacements. Martin suggested I give the expedition organisers a call to see if they would consider me. I wasn't quite sure about it – we had history – but he encouraged me, reminding me of how far I'd come.

After leaving the gym I thought it over for a few hours, but really

UNEQUIVOCAL

I think I'd already made my decision. That afternoon I found myself reaching for my phone. If the last few months had taught me anything at all, it was that you never knew what was going to happen.

*****

Walking With The Wounded, by now a very familiar name on the military charity scene, was founded in early 2010 by Ed Parker and Simon Daglish, who started putting together an unsupported expedition to the North Pole. Both had military backgrounds – Ed had served with the Green Jackets and Simon had been to Sandhurst – but they had since gone on to become a wine merchant and a director at ITV. To raise money for a cerebral-palsy charity that cared for his son, Simon had walked to the South Pole a couple of years previously and, in what looked like a bit of a midlife crisis, his good friend Ed decided that he also wanted to do something punchy. The two of them had just started making preparations for a trip to the North Pole when Harry Parker, Ed's nephew, was wounded in Afghanistan and returned home missing both his legs.

Harry's injury changed everything. Visiting him in hospital, Ed was overwhelmed by the fighting spirit he encountered in the wounded soldiers. *Why not do it for these guys?* His first thought about using the expedition to raise money for a wounded veterans' charity quickly turned into a new one: *Why not do it* with *these guys?* It was an entirely new way of thinking at that time, when the shocking injuries that many soldiers sustained in the bloody years of 2008 and 2009 were only just starting to come to public attention and military charities were slowly on the rise. The focus was still very much on supporting the wounded with a definite lean towards pitying us for our new disabilities. That was actually quite the opposite of how we felt – even in my hospital bed I was determined to go back to Afghanistan – and I've always admired Ed and Simon for being able to put themselves in our shoes. Unlike most people, they understood that as wounded soldiers we didn't want to be pitied or assumed to have limitations. What we most wanted to do was to challenge ourselves to greater things.

It was this understanding that led to the birth of Walking With The Wounded, a charity that would kick off with an expedition to the North Pole. Entirely unsupported (meaning that all kit and supplies would be man-hauled across the ice), it was going to be the first time a wounded team had ever attempted such a feat. A world first and a wounded first. The pull was irresistible.

I first heard about the expedition at a regimental dinner in the sergeants' mess. I had been invited along with a few other wounded soldiers and a car was sent to collect me from Headley Court. During the evening one of my officers mentioned it to me as a potential opportunity – he'd heard on the grapevine that a crazy-sounding expedition was in the offing and he thought it would be right up my street. When he offered to send me more information I didn't hesitate to say yes.

This was early 2010, just a short while after I'd returned from South Africa. Although I was walking again I was still relying heavily on a stick and I knew I had a long way to go until my leg was fully healed. Yet when the information came through about the expedition – followed by a call for applications via the Headley Court network – it sounded easy.

It seemed that getting to the North Pole involved walking ten or twelve miles a day, a distance I had been able to cover during a TAB in around two hours, even with a full load of kit. That would definitely be something I could manage in a few months' time.

UNEQUIVOCAL

It just goes to show how much of a military mindset I was in that I applied for the North Pole expedition when my arm and leg still weren't fully healed and I had a colostomy bag. At the time, none of those things occurred to me as a potential problem. Filling in the application forms, I was confident in my abilities, and I felt even more certain when I was invited to London for an interview.

The interviews were being held at the Rifles Club, so through Headley Court I organised a taxi to get me to central London. When I got there I was surprised to see a couple of familiar faces, and yet more arrived throughout the course of the day. Guys I had been sitting with at breakfast only a couple of hours before turned out to be there as well – everyone had been keeping their applications secret in the hopes that it might better their chances. It was a bit like being back at school, no one wanting to talk about something really cool in case everyone went out and got it too. In the end, though, it had only cost us all more money to get there on our own instead of sharing a taxi.

Eventually I was called and walked down the corridor to the interview room. On the way I suddenly realised that I was leaning on my stick – probably not the best first impression to make if you're applying to walk to the North Pole. I left it propped outside the door and made myself walk as straight as possible.

Waiting on the far right of the room was a group of guys: Ed, Simon, Henry Cookson and Inge Solheim. Henry is an adventure specialist and had taken on the role of logistical manager for the expedition, while Inge is a Norwegian polar guide who eventually led us to the Pole. There was also a prosthetics specialist, a doctor and a physiotherapist, who later ran through a series of tests with me.

The interview wasn't particularly difficult – the questions were all about my injuries and military career, my motivation for going

Say cheese!! Four-year-old me posing for my picture to go on the wall at Kabouter Pre-School, Witbank. Wearing my favourite outfit so starting the year on a good foot!

Two-year-old me sitting on my grandmother's lap – next to us is my sister Lizanne in her favourite dress. At the back standing tall are my cousins, Tommy and Elzet. This picture was taken over the Christmas of 1988. We always spent time on my uncle and aunty's farm as a family

12-year-old me at Laerskool Taalfees, Witbank, having just been selected as a school prefect (as indicated by the badges on my left collar) and receiving a certificate for outstanding performance in sport, leadership and discipline

Together with my mum Aloma and sister Lizanne at my passing off parade in 2008. An extremely proud moment in my life, passing off the square and becoming a Paratrooper. The start of my military career. The next stop is Brize Norton for jumps school

Ready for vehicle/mobile operations somewhere in Afghanistan in 2009. Weapons are clean, rations are paced and we carry enough fuel and water to live and survive in these vehicles for weeks in the desert

My first tour to Afghanistan. A young soldier not long out of Basic Training myself, I found myself training new Afghan recruits. We had to be on high alert all the time, it was hard work and tough at times but I loved every moment of it

Sun's out, guns out. Working closely with the Afghan Special Forces, we took the opportunity to teach them very important skills when we had some free time between operational missions

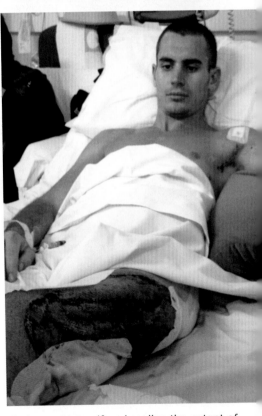

Selly Oak Hospital, 2009. The first time I look down at myself and realise the extent of my injuries. I had lost my left arm just above the elbow as well as suffering a collapsed left lung and shrapnel wounds to my left side that left me with a colostomy, a third of my left upper thigh was blown off, I had suffered a fracture to my left knee, a fasciotomy on my left calf and a broken left tibia and fibula

The stump was extremely sensitive so my sister gave me her travel pillow to rest underneath it to help support it

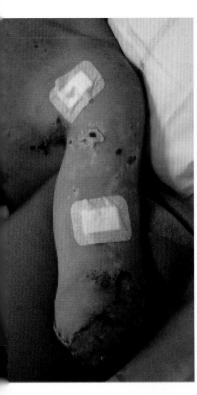

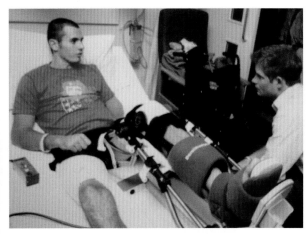

On Ward 5 we received a visit from both Prince William and Prince Harry. This was the first time I had ever met a member of the Royal Family. Harry sat and spoke to me, he listened intently to my story and showed great respect to everyone in the ward. This was the first time I met Harry... it would certainly not be the last

My blue steel look! This picture from 2011 was taken just days before we set off on what would be my first ever epic adventure. I recall being rather nervous but also extremely excited. I also remember clearly just how very cold it was... as a South African this was a cold I had never felt before!

Multiple days into our 2011 North Pole expedition, crossing endless rubble fields. The cold started taking its toll and I had to cover my nose with white zinc oxide tape

Another long cold day on the ice. Temperatures have dropped well below -30. The terrain is extremely difficult to cover and it has slowed our progress down significantly. With low temperatures and high winds it is important to cover up. Our sleds weigh anything between 95 and 110kg and dragging them over boulders of ice is extremely difficult

It was a great privilege to have been nominated and selected to be a London 2012 torch bearer. It was at these Games as a spectator that I was inspired to become a Paralympian myself

Here I am showing off my new ice axe arm in the Hyatt Hotel, Nepal. The arm was developed by myself and the wonderful prosthesis team at Headley Court. The prosthetic fitted nice and comfortably and had electric heated pads on the inside to keep my arm (stump) nice and warm against the cold. The heat pads were powered from a battery pack that was situated on my chest with a custom pocket sewn onto my base layer to keep it warm and working for longer

This picture was taken at the summit of Mt. Manaslu at 8163m. Above 8000m we are in the death zone. This was my first exposure to extreme altitude and we started using oxygen from Camp 4, situated just below 8000m

Pretending I know what I am looking at. Glancing over a vast map of the Nepal mountain ranges. This was a picture taken in the comfort of the Hyatt Hotel before we departed for Everest Base Camp

Putting the ice axe arm through its paces. Training and brushing up on our skills and getting used to the kit and equipment we would be using during our Everest summit attempt

On our way down after a successful summit of Mt. Manaslu in Nepal (the 8th highest mountain in the world). A few days before our summit (situated at Camp 2) we experienced a rather large earthquake. In this picture you can see some of the effects of the earthquake as the crevasse we have to cross has opened up even further during the quake, leaving the ladder dangling and only connected by the two ropes

At the 2016 Invictus Games in Florida. I have just won the Individual Time Trial for the cycling events and was presented my gold medal by Prince Harry. Humble and down to earth, Harry was very happy for a brief catch-up and posed for a picture with both myself and my sister, Lizanne van Gass

Somewhere on a ridge between Camp 4 and Camp 5 on Denali in 2013. Denali is one of my favourite mountains. Once we reached the higher camp, Henry and I felt strong and decided to push all the way to the summit. We summited Denali at 23:30 that evening and made it back to the high camp just after 03:00

Watching and waiting at the Izu Velodrome in 2021. Everything is done, there is no more I can do, the moment has come. I have done this exact warm-up over a hundred times – listening to Lenny Kravitz in my headphones – but this time it matters more than ever

I have just finished and won the C3 Individual 3km Pursuit... my first Paralympic medal and a gold one at that. I grabbed a GB flag from a fellow teammate that was watching the race from the stands although I instantly regretted this decision as the flag nearly went into my front wheel! In the picture is the back of my coach John Hewitt clapping and whistling. Winning your first gold medal is a truly amazing experience

Myself and teammate Fin Graham shortly after the podium and medal presentation. Fin was a very worthy opponent and he pushed me all the way during the race. It was a Great Britain one and two and a privilege to compete with and against him

Receiving my MBE for services to cycling at Windsor Castle, presented by Prince Charles, in May 2022. The most wonderful day and in the company of my wife – and constant support – Kathryn

on the trip and my plans for the coming year – and I also felt I did fairly well in the physical tests. I was acutely aware of my colostomy bag, which of course I mentioned, and Ed also asked me to pull my trousers down to show them the damage to my left leg. I saw the shock on his face when he saw the raw-looking wound and tissue damage, but I did my best to ignore it. Walking out of the room and collecting my stick, I was pretty confident of my chances.

Several days passed with no news. Eventually I asked a couple of my friends who had applied, but none of them had made it on to the team. Maybe that was good news for me. But still I didn't get a phone call and so eventually I wrote Ed an email to ask him when I might hear. His reply was quick – he was terribly sorry, he'd been trying to get in touch but he seemed to have the wrong number for me. I gave him the right one and he called straight away.

It was bad news. I hadn't been selected for the team. Ed told me I'd been the most severely wounded applicant they'd seen and that they just didn't feel I was strong enough yet.

The colostomy bag was also a concern – changing it in sub-zero conditions would not be funny – and they didn't want to return me even more injured than I already was. He was kind, but it was still a no, and I hung up feeling disappointed. Already in quite a fragile state of mind, I felt that I had failed. Again I heaped the blame on my colostomy bag, another thing that made me even more determined to have the reversal procedure as soon as possible.

Over the course of the year the disappointment faded and I heard little news of the expedition. I was busy learning to ski, spending more time in St Athan and running half and full marathons in Lewa and Washington, so when I met Martin in the gym that November his suggestion took me totally by surprise.

Ed, however, seemed to be expecting my call, and we arranged to meet up with Simon in London for an in-person chat.

When I talk to Ed about it now, he says I had stayed on his mind since the day of the interviews for the sheer confidence – or craziness – I had shown in thinking I was physically up to the challenge. Back in January I certainly hadn't been – even I could see that by then – but towards the end of the year I seemed like a different person. I had become a member of the CSDST and trained regularly with Martin, who had mentioned me to Ed when they suddenly found themselves needing to make up numbers. One team member hadn't been quite as suited to the expedition as they'd thought; a second had been pulled out by his regiment. Even though I was memorable to Ed for not quite the right reasons, he was impressed by Martin's description of how far I had progressed.

Back in London I met up with Simon in a pub – Ed had to cancel at the last minute – and learned more about the expedition and what stage of preparation they were at. As they were still looking for two team members I suggested a friend from St Athan, Steve Young.

Steve was a sergeant in the Welsh Guards who had been injured in Afghanistan when his vehicle drove over an IED. The blast had badly broken his back and we had become friends doing rehab in the gym. I wasn't sure if he would be eligible – he hadn't applied for the expedition in the first place – but he'd run the Lewa Half-Marathon alongside me so I knew that he was fit and capable. Most of all, he had immense grit and determination. To this day I have rarely seen anyone deal so bravely with the amount of pain Steve did.

Taking a chance on both of us, what was left of the team invited us down to Devon for a training weekend on the Jurassic Coast. The only person I hadn't yet met was Guy Disney, a leg amputee, but Steve was new to the entire team. He got along with everyone instantly – army humour came into play and soon all five of us, including Simon and Ed, were ripping into him for his thick Welsh accent, pretending not to understand a word he said. Not being officers like Guy and Martin, the two of us added balance to the team. The sense of hierarchy in the army is strong, even outside a classic military context, so it was only natural that we should form closer bonds based on our ranks. At the same time, we all got along incredibly well together – never before or since have I had the privilege of being part of such a strong team. Although some of us were louder than others, no one ever threw his weight around or put his needs first. From that very first training weekend, we all pulled together.

Pulled together in quite a literal sense, because one of our main forms of training was dragging tyres. As well as the weight of the pulks (sledges) they represented, we had to get used to the resistance and spending long hours on our feet. Walking ten miles in the Arctic wouldn't be taking the two hours I had originally imagined – with heavy pulks dragging behind us and incredibly difficult terrain beneath our feet, we could reasonably calculate spending eight to ten hours a day on the move.

The going would be tough, but it was a challenge I relished. After moving from one sport to the next in quite quick succession, joining the CSDST but faced with leaving the army, becoming a member of the North Pole expedition gave me a newfound and much-needed sense of purpose.

*****

Following the training weekend on the Jurassic Coast, the six of us took part in the Soldier 30:30, an endurance race on Exmoor organised by two ex-Special Forces soldiers. Known for being incredibly tough to complete, it's an exercise in navigation as well as stamina. Setting off in an early-morning fog, Guy and Martin were in charge of the map and, in classic officer form, had us lost within the hour. Steve and I took over and did a far better job, and for most of the day we made great progress.

Because it was raining things were especially tough for Guy with his prosthetic leg – the ground was incredibly soft and boggy – but he kept going without complaint. All the same, when we got to a checkpoint in the afternoon the organiser manning it said he would have to pull us from the race. Looking us up and down, he said he didn't think we were capable of getting to the next one before the cut-off time.

It was a simple assumption made on the basis of our injuries, a reaction that we encountered again and again in preparing for the expedition. Even within the military there was an enormous amount of pushback – people simply didn't believe we were strong or capable enough to go. What few of them realised was the extent of the thought and thoroughness that was going into our preparations, or that no one knew our abilities better than we did.

Another factor people rarely considered was the depth of our determination. While Ed and Simon's top priority was not letting us sustain further damage, they were also 100 per cent behind us in letting us show the world what we knew in our hearts we could do.

Ed had stern words with the organiser, who eventually let us continue. We made it to the next checkpoint and halfway to the next before darkness started to fall and we were forced to stop. Although we were aching and exhausted, we were still desperate to finish, but in the end we had to admit that safety came first. Out of the twenty-five teams that started, only three finished, with our team the closest to taking fourth place.

That weekend was just one of many training sessions we would do together. Sometimes they involved walking along stretches of British moor or coastline, other times Guy and Steve would come out to join Martin and me on a CSDST training camp somewhere in Europe.

As the 2010–11 skiing season progressed, the two of us were spending more and more time at training camps and competitions, which were the perfect places for practising walking on Nordic skis. Our instructors were full of enthusiasm for the expedition and we worked out a nice arrangement that allowed us to spend four half-days a week training for the North Pole.

Nordic skis are quite different to normal skis: they're very thin and straight rather than tapered, with flat edges that mean you have to step instead of leaning to make a turn. For the first fifteen minutes after strapping them on each day there was utter chaos, with Martin and I falling all over the place as we tried to move in them like the normal skis we'd had on earlier.

Many moments of hilarity accompanied that learning process, and I was also fascinated to get a glimpse of life in the mountains, where ski touring was a daily activity for some. We followed tracks to incredibly beautiful areas that were so remote we'd never have seen them otherwise. The days were long and intense but I loved every minute of them.

At the beginning of 2011 I moved to London to begin my resettlement, the eighteen-month phase that would transition me from the military back into civilian life. When I wasn't away skiing I was dragging tyres around Green Park or Blackheath, first one and then two stacked on top of each other.

I struggled initially with the harness I'd been given, which made me hunch forward too much, but eventually worked out that I could attach it to a backpack and pull with both my back and hips. Almost every morning, after a big breakfast, I'd set off to drag my tyres for three to five hours, and after lunch and a bit of a rest I'd head to the gym to improve my upper-body strength.

At almost every opportunity I would be on my feet, walking across London instead of taking the bus or not sitting down if I was on the tube. Dragging tyres definitely attracted the most attention – people would come up to me to ask what I was doing or literally throw money at me in the street: 'Whatever it is you're doing, put that in the kitty!'

Just as I had found a way of pulling tyres (and eventually a pulk) that suited me, we all had to figure out ways to adapt the circumstances to suit our injuries. Each of us had been wounded in different ways – Guy missing a leg, Martin with a paralysed arm, me missing an arm and Steve with a broken back – so we all had very different needs and had to adapt our kit and roles within the team accordingly. We went down to the Institute of Naval Medicine in Gosport to get advice from their prosthetics experts and go through various tests that simulated the conditions we might be facing.

The temperature was always going to be a big concern for me as the stump of my arm gets cold incredibly quickly, so I needed extra layers around it and hand warmers inside the sleeve of my jacket to make sure I didn't get frostbite.

A major test of our preparations came in late January when we set off for a training session in Norway. Inge was with us and we did a trial run of what the expedition would be like, spending five days unsupported out on the ice, skiing for most of the day and setting up camp in the evening.

That weekend came as quite a shock. Although I was pretty good at pulling a heavy pulk and managing my skis, when we stopped for the day I felt useless. With only one hand each, neither Martin nor I could be much help in putting up tents or setting up stoves to boil water – a hard fact to accept given our hands-on military mentality. I was desperate to do what I saw as my fair share of the daily tasks, but instead I spent a lot of time either getting in the way or hanging around frustrated as the others worked on my behalf.

Everything needed to be done incredibly quickly because of the cold and I felt miserable as I watched my teammates struggling. Things only got worse when a storm came in and we had to make camp even faster than usual.

Aside from the tents and stoves, Martin and I found ourselves relying on the others for even the most basic tasks – doing up zips or tying laces. Although I had worked out a system for tying laces with one hand, trying to replicate that in sub-zero conditions where it was risky to take my hand out of my glove for too long was almost impossible.

Those few days were a real eye-opener in showing me that I did have limitations and making me aware of exactly what they were. At times I even doubted my place on the expedition – I felt that I wasn't worthy, even a nuisance – but this was where our strong team bond really kicked in. Ed in particular was fantastic about working out the logistics of who could do what and how; he really felt a duty of care for us all. He trod a fine line in making sure that tasks were completed as efficiently as possible but that none of us ever felt left out or worth less than anyone else. I might not have been much use in camp, but I was a great man-hauler and compensated by taking extra weight. There were other things I could do too, like help Steve with the physio exercises he had to do every day for his back.

It took a slight adjustment in my mentality, but eventually I learned to recognise situations in which I really needed help, then to ask for and accept it. It might sound like a small thing, but for me it was a huge mental leap and one that helped my recovery immeasurably. As important as it was to stay determined and independent, it was also essential to learn that I wasn't alone.

*****

When we returned from Norway everything seemed to start moving very quickly. The expedition was building serious momentum and it was all I did or thought about. It affected every single aspect of life, including what I ate. In fact, food was such a significant element of the build-up that when I wasn't training I was stuffing my face.

The experts at the Institute of Naval Medicine had worked out that we would be burning roughly ten thousand calories a day on the expedition, but despite carrying the most calorie-rich meals we could find, we would only be able to replace six or seven thousand. That meant that before we set off each of us needed to weigh a minimum of eighty kilos, with enough reserves of body fat to ensure our survival. For me, who weighed in at seventy-four kilos and was doing a punishing daily training regime, this was a problem. It was time for Operation Get Fat to commence.

At first it was wonderful – I'm not going to lie. For the only time in my life I was able not just to eat as much as I wanted, but had actively to try to eat as much as I physically could. On team training exercises we would go out for an evening meal and start with an entire pizza each, followed by a main dish like steak and chips. When it came time for dessert we always got competitive – most of us were capable of eating four or five in one sitting. And that was just the evening.

Throughout the day I was constantly eating: enormous breakfasts and lunches, Chinese takeaway as a bedtime snack, fistfuls of dry cereal or hummus and carrot sticks when I woke up hungry in the night. Each morning I would get out of bed starving, faced with a day of intense physical training during which I was also trying to get fat.

By the time we were nearly ready to leave I was sick and tired of Operation Get Fat. I spent a long time hovering around the seventy-eight-kilo mark and struggled to eat enough of the right fats – even though we had to eat a lot it wasn't a licence to go to McDonald's every day. The extra pounds I was putting on didn't help my performances for the CSDST either, and as someone who had always watched his weight it went against my nature.

There are some pretty terrible photos of me wearing a ski-team skinsuit from around that time, but fortunately the chubbiness didn't show up too badly during the most important photo shoot I had. Publicity for the expedition was building and we had a few incredible sponsors, like fund manager Artemis, on board, so very often there was a talk, gala or sponsorship event to attend. They were all fantastic and provided the added bonus of helping me with my resettlement – every event I went to got me outside my army box and talking to other people. It was the photo shoot for GQ, however, that really sticks in my mind.

Back when I was in hospital in Selly Oak, Prince Harry had paid a brief visit to Ward S5 and spent a few moments by my bed. I don't really remember it – I was pretty out of my mind on painkillers at the time – and still less did I expect that a couple of years later I'd be walking part way to the North Pole with him. Having heard about the expedition, Prince Harry had very kindly agreed to be our patron and even come to join us on the ice for a few days. A photo shoot for a feature in GQ was our first opportunity to meet him.

Growing up in South Africa, I'd never heard of David Bailey, so when we were told he'd be taking our photos I wasn't terribly bothered. But Ed and Simon were hugely excited and when I realised just how famous he was I was also pretty impressed.

Our photo shoot took place in a draughty aircraft hangar not far from where Prince Harry was doing his Apache helicopter training and involved all of us dressing up in the new kit we'd be wearing for the expedition. One of the best items was a huge, thick red Helly Hansen jacket with a fur-lined hood and our sponsors' logos on the chest.

David took photos of us individually and as groups, telling filthy jokes to make us smile and occasionally breaking off to talk about Afghanistan, where he'd been a few years before to take photos of both soldiers and civilians. He knew some of the places we mentioned and could relate to us on a level I hadn't expected.

About halfway through the photo shoot Prince Harry arrived. He put us all at ease instantly, telling us to call him 'H' and getting very close to us on David's request. For one picture Guy and I almost had our faces in Harry's armpits, a moment that was more than surreal. But by the end of the day we were all laughing and joking together, which came as a big relief. We'd found our final team member – although he only had a short time to spend with us, Harry had slotted in just like any one of the other boys.

There were still weeks of training (and eating) to go, but now none of us could wait until the moment we finally set foot on the ice.

X

ON TOP OF THE WORLD

The Arctic was the most beautiful place I'd ever seen.

Thanks to being part of the CSDST, I had become pretty well acquainted with snow and ice by the time we arrived there in April 2011, but the landscape was different to anything I'd encountered before. The sunlight falling on the ice made the most spectacular colours, brighter and lovelier than I'd ever known they could be. It was impossible to photograph, but there was beauty underneath all that white. I felt I was seeing nature at its very best.

Arriving in Longyearbyen, the main town in Svalbard, we met up with Inge Solheim, our polar guide, and also Petter and Rune, two of his colleagues who would be pulling pulks for Alexis and Rob, our film team. Although in the documentary that was made about the North Pole expedition the public only ever saw a team of seven – me, Steve, Guy, Martin, Ed, Simon and Inge – we were actually a team of eleven.

Twelve with Prince Harry, who walked with us for the first few days. Petter and Rune proved to be absolute machines on the ice, each of them dragging two fully loaded pulks. With tents, stoves and enough food and fuel for three weeks, our pulks weighed around a hundred kilos each.

Packing properly was very important, so we spent a few days in Longyearbyen in a rented warehouse where we could spread out all our kit and equipment. We packed and re-packed our pulks, trying to get all the heavy things at the bottom to make them as stable as possible and keeping lighter things like clothing on top for easy access. Because the expedition was entirely unsupported we had to carry everything we'd need to survive for three weeks on the ice, so there wasn't much room for personal items. Food was really the only individual luxury we had.

Eating a proper meal from our ration packs involved setting up tents and stoves, so we would only be doing that for breakfast and dinner. Lunch and snacks would have to be eaten on the go: hot soups in thermos flasks and a big bag of trail mix with added bits like biscuits, chopped-up chocolate, peanuts, raisins and sweets. Each of us personalised these packs with extra items we had bought: Simon added Green & Black's chocolate to his, and I filled mine with M&Ms. I loved M&Ms, but four days into the expedition I hated them. At temperatures of minus forty they froze into rock-solid lumps that could break your tooth or be used in a slingshot.

After a few days of preparation we were ready. Harry had arrived shortly after us and had also sorted out his kit. He was so nice and normal and never expected to be treated differently – he made his own ration bags, packed his own pulk, and spent a night in a tent with Inge to learn things like how to set up the cooker. He was very hands-on and always game for a laugh, which we did have a few of when locals recognised him and his two security men had to spend the evening keeping them away.

The media build-up in the UK had been huge and the press came with us to Longyearbyen. It was a strange time – although on the TV documentary it might have looked like we were alone, we definitely weren't. To add to the mounting nerves, both Steve and I caught flu, and then we were given some bad news. Poor weather conditions meant that we weren't allowed to fly up to the ice camp at Barneo, from where we would be taken to our starting point. Our start date had been 30 March; now it was indefinite.

The wait was incredibly frustrating. Longyearbyen is a small town and there was very little for us to do except sit around in the hotel watching the film *Step Brothers* on repeat, or spend time in the warehouse re-packing our pulks again. Once, we visited a friend of Inge's out at his cabin, and local Search and Rescue also took me, Guy, Martin and Steve polar-bear-watching in a helicopter – a pretty cool experience.

Finally, after a delay of five days, we got the good news we'd been waiting for. Flights to Barneo were operational again and we were going to be on the first one.

Suddenly the lethargy we'd fallen into vanished and that day was a scramble to get ready. Steve and I had recovered from our bout of flu but Ed had just caught it, so he was feeling pretty terrible as we boarded the plane. The excitement and nerves had reached fever pitch. It was 4 April 2011 and the first Walking With The Wounded expedition was about to begin.

*****

It took the pilot three attempts, but eventually he managed to locate the landing strip. The plane hit the ice with an almighty bang and when the door opened cold air rushed in. It had been so hot in the cabin that we'd all stripped off, but now we were struggling to put our layers back on.

As I stepped out, my face said it all: this cold was serious.

Barneo is a temporary Russian ice base that is rebuilt every year roughly one degree away from the North Pole. Because the ice melts so rapidly, the base only exists for about a month, which gave our expedition a limited window of time. The delay we'd experienced in Longyearbyen had cut five valuable days off that, and we were all very aware that we'd be racing against the clock. If we even made it to our starting point, that is – looking at the old Russian helicopter that would be taking us the rest of the way, I think each of us feared for his life. Harry had just passed his Apache helicopter training so he did a quick walk-round and made some checks. 'Yeah,' he said when he came back. 'I'm not really sure we should be sitting inside this thing.'

The twelve of us and all our pulks – which between them weighed well over a tonne – crammed into the ancient helicopter and lifted off. We were flying away from the North Pole to a latitude of 87° 44', which gave us roughly 165 miles to cover on foot. Looking down, I saw the vast, white desert we were going to cross and for the first time I could really see its scale. It was hard to understand just how enormous it was – acres and acres of snow and ice traversed by stretches of open water known as leads.

I tried to map our route backwards in my head, even though I knew that the ice is constantly moving so this wouldn't actually be of any help. Mainly I was just fascinated by the beauty of the landscape.

The helicopter landed with another bump and we quickly unloaded all our kit, grateful to have survived the journey. The pilot waved goodbye cheerfully and took off. We stood there watching as the noise of the engine disappeared and the helicopter got smaller and smaller. We were alone in a silent world of endless white. It was a moment I'll never forget: the moment it all became real.

The Arctic has twenty-four-hour daylight during the summer months, but despite the bright sunshine Inge insisted we get some sleep. It was 4.30 a.m. and we'd been on the go all day. I wondered if it was really worth the effort of putting up the tents for about three hours' sleep, and I could see Inge getting quite stressed by the amount of faffing going on. It was a shock to the system to realise how long it took to do everything, and despite the fact we'd re-packed our pulks about fifteen times, no one seemed to know where anything was. All the things we needed were somehow weighed down at the bottom under spare fuel and emergency supplies, so the whole process of making camp took far longer than it should have. Inge is a man of few words, but he made it clear that we needed to do better.

The adrenaline made it hard to sleep and we all had a restless 'night'. After a couple of hours we were up again, striking camp and ready to take our first steps towards the North Pole. Looking back, most days of the expedition have blurred into one, but that first one will always remain with me as a day that was seriously, shockingly hard.

We had trained a lot for the expedition. Walking With The Wounded was a new charity and Ed and Simon had found themselves facing a lot of pushback from the military, with the general consensus being that we didn't know what we were doing. To prove that we were serious – and make sure that we could actually achieve what we set out to – they had taken every little detail and risk into account, while each of us had worked incredibly hard on his physical condition. But no matter how many hours you spend on Nordic skis or dragging tyres around Green Park, the one thing you can't do is replicate the Arctic anywhere else in the world.

The open-water leads, the pressure ridges (where two sheets of ice press against one another with such force that the edges buckle into a high ridge), the rubble fields of ice boulders and even the texture of the snow were all things we could never have encountered before, even if we'd tried. That first day, we met them all.

It was a total shock to the system. From the first step I took, my pulk was heavy and kept sticking to the ice. My breath was coming heavily and steaming up my glasses, so I kept having to stop, take them off and wipe away the moisture. I swapped them for my ski goggles, which weren't much better, but at least I had got rid of the material below the glasses, which had been flapping annoyingly around my face. Everyone was having problems with their goggles fogging up and freezing over, so every few minutes we had to stop for someone to sort himself out. During one of these breaks, Inge came down the line (we skied in single file) to check on us individually.

'Woah, Jaco!' he said when he got to me. 'You need to cover up your face! You're going white on the left side, on your cheek.' Skin turning white is the first sign of frostbite. I couldn't believe it. We weren't even halfway into the first day of an expedition due to last three weeks and already I was in danger of frostbite. I covered up my face but now I could feel a distracting numbness in my cheek, which made it even harder to concentrate on finding a rhythm.

Each time we came to a rubble field or pressure ridge we had to help each other lift the pulks over. Coming down the other side, they would either get stuck or speed up and run into the backs of our legs, pulling us over or dragging us down the slope. It was incredibly hard work – just the amount of power needed to lift a pulk over a large boulder was immense – and we hadn't worked out our technique yet.

Everyone was very hands-on with helping each other, probably none more so than Harry, who was always the first to take off his harness and help push someone else's pulk over a ridge. He also proved to be extremely good at skiing, almost annoyingly so.

At the end of that first day we were all completely shattered and very frustrated. We had put in a disappointing performance, doing far less than the fifteen miles we needed to cover each day to reach the Pole before the base at Barneo closed. Inge was visibly unimpressed and told us straight up that we needed to try harder, to concentrate and look out for each other. Although I don't think any of us ever doubted that we would reach the North Pole, that first evening we all felt uncertain about *how* we would achieve our goal.

Might we have to give up the unsupported element of the expedition and get help carrying our food and fuel? Would we have to get helicoptered in to a point that was closer to the Pole and finish walking from there? Time was against us, and if we could only manage to walk eight or ten miles a day we were never going to finish.

Keeping the rest of us out of it, Ed and Simon had serious conversations with Inge that evening and over the next couple of days. Even though he was concerned, Inge was prepared for us to keep going as planned, at least until the end of the first week. Day One of a new challenge is always tough and he knew how determined we all were to succeed. In a way, I think, the frustrations of that first day helped us.

We had seen for ourselves where the difficulties lay and worked hard to overcome them. The next morning we woke up with fresh determination and a bit of positive news: because of the way the ice was moving, we had drifted three miles closer to the North Pole.

The drift was a factor we hadn't really taken into account but which ended up working in our favour. Inge, who is a very experienced polar guide, had worked out that our chances of a good drift were best if we approached the Pole from the Russian side, which is why we had ended up flying through Barneo. In fact, none of the teams that started from the Canadian side that season were successful because of bad weather and unfavourable drift, so his decision proved to be the correct one. Apart from a couple of days when we drifted away, most mornings we would wake up to find ourselves a mile or two closer to the North Pole than we had been when we'd made camp. It wasn't far, but each time it happened it was an incredible morale boost that really set the tone of the day.

On 6 April Harry was due to be picked up by helicopter to fly back home for his brother Prince William's wedding, but a crack in the ice sheet that was the runway at Barneo meant his flight would be delayed.

We were thrilled to have him with us for another day – he had slotted into the team so naturally and was great fun to be with. He and Inge shared a tent but in the evenings he would come to mingle with us, often bearing a slice of ice-cream cake that he had brought with him from Longyearbyen and hidden in his pulk. Little things like that and his general way of being made us feel very at ease around him, and when the runway finally did re-open on the evening of 7 April we were genuinely sorry to see him go.

After the rush of goodbyes and getting his kit loaded on to yet another dangerous-looking helicopter, we were left with that feeling of loneliness again. It was a very sad moment to lose a teammate who had, in one way or another, been there since the beginning.

*****

We were a man down, but there was no time to really dwell on it – four days into the expedition, it was time to get serious. After the struggle of the first few days we had finally found our rhythm and started to cover an impressive number of miles. We had become more confident about crossing open-water leads, jumping over without slipping and pulling the pulks across after us, and we were even starting to smash through the pressure ridges without a lot of fuss. Knowing that we were making progress boosted morale, and that in turn gave us more energy to accomplish some very big days.

In general we would walk from about nine a.m. until six p.m., with five-minute breaks every two hours to have something to eat and drink. When we stopped we instantly had to wrap up in thick down jackets to prevent us from getting cold, but for walking we wore fewer layers to try to avoid sweating. If we sweated too much it would freeze inside our clothes, so we were in a constant battle to maintain a regular body temperature. I kept checking the stump of my arm to make sure the blood was still flowing to it – that and the small patch of white skin on my cheek were two of my main concerns.

All of us felt aches and pains while we were walking – towards the end of the expedition Guy's leg was in a bit of a mess from where his prosthetic had rubbed the end of his stump – but Steve was in by far the worst pain.

He carried a lot of painkillers and high-intensity heat pads with him, and one of my main jobs when we stopped for a break or had made camp at night was to help him with his physiotherapy exercises. He would lie on a mat and I would help to stretch and pull him into different positions in an effort to relieve his back. Like most of us, though, he shut up and got on with it. Only Ed and I really saw when he was struggling because we shared a tent.

Being in a tent with Steve was a serious luxury – as a platoon sergeant in the Welsh Guards he was really good at looking after people. Mornings began with Steve starting to rustle, and as he crawled out of his sleeping bag Ed and I would pull ours up over our heads. We only crept out when Steve had got the burner going and started to boil water for a brew.

During the day we rarely talked much. When we stopped for a break we would check in with one another, and some days were chattier than others. Each of us had different ways of coping with the long, silent hours of walking. Guy listened to his iPod, which he had loaded with audiobooks, and Martin loved his house music. I was fifty-fifty between listening to music and just walking along with my thoughts. It depended a bit on our surroundings: when we came to rubble fields we needed to communicate, but when there were long, flat sheets of ice it was good to listen to a bit of music to take my mind off feeling cold or tired.

At other times it was lovely just to hear the wind and the sound of skis gliding over the ice, and to be alone with my thoughts in the little world behind my hood and goggles. The beauty of the scenery was breathtaking, in part because of the scale. It was possible to get really close to a snowflake or ice crystal and see all its incredible detail, but at the same time I felt tiny and insignificant in the midst of all that white. It was the perfect place to reflect on life and do some serious thinking.

Inside our tents in the evenings we did talk to one another. Ed, Steve and I swapped stories of our experiences in the army – back in his day, Ed had done a couple of tours of Northern Ireland so he was particularly fascinated to hear what it was like to serve in Afghanistan.

We all wrote diaries, but most of the evening was spent cleaning ourselves with baby wipes as best we could, melting snow for water and food, and trying to dry our clothes. Ed is a big boy who sweats a lot, so there was moisture everywhere.

Our tent looked like a Chinese laundry with clothes hanging out to dry all over the place, and every time Inge came in he would go nuts.

'The tent needs to be dry, you're going to get cold!' He told us time and time again, but we couldn't do anything about it. In the night the moisture would freeze and when Steve got up in the morning and touched the side of the tent all the ice came crashing down on our heads.

After Harry left, Inge was in a tent on his own, so to ease things for everyone – the tents were *very* crowded – we took it in turns to spend a night in Inge's tent. It was like a hotel; no one wanted to leave. You could put your hand anywhere on the canvas and there was no moisture, but the main thing that impressed me was how warm it was. Tea and food would appear as if by magic and the night I spent there I finally slept properly. I tried to behave well so that he would keep me, but after my one-day holiday I was sent back to the Chinese laundry.

Despite the fact that we were eating a lot, my metabolism had started racing by about Day Five. In the evenings I was absolutely starving and during the day I could barely manage an hour and a half of walking before I felt my energy levels drop. I started keeping trail mix in my pocket so I could eat on the move, and in the evening after my freeze-dried dinner I would finish whatever I had left over. There were usually a lot of M&Ms in there, but at least in the warmth of the tent they were edible again.

When I wasn't eating, I was thinking about food – as I walked I would fantasise about the meals I would have when I got back home. Strangely enough, I wasn't that excited about the idea of a burger and chips, like some of the others were. The one thing I really craved was broccoli.

During the final days of the expedition I felt much better because

UNEQUIVOCAL

I was able to start tapping into our extra food reserves. We had brought enough supplies for three weeks, but thanks to the drift and our walking speed we were on track to reach the Pole after just two. We had got so used to this new way of life and being a little group of eleven people out there in the wilderness that when we came across a set of ski tracks on Day Ten we were absolutely amazed. It was the strangest feeling to think that someone else was out there and had even walked this way. My instinct was to follow the tracks and see where they led, but the compass showed North to be in a different direction. The ice had twisted since the other team had passed, so we crossed the tracks and continued towards our North Pole.

The long days, broken nights and constant having to look after our bodies were starting to take their toll. Each of us struggled with pain or tiredness, but I think the one thing that really got us through was how strong a team we were. If someone was having a bad day, the rest of us were there to help – perhaps by carrying some extra kit or just being there for a chat during a break.

Ed took a hard fall a few days before the end and passed out because of the pain. I pulled his pulk for the rest of that day and Steve gave him a heat pad in the evening. Although our closest bonds were in our tent groups, we all knew that we were there for one another no matter what.

Having that incredible level of trust and respect – and the ability to take the piss out of each other brutally – gave us an amazing amount of strength on a team and a personal level. It more than paid off: we ended up going further and faster than any other team that season.

*****

ON TOP OF THE WORLD

We reached the North Pole on Saturday 16 April, having covered 165 miles in twelve days. That day we woke up knowing we had the final ten miles to walk, but aware that anything could go wrong. Not knowing exactly where the Pole was probably helped us – we could almost pretend that it was just a day like any other. Only Inge, who was holding the GPS reader, actually knew its location, and he called out when we had about a hundred yards to go.

We had never planned it this way, but the six of us fanned out to walk the last steps next to one another, rather than in single file. As Inge watched the reading on the GPS monitor he shouted, 'Eighty-nine point nine nine nine nine nine... ninety point zero. We're there!'

It was an amazing moment.

Because the Arctic ice is constantly moving there is nothing to mark the geographic North Pole – no flagpole or statue or giant research base. Our North Pole was nothing but a patch of snow and ice, and yet that was what made it so special: it belonged only to us. No matter where that piece of ice drifts to, it will always be our North Pole and no one else's.

We were on top of the world in more ways than one. After a rocky start we had made it to the Pole in unexpected time. We celebrated with lots of photographs – each of us had brought various bits along, like Steve's Welsh flag and my Parachute Regiment one. I had also been given a fold-up dartboard by Gary Palmer, a friend of John McDonald's who ran the company Target Darts, so Steve and I set it up and had a quick game at the Pole.

We stuck a ski pole in the ground, all put our hands on it and 'ran around the top of the world' as fast as we could, and rounded off the day by opening a bottle of whisky and a box of cigars. Then, exhausted but elated, we set up our tents to spend a final night on the ice.

UNEQUIVOCAL

The sense of achievement was unreal, but at the same time I felt a great sense of loss. The North Pole was all I had worked for, such a big part of my life, and to a great extent my sole purpose over the last few months. I knew I would be going back to London to continue the process of leaving the army, and I wondered what exactly it was that I was going home for.

I'd be living on an army base that wasn't even mine, alone in a room on a block where I knew no one else. Before, I'd spent hours every day dragging tyres through London parks, but to work on my fitness now I could just go to the gym. There was no need to fill my days with what I'd filled them with until now. As proud as I was of our achievement, when I thought about the future I was overwhelmed with sadness that the expedition was over.

The strange mix of emotions was made even worse the next morning when a Japanese team suddenly skied on to the Pole, closely followed by the helicopter that had been sent to take us back to Barneo. Although we were all quite pleased to see the helicopter – we were tired, cold and desperate for proper food and clean clothes – it had brought along four rich South Koreans who climbed out, had their photos taken at the Pole, and promptly got back in again.

Having just man-hauled a tonne of kit and equipment for over a hundred and fifty miles, we could hardly believe our eyes.

The past twelve days seemed all the more unbelievable when the helicopter took off and we found ourselves flying over the ice we had just crossed on foot. Again I was struck by the incredible scale of the Arctic: with the open-water leads criss-crossing through the snow, it looked like a giant maze.

I found it hard to believe that just the day before we had been down there somewhere, trying to find a way through the rubble fields and hauling our pulks over high pressure ridges. Throughout the half-hour flight to Barneo and the plane journey back to Longyearbyen, it all started to fade like a dream I had just woken up from.

Getting back to civilisation did feel amazing. Every time I go on an expedition it's the same – after weeks spent living in a tent you really do appreciate the finer things in life. Standing under a hot shower was incredible and our hotel beds felt like the softest things in the world.

We couldn't wait to have proper food either, and the burger and beer I had that evening were probably some of the best I've ever tasted. Longyearbyen didn't have a lot in the way of broccoli, though, so I would have to wait another few days before being able to satisfy that particular craving.

We spent four days in Longyearbyen before flying back to London via Oslo, during which time we all became desperate to get out. Having reached the Pole and gone through the strange emotions that accompanied it, we wanted nothing more than to leave the Arctic behind us.

We were simultaneously exhausted and feeling like we had to blow off steam, which resulted in some pretty wild evenings in the whisky bar and long days spent in bed. Oslo was a much better place to be and on the night we spent there I finally got my broccoli along with a beautiful piece of salmon. It was one of the greatest meals of my life.

Everything in Oslo seemed so much brighter. We had finally left the world of whiteness behind and it was hard to take in all the colours. I remember being particularly struck by how green the trees were and also by what I could smell.

In the Arctic it was so cold we had lost almost all sense of taste and smell, but on the streets of Oslo I could smell a woman's perfume from six metres away. Every meal was intense and even the airport blew me away with the sheer number of people around us. My brain struggled to cope with the sudden change: for two weeks we had been the only twelve or eleven people in the whole world.

*****

Even before we left Longyearbyen we were already talking about what we would do next. It didn't take longer than a couple of days of good food, warm showers and proper beds before we were willing to push ourselves beyond our comfort zones again. It would be a few weeks or even months before we truly saw what an incredible impact Walking With The Wounded had had, but even at that early stage we knew it was something we needed to keep going.

What started in 2009 as a plan for two friends to walk to the North Pole had turned into something that had the power to change public perception of the wounded and make a real difference to people's lives. I think that before we did the expedition there was a great deal of sympathy for wounded, but it was sympathy that was misdirected.

I often felt belittled by people constantly wanting to help me – of course they meant well, but to me it seemed like they were saying I couldn't do even small things like making a cup of tea on my own. A lot of my friends struggled with that too, and it could lead to a build-up of tension within people and families that was hard to know how to deal with. But with our expedition to the North Pole, we had shown that it was possible for wounded men and women to crack on and do whatever they wanted.

Each of us had very different injuries, but together we had achieved something extraordinary.

Although Walking With The Wounded has always had a military

focus, the ripple effect it produced went much further. Letters, donations and little gifts came pouring in after the expedition, and the charity raised so much money beyond sponsorship that it was eventually able to start offering its own services, rather than just distributing funds to other charities.

Even people who had nothing to do with the military were inspired, like the elderly lady who wrote to us to say that she had been bed-bound for eight years, but after watching the expedition documentary on television she had managed to get up one morning and pick up the post from her doormat. It was an amazing feeling to know we had done something positive for so many people.

All that was still to come, though, and my main thought when we got back home was what the future would bring. There would be a busy period of catching up with family and friends, but it felt like my whole life for the past few months had been building up to this one thing.

Now that it was gone, my life was empty, and I had no distraction from the painful process of losing the army, the career I had loved more than anything in the world.

So it was with absolutely no hesitation that towards the end of April I told Ed I was on board for a new expedition. We had already stood on top of the world at the North Pole, but this time we wanted to see the view from a different angle.

We were going to climb Mount Everest.

XI

ESCAPING EVEREST

Although I had been one of the first to put my hand up for the Everest expedition, I had to accept that I wouldn't actually have the chance to summit the world's highest mountain.

Getting a permit to climb Everest is incredibly expensive, not to mention all the training and kit that goes into it, so it was beyond Walking With The Wounded's means to send more than about six people to the very top. The summit team would be selected from a larger pool who would first climb Mount Manaslu, another 8,000-metre Himalayan peak and the eighth highest mountain in the world, but this was as far as I would be getting. Having just walked to the North Pole, it was time to give someone else a chance to reach an extreme goal.

I would be lying if I said I didn't feel a bit disappointed, but I was mainly just grateful to be involved. The North Pole expedition had been a serious boost for my confidence and made my outlook on the future so much more positive. I had the feeling that despite my injury, I could do anything I wanted. The only question was: what? With the North Pole behind me and only a phased withdrawal from the army ahead, I was relieved to have a new challenge to channel my energies into.

Things started moving very quickly. We returned from the North Pole in late April 2011, and by the end of July I was on a plane again – this time to France. In a similar process to the North Pole expedition, Ed and Simon had held interviews at the Rifles Club in London and put together a pool of candidates: Francis, Dan, Andy, Karl, David, Mani and Chris. Martin Hewitt was definitely on the team and, despite having missed an initial selection weekend in Snowdonia, I was also allowed to proceed to the next stage: a week of mountaineering in the Alps around Chamonix.

It was my first experience of mountain climbing and I instantly fell in love. Though different to anything I'd ever done before, I loved the physical and mental challenges involved as I pushed my body in new ways and got my head around unfamiliar equipment. For the first two days we were only given kit lessons – how to set up a harness, how to clip into a safety rope using a jumar (a handheld metal device that grips climbing ropes) – and then we went up into the mountains to practise technical climbing. After that we moved on to a glacier, where we learned how to walk in crampons.

That day involved lots of falling over as we tried to walk normally and ended up getting the teeth of our crampons stuck in our trousers. We also spent a while doing crevasse rescue drills and learning safety techniques, like how to use an ice axe to stop ourselves sliding down a mountain face.

As with the North Pole team, the nine of us had all suffered different injuries, so a lot of time was spent working out how to adapt kit to our individual needs. Martin and I, for example, had to climb one-handed, which meant finding a harness that wasn't too fiddly.

Clipping in and out of the safety ropes was also a bit of an issue. To get the dexterity needed to work a jumar you have to take your hand out of your thick top mitten, and as we were always using the same hand our fingers got cold much faster than everybody else's. It wasn't too much of a problem in the Alps in summer, but to climb at eight thousand metres with an extremely cold wind blowing we would need to find a good solution.

The aim of the week was to summit Mont Blanc, Europe's highest mountain, but due to bad weather we had to change our plans. Instead we drove through a road tunnel into Italy and climbed Gran Paradiso, a 4,061-metre peak. It was a fantastic trip and I loved every minute of it, starting with the walk from the car park at the bottom to the mountain hut where we would be staying. The first part of the walk was through dense forest, with the landscape gradually becoming more barren until we reached the snow line, which was surprisingly low for that time of year. Lots of people walk up to the hut for lunch and back down again, but we stayed the night in simple rooms and got up at five o'clock for a summit attempt.

Watching the sun rise as we gained height was beautiful, and for the rest of the day the sky was clear blue. The climb wasn't very technically challenging, although just before we got to the summit there was a sheer rock wall we had to shuffle along, with our chests and faces pressed against the mountain and our backs to a steep drop.

To get on to the peak itself we had to jump across a chasm, which was a bit hairy, but finally we made it to the summit where there was a little statue of the Virgin Mary. It was about eleven o'clock by that stage, so after spending a bit of time admiring the view we headed back down to the hut, had something to eat and drink, and basically ran down the rest of the way. It was my first successful summit and from then on I was hooked.

Even though Gran Paradiso was supposed to be part of the selection process, everyone in the group had done really well. Our climbing guides, Russell and Adrian, who would be leading the expedition to Everest, had a chat with Ed Parker and Simon

ESCAPING EVEREST

Daglish, who decided that all of us would be allowed to tackle Manaslu. It was great to know that everyone was going – we had bonded really well in Chamonix and formed a good team with various different characters. Knowing that I wouldn't be climbing Everest, Manaslu was a rare opportunity for me to get experience of an 8,000-metre peak and I couldn't wait to get going.

*****

We flew to Kathmandu in late August 2011 and met up with the other members of our climbing group. We were doing both Everest and Manaslu with the company Himalayan Experience (HimEx), which is run by mountaineering expert Russell Brice. His track record for safety and successful summits of Everest is legendary, so we felt that we were in very good hands.

Various other people had signed up for the HimEx summit of Everest in April the following year, including Sergei, a Russian billionaire, and Pierre, a French guy who worked for Formula One. Also with us were Monica, the expedition doctor, climbing guides Adrian and Harry, and Henry Chaplin, who was leading the expedition for Walking With The Wounded this time, as various family and work commitments meant Ed Parker was unable to come on the trip.

And of course we had a film crew: Alexis, who had been with us in the North Pole, and Petter, the Norwegian polar guide who had pulled his pulk for him. Petter had quite a lot of mountaineering experience so this time he was operating a camera too.

I had never been to Iraq, but I was struck by how several of the guys who had served there said that Kathmandu reminded them of Baghdad. For some of them it brought back almost too many memories, so we were all quite glad when after a couple of days of sorting out kit we flew up to the mountains to start our walk-in. Most of our kit was transported to Manaslu Base Camp for us, so for the five-day trek we only needed a daypack with a few warm layers for the evenings.

The helicopters dropped us in a farmer's field where some more guides and Sherpas were waiting for us, and we started to follow the river. For five days we walked upstream along the valley floor, through green fields and little villages with lots of trees. We often stopped at a teahouse for a cup of sweet tea and something to eat, and wherever we went people would try to talk to us even though there was a language barrier. Some nights we spent in teahouses and others in tents, until the final night when we reached a big campsite at the end of the valley.

To acclimatise, the next day we walked up through the forest to Base Camp, gaining height very quickly on a series of switchbacks, and headed back down after lunch to sleep on the valley floor again. About halfway down was a lake of crystal-blue glacier water that ran straight off the mountain, which the guides told us had healing powers. Obviously we were all missing bits or covered in burn scars, so we were encouraged to swim. It was a hot day, but when I jumped in the water was so cold I could hardly move. It was beautiful, though – a really special experience.

We passed the lake again the following day on our way up to Base Camp, where we settled in for a long stay. Russell had a great set-up: a comms tent and a medical tent, another one for his office, cooking tents and two or three big yellow dining tents, and a lot of little white pods which we would be sleeping in. At Base Camp we each had our own tent because there was so much equipment to store, but higher up the mountain we would start sharing.

For the first few days in Base Camp we were encouraged to move around a little bit to acclimatise, but not do so much that we tired ourselves out. We practised the techniques we'd learned in Chamonix on a nearby glacier, and walked up and down to a viewpoint about two hundred metres higher. Our first proper challenge was to go up to Camp 1 and back down again in a single day.

We always stopped and waited for the rest of the team when we got to our destination, but when walking or climbing everyone went at his own pace. I was usually at the front along with Francis, a doctor who had been shot through the bicep on patrol in Afghanistan. Both of us climbed quite quickly and often fell into the same rhythm.

That first day was incredibly tough. Between Base Camp and Camp 1 was a section called the Hourglass, which was a sheer wall of ice about eighty metres high. It got its name not from its shape but from the length of time it took to climb it: they say no matter how experienced a climber you are, it will always take about an hour. By the time I got to the top I was shattered, and from there it was still another two hours of walking to reach Camp 1.

Going back down was even worse: the only way I could tackle the Hourglass was to wrap the rope around my arm and go face first, a bit like abseiling but looking down. It was terrifying.

Everybody really struggled that day – the altitude and the physical effort of climbing were a real shock to the system. Some of the guys, including Martin, Dan and Andy, suffered really badly from altitude sickness, and although I still felt OK I was absolutely exhausted.

From then on we tackled the mountain in stages, walking up to a higher camp and coming back down to sleep at a lower altitude. This was the first time we really understood the importance of acclimatising. I had always wondered why it took so long to climb a mountain, but now that I was experiencing it for myself I realised how essential it was to do things slowly. By the time we had gone up to Camp 2 and back down a couple of times, I was starting to adapt and things were getting easier. Even the Hourglass didn't seem as difficult.

We were staying at Camp 2 when the earthquake struck. Francis and I were in our tent at around seven o'clock in the evening when we felt something like a phone vibrating under our sleeping mats. It got more and more intense until there was a big rumble and the entire mountain started to shake. We all clambered out of our tents and watched as a series of avalanches was released from higher up. Camp 2 had a slightly strange position on a raised mound between a crevasse and the mountain face, and only now did we realise why Russell had chosen to put it there.

As the avalanches came down the mountain they were diverted by the mound, so they spilled around us on both sides and straight on into the crevasse. There was no denying that the man was an expert.

Although we were quite literally shaken, everyone was OK, but the avalanches had made it impossible to continue. We would have to return to Base Camp while the guides and Sherpas checked that the route ahead was still safe.

Almost as soon as we left Camp 2 we found that the nearby crevasse had widened and the ladder we used for crossing it had come away from the edge. We had no choice but to walk across, holding the safety rope for balance as the ladder bounced in thin air. We all survived the descent, but David 'Wisey' Wiseman nearly didn't – further down the mountain he stepped on a snow bridge over a crevasse that collapsed beneath him. Fortunately he was clipped in to the safety rope so ended up dangling in his harness on the end of a six-metre rope, but when he fell the slack between us vanished and I almost got pulled in too. The guides were very quick to haul him back out and he took it very well, but it was quite a shock to see how fast someone could fall away.

Back down in Base Camp, the weather turned. The summit window we had had before the earthquake had disappeared, and it was starting to look doubtful that we would ever manage to reach the peak. Some of the other guys started making plans for a short trip to Thailand while we waited for our flight home from Kathmandu, but all of a sudden their dreams of lying on a sunny beach were shattered. There was another big change in the weather and a new summit window appeared.

I was very excited to be finally going for it. We passed through familiar territory, Camp 1 and Camp 2, but this time we went further to the new heights of Camp 3. That camp was horrendous – it was basically suspended from the side of the mountain, with the tents on a steep edge just half a metre from a drop. Every time we got out of our tents we had to put on our boots and crampons, so going for a wee or collecting snow to melt became a real schlep. I felt particularly exposed with only one arm and the wind battered the tents all night long. Even though we were going higher, it was a relief the next day to move on to Camp 4.

Camp 4 was so high that we were given oxygen: one bottle to sleep on and a fresh one for summit morning. I was late starting because there was a problem with my oxygen flow, but once I did get going I felt absolutely amazing. It was as though I'd run a marathon the day before and woken up to find that someone had given me a brand new pair of legs. I felt so fresh and fit; there was oxygen flowing through my body and all my muscles were able to function. I set off at quite a fast pace and overtook a lot of the others, eventually reaching the summit just behind Karl and Wisey.

The summit of Manaslu is very narrow so can only hold two or three people at a time. One of the guides, Adrian, stayed up there to help us and I climbed up with my Sherpa, who was with me the whole time to assist when my fingers became too cold to clip in and out of the safety ropes. The scramble up was quite slippery so I really had to concentrate, but when I got to the top I was absolutely blown away. We had approached via a ridge on the back of the mountain, and on the other side there was nothing but a sheer drop. I was standing looking down on five thousand metres of nothing, more than eight thousand metres above the world. It was a beautiful day and the mountains in front of me seemed to go on for ever – an absolutely stunning view. I felt such a sense of relief and achievement to be standing there. For all I knew, it was the highest I would ever get.

*****

A couple of months later, in November 2011, I was just getting ready to run the New York Marathon when my phone rang. It was Ed Parker, calling from London, and he wasn't very pleased to hear that it was costing him a lot of money.

'Oh shit, you're in New York?' he said. 'Well, I just wanted to tell you that you're on the Everest team. We'll talk when you're back. Bye!'

It was the last thing I had been expecting.

Manaslu had been both incredibly hard and utterly exhilarating, but as far as I had been concerned that was it for my current involvement with Walking With The Wounded. When I got back to London, however, I met up with Ed who told me that the final selection had revealed they didn't have enough people for the summit team. Some suffered too badly from altitude, while others simply weren't strong enough. Along with Francis, I was one of the most confident climbers, and Ed was very keen to see at least one person get to the top of Everest. Not that he wanted to put me under pressure or anything... I was totally surprised but completely elated. Not even two years had passed since I had taken my first independent steps after being injured and I was being given the chance to climb the world's highest mountain. It was a challenge I had never even dreamed of.

After a few months of build-up, we arrived at Heathrow on 28 March to find a surprise waiting for us. Not only were Ed and Simon there with the media to see us off, but Prince Harry had come to pay us a visit. He was still the patron of Walking With The Wounded and came round each of us in turn to have a quick chat and say good luck. Of course Martin and I knew him well so we were able to have a joke, but Karl, Francis and Wisey, the other three members of the summit team, were all a bit star-struck.

Getting to Everest Base Camp was similar to going to Manaslu. After a few days in the Hyatt Hotel in Kathmandu, we boarded a helicopter to the Himalayan town of Lukla. The airport there is one of the most dangerous in the world, with a very short runway built into the side of a cliff, so we were quite relieved not to be on a plane.

From Lukla it was around a ten-day walk to Base Camp, through lush green fields and rolling hills dotted with little villages. The path is pretty well trekked – lots of tourists do the walk to Base Camp, stay there for a night and then go back down – and although life in the mountains was clearly very tough, I was impressed by the infrastructure. Lots of teahouses advertised internet or Western toilets and there were loads of cute little kids who rushed out to try to practise their English. The valleys were connected by long swing bridges, cables suspended several hundred metres above the valley floor, and we were constantly passed by caravans of yaks carrying supplies up the mountain. It was the first time I'd seen these animals and I found them phenomenal – they have massive horns and just know exactly where they're going. They cruise up the mountain under enormous loads and there's nothing for it but to get out of their way. I would watch them and feel that I was in their world now, not mine.

As well as the yaks I was amazed by the monasteries and prayer wheels, which we would spin for good luck as we passed. It was a completely different culture with a lovely feeling to it. I also loved the teahouses we stopped to eat or sleep in – we could sit outside and chat to the locals while drinking enormous mugs of really sugary tea. I've always had quite a sweet tooth so it was heaven for me, especially when there was cake to go with it.

We all walked at our own pace again and got to know yet more members of our group, including Alec, a Canadian, and Annie Doyle, who was trying to become the first Maori woman to complete the Seven Summits challenge, an ascent of the highest mountain on each continent. Henry Chaplin, who was standing in for Ed, had even brought his family with him. His ten-year-old daughter walked all the way to Base Camp without a fuss.

The camp itself is enormous – a series of tented villages that each belongs to a climbing operator. Our area was one of the first and biggest, with yellow-green tents for sleeping in and an enormous white yurt in the middle. This was the Big Dome, and it served as Russell's office, a comms centre, a party zone and a chill-out area.

There were sofas and a few tables that were always full of sweets and crisps, several laptops which we could pay to access the internet on, and probably the world's most expensive bar where beer cost about fifteen quid a bottle. Everything had to be carried up on a yak, so it was ludicrously expensive, and the remote location meant that internet and communications were all via satellite.

ESCAPING EVEREST

Accidentally downloading an email from Argos could cost about £40.

Base Camp would be our home for the next three months, so it was worth spending a couple of days getting comfy. The tents had been pitched on stony ground so it took several hours and a lot of shifting of rocks to create an area that was even vaguely comfortable to sleep on.

As with Manaslu, we had our own tents at Base Camp but would be sharing higher up, and in general we were free to do what we wanted. Every couple of days I would walk an hour and a half down the mountain to the nearest village, where there was a little café with cheaper internet. I enjoyed the feeling of getting some exercise – all that sweet tea and the snack tables in the Big Dome were having an effect – and also getting away from the claustrophobia of Base Camp.

Get a group of army guys together and tell them to hurry up and wait, and you're going to end up with a lot of mischief. Even though we could walk to the village or do occasional training climbs on the Khumbu Icefall, we spent a lot of time at Base Camp feeling quite bored. One day Wisey, Karl, Francis and I made a cardboard sign advertising a book – *Giving It Big Licks* by the 'famous climber' Martin Hewitt – and put it at the entrance to the camp where all the tourists and day-trippers came in. It took Martin days to work out why people kept coming to his tent to ask for an autograph, while the rest of us sat around pissing ourselves laughing.

Another time Wisey and I streaked through Base Camp, looking exactly like Will Farrell in the comedy *Old School*. It was hilarious (and cold) but ended up being not so funny – a few of the other outfits' Sherpas were quite offended and wanted to have us thrown off the mountain. Russell managed to negotiate on our behalf and it taught us a valuable lesson about respecting other cultures.

Sometimes what seems like a laugh to one person can actually seem very disrespectful to another.

Throughout the whole time we were at Base Camp there were concerns about the weather. It was unusually warm that season – we were able to sit outside tanning – and avalanches were falling constantly. Even Russell, who had been coming to Everest for twenty years, said he'd never seen anything like it. The warmth was also making the Khumbu Icefall extremely unstable. It naturally moves at a rate of around one metre a day, but with the sun baking it all the time it was flowing even more strongly. Almost every day our Sherpas had to put in new guide ropes and ladders to replace routes that had collapsed into the ice, and a team of our guides led by Harry and Bruce went to check out the situation for themselves.

While we were waiting for the Icefall to settle and a summit window to appear, we completed our acclimatisation phase by climbing Mount Lobuche. A 6,119-metre peak near the Khumbu Glacier, Lobuche is often used as a practice mountain for climbers hoping to summit Everest. It took us two days of tough climbing to reach the top, which is roughly at the same height as Camp 2 on Everest, and we then spent three nights up there to get used to the altitude. Francis and I were the first to reach the top and were filmed coming in by our Norwegian ninja, Petter. It was a really good moment that filled me with confidence for Everest.

While we were away on Lobuche, our summit date for Everest was fixed. We would be setting out five days after returning to Base Camp in the first week of May.

A couple of days beforehand, our guide, Harry Taylor, summoned us into the Big Dome and sketched out our route through the Khumbu Icefall on a whiteboard. We would be climbing in the middle of the night when the temperature was at its lowest and the Icefall at its most stable, so it was important that we memorised where to go to avoid getting confused in just the light of a headtorch.

I spent the afternoon before we left packing and re-packing my kit. Just like the first time I'd gone to Afghanistan, I really struggled to know what to take. To keep things as light as possible I decided to take just three pairs of socks and base layers for seven days, but the gloves were a different problem – we had five different kinds to wear. There were gloves everywhere in my tent, and I only have one hand. Goodness knows how people with two manage to cope.

Finally I had my kit sorted and after dinner I lay down to get some sleep. It didn't work, of course – I spent most of the time worrying about whether I'd eaten enough to get me through seven hours of climbing and if my stump was going to get too cold despite the hand warmers I'd sewed into the shortened end of my sleeve.

The thoughts continued whirling around my head until eventually I decided just to get up and get dressed. By the time midnight came I was hanging around outside my tent, ready and waiting to go.

It was a twenty-minute walk through Base Camp to the bottom of the Khumbu Icefall. I was extremely nervous when we set off, but by the time we started to climb I had settled down and was focused on Harry's instructions although I was still aware that the ice around us was constantly shifting.

It was never completely silent, but the big crack Francis and I heard as we were coming over a ridge a few hours into the climb was something new entirely. We looked around wildly but there was nothing to be seen – our headtorches only showed us so much. It was probably just the ice settling, we agreed, and continued to climb. The second, bigger crack came two minutes later, this time followed by a boom. A fall.

'Avalanche! Avalanche!' I didn't need my Sherpa to tell me. We'd been hearing them for weeks, only this time the sound was much closer. As it built in noise and intensity, I had absolutely no doubt. It was coming for us.

The decision to sprint to the massive ice boulder I had glimpsed to my right was a split-second call that saved my life – and probably Francis's and my Sherpa's as well. Just as they stooped down behind me the avalanche passed, not more than two or three metres away. An enormous wave of ice and snow and everything it had dragged with it ripped past us, heading down the mountain at terrifying speed. It was gone as soon as it had come, in a matter of seconds, leaving behind a fog which settled on us slowly along with the shock.

Nobody had been hurt, but it was an incredibly close call and a grim reminder of the power of the mountain.

'Let's just get out of here,' Francis muttered. We were all too stunned to speak much and continued climbing as fast as we could in silence. I felt very disorientated and, whether from the shock or the cold, was starting to shiver. Not long afterwards, I had to ask my Sherpa to start helping me each time I needed to clip in or out of a safety rope – I just couldn't get my fingers to work. Bruce, who had been just behind us and dived the other way, was also visibly shaken. After that avalanche, I don't think any of us really recovered.

The temperature seemed to drop as soon as we reached the top of the Icefall and found ourselves in a valley. The terrain was absolutely crazy, with mazes of crevasses that we needed to cross by jumping or using ladders. I followed my Sherpa the entire way – he'd done it so many times before that he knew exactly where he was going. (In general, the Sherpas were completely amazing, as were the Icefall Doctors, a team specially employed by the Nepalese government to assess and create safe routes through the Khumbu Icefall. By the time we returned from Lobuche, seven of our Sherpas had already summited Mount Everest at least once that season.)

I was getting absolutely exhausted from having to concentrate and there was a headwind cutting right through my clothes. I tried to keep my head down and cover my face as much as possible, but all the while I could feel my arm getting colder and colder. I swung it round desperately to try to get the circulation going, but neither that nor the hand warmers seemed to be having an effect.

Francis was still near me and we kept leap-frogging one another on the long walk up that valley. Sometimes I would manage to find a good rhythm and stride ahead, but then a hidden crevasse would slow me down or I got tired and needed to take a short break. Francis would overtake me and I would spend the next while trying to catch him up. Sometimes we tried to speak to one another, but our faces were so cold that our jaws were frozen. Finally, after what felt like forever, we saw a glimmer of Camp 2 in the distance.

It was then that the real torture began. As we walked I was put in mind of something Simon had told me when we were on the way to the North Pole. A few years before he had been to the South Pole, where there's a large American research base. They had seen the lights and even buildings on the base from so far away that it had taken them a whole day to get there. That was what Camp 2 on Everest felt like – I walked for an hour and it still didn't seem any closer.

Time was moving so slowly and I thought the walk would be never-ending. And when I finally did pass the first tent, I saw how huge the camp really was. It took another twenty minutes before my Sherpa and I arrived at the HimEx area.

I was completely knackered, but most of all I was cold. Lots of our Sherpas were already there getting things ready, but because we had made such good time our sleeping tents weren't warm enough. Francis and I went into the cooking tent where a fire was always going, and I stood there with my hand almost in the flames under a pan, desperately trying to warm up. The Sherpas could see how cold we were and bundled us into a corner, piling us with warm gear and their own sleeping bags, which they opened up like duvets. We huddled together, still unable to speak. Not even in the Arctic had I ever felt so cold – it was the first time I can truly say I was chilled to the bone.

One by one the others started to trickle in, and our group in the corner got bigger and bigger as people huddled up close for body heat. Everyone was feeling quite emotional – we were all tired and cold and wondering if we could actually do this, as well as feeling desperately relieved to have reached the next camp – but Karl was the first person to properly break down. He came into the tent, took off his rucksack, sat down in the middle of the group and burst into tears.

Someone gave him a hot drink and we all grouped around him as he cried and cried. 'It was so hard,' he kept saying. 'It was so hard.' It was quite humbling to see him – a young, fit guy with long hair and tattoos, who had suffered severe burns to his head, chest and arms while trying to escape from a tank that had been petrol-bombed. For me, that was a measure of how hard Everest really was.

*****

Camp 2 is located in a very safe place, well protected from any threat of avalanches. The surrounding area is flat and wide, with a clear view of Everest straight in front and the route to Camp 3 on the right-hand side. We could see a sheer wall of ice we would have to climb, and then a long traverse on a narrow glacier known as the Yellow Band. It was good to know where we were going, but looking at the route didn't exactly fill me with optimism.

We were due to spend two nights at Camp 2 before moving on, but the weather conditions were against us so our stay was extended. I was sleeping very badly, plagued by flashbacks to Afghanistan that had been triggered by the sound of the avalanche. It was a very specific sound that I had only heard once before: the night in the Afghan desert that a rocket-propelled grenade had nearly taken my life. That night too there had been a big crack in the dark, followed by a steadily building roar and the knowledge that something was coming for me, something I might not be able to escape. I knew I had been lucky on Everest – perhaps luckier even than in Afghanistan – but I would lie there in the dark, unable and unwilling to close my eyes.

During the day I felt safer, but the tents were too bright and hot to sleep in, so as a result I was getting very fatigued. I knew I was on a team with other people who had suffered from PTSD, and I could see how one person in particular had been very affected by the shock of the avalanche.

Still, I didn't speak to anyone. I had no idea how to deal with the flashbacks and what I was feeling, so I simply said I couldn't sleep and that it was probably the altitude. Looking back, I don't know why I didn't talk about it. Perhaps it was my mentality of just getting on with it, or maybe it was because I didn't really want to confront it properly. After the third night I started to feel more settled, but the flashbacks and stress had left me utterly exhausted.

We were sitting in the dining tent one afternoon when a Sherpa rushed in. 'Is your radio working? We need a doctor!' he said.

Francis, who of course is a doctor, went with him. There were extremely high winds further up the mountain and a Sherpa had been hit in the face by a flying piece of rock. It had fractured his left jaw and ripped up his cheek, and although his colleagues had managed to get him down as far as Camp 2 they were worried he wouldn't make it.

Francis and a few of the other medics in camp managed to patch him up and stop the bleeding, and a helicopter was called in. The altitude and low temperatures can make it very dangerous to land a helicopter on Mount Everest, but in this case they were able to evacuate him.

We later found out that thanks to the medics' efforts the Sherpa survived, but at the time it was quite shocking. We had all been thinking that if we made it through the Khumbu Icefall we would be absolutely fine, but that day we realised there was an awful lot more to Everest than that. Looking back, I think what happened to that Sherpa was the final nail in the coffin of our expedition.

That night there was a conversation between Camp 2 and Base Camp in which the decision was taken for us to go back down the mountain. The high winds were simply too dangerous and we had missed our original summit window, so it seemed to make most sense to return to a lower altitude and wait for another opportunity. Going back down in daylight, it felt like a different world.

A dump of snow had filled in many of the crevasses we had crossed in the valley and I followed behind my Sherpa, stepping exactly in his footprints. I didn't want to move so much as a centimetre to the left or right – the tiniest mistake and I knew I could be going. Compared to that, the Icefall was surprisingly not scary. Looking at it in the sunlight rather than the beam of my headtorch, I couldn't believe we had managed to climb up the way we did. At the same time, it was breathtaking – the scale of the area was just phenomenal. The light shone through sheer pieces of ice in beautiful blues and greens, but there was also a harshness to it, a sense of danger lurking.

ESCAPING EVEREST

It was a relief to be back in Base Camp. We were really tired and quite emotional – a mixture of happy and disappointed. Although at that stage we knew we would go back for a second try, I think all of us had secretly wished for a perfect summit, to get right to the top on our very first attempt. But we were soon distracted by the comforts of camp life, starting with the shower tent. The Sherpas had rigged up little cubicles with big plastic containers attached to a hosepipe and a pump for building up water pressure. We were normally allowed one shower a week, and that day was one of those occasions.

The feeling of warm water on my skin was so amazing. After days of climbing and sweating and only having baby wipes to 'wash' myself with, it was such a relief to feel properly clean. The fresh kit I put on was unbelievably soft, and once I had washed my hair as well I felt like a new person.

The next day we spent washing clothes and doing general administration, and for the evening Russell announced that he was going to throw a big party. Our Big Dome parties were legendary and this was probably the best one yet. Everyone from our camp was involved and we extended invitations to a few people we knew from other outfits. Even Kenton Cool was on the guest list, a famous mountaineer who had summited Everest several times and whom we liked to annoy by refusing him access to our parties.

We had a plentiful supply of whisky, the fifteen-quid beers were flowing, and we connected somebody's iPod to several speakers. Things got a bit out of hand when Martin took over the role of DJ with his beloved Scouse house music, but fortunately Francis was around to take over with some less extreme tunes.

After the last few days we really needed to blow off some steam and we were grateful to Russell for giving us the chance to do it. Strangely enough, no one actually noticed that Russell himself was the only person missing from the party. The next day we all woke up hungover to the max, only to find Russell calling us to a team meeting in the Big Dome. The remains of the party had been cleared away and we sat down on the sofas while Russell stood in the middle. As he gave a little speech, his eyes filled with tears.

While we had all been partying, Russell had been on the phone to Ed. The weather was really troubling him, as was the fact that a couple of Sherpas had already died or been injured on the mountain, and Ed was keen to get a clear picture of how things stood.

When he asked Russell if there was any seed of doubt that we would all make it up and down again unharmed, Russell answered very honestly that yes, there was. He's one of the few Everest operators to have a 100 per cent track record – none of his clients has ever died on the mountain because he is willing to step in and make those tough calls.

When it came to our group, some of his clients and guides had families and children, and the last thing he wanted to do was send any of us home more injured than we already were. For Ed, safety was the bottom line. As soon as he heard that our safety was even the tiniest bit in doubt, his mind was made up. He was pulling us off the mountain. The expedition was over.

'I'm just so sorry,' Russell said when he finished. Tears were rolling down his face; it was clearly breaking him to give us the news. When I asked Ed later if he had found it a hard decision, he said no. Dislocated from it all in London, it was easy for him to look at things objectively and make what turned out to be the right decision. At the time, though, I couldn't understand it.

Like most of the rest of the team, I think, I felt like I had been stabbed in the heart. At this point we had been away from home for close to two months, had trained for nearly an entire year and put in a huge amount of personal effort. On top of that, Martin and I in particular were still flying from the success of the North Pole and found it very hard to accept that we would be going home having failed our next mission. It was a truly sad moment and very, very difficult.

Martin and I were so unwilling to accept the decision that we teamed up with Sergei to try to attach ourselves to a new group. We talked about approaching Kenton Cool, or maybe just hiring a couple of Sherpas and setting out on our own. We had all the kit and we were sure we could get oxygen and fuel from somewhere. We had come all this way and put in so much work – surely we had to give it one more go?

Word got out that we were planning a coup and Ed asked Henry Chaplin to stop us. In the end, though, it was Harry Taylor who stepped up and brought the full weight of his many years' experience to the table. He sat down with the entire group for a conversation I'll never forget.

'I've summited Everest,' he told us, 'but how long do you think it took me?' We guessed three attempts. 'Six,' he said. 'Six times I came back, and in those six times I saw friends die or I came away with injuries. Only on my sixth time did I make it. I came back again and didn't make it last time, and we're here on my eighth time now. It's just the way it is – don't force it. You're only going to regret it, or your family's going to regret it because you'll be dead.'

That hit a nerve. Our families had already been through so much with our injuries, and even if we thought we were confident enough to make it, we knew we couldn't put them through the pain of yet more injury or, even worse, death. I also realised that our sponsors and the public hadn't supported us and donated money just for us to kill ourselves doing something stupid. It might seem like a failure, but Walking With The Wounded would be far better served by us taking the sensible option of going home when all the signs were bad. We knew it was the right thing to do, but it was with heavy hearts that we turned away from our dreams of summiting.

With the decision taken, Sergei and a couple of Russell's better-off clients organised a helicopter to fly them out, but we spent another two days in Base Camp before setting out to walk back to Lukla. Partly because it was downhill, partly because now the expedition was over we were just desperate to get home, we basically ran down the valley and covered the distance in just three days.

It was a different route to the one we'd taken up, with scenery that was just as beautiful, although we didn't have much time to appreciate the greenery or teahouses. At Lukla Airport we sat and waited for our flight, looking at the wrecks of planes that had overshot the runway and crashed into the mountainside. It wasn't the greatest confidence booster, and when a tiny cargo plane laden with sacks of rice flew in we weren't best pleased to learn that we were getting on it.

After helping to unload the rice we climbed on board and strapped ourselves in. The pilot made a few checks and fired up the engines, backing up along the runway as far as he possibly could. He put the brakes on and revved the engines hard – the noise was deafening – before suddenly releasing the brakes and letting the plane race off along the runway. Just before it ended he pulled up a little and we shot over the edge of the cliff into empty space. *Oh my soul*, I thought as the plane dipped, but the engines held and we were soon flying away from the mountains. It was a very bumpy journey but quite an incredible experience.

In the Hyatt Hotel in Kathmandu I ordered a mojito. All the boys were drinking beer, but that's never been my favourite. After standing under the shower for twenty minutes and lying down on a bed that felt like a cloud, we were in the restaurant eating steak and chips and I felt in the mood to celebrate. The taste of that mojito was so good that everyone wanted one, and for the next couple of days while we hung out at the pool the poor barman did nothing but crush ice and mint leaves for us.

Coming back from an expedition is always a time at which you really appreciate the little luxuries in life. The taste of a cocktail or the feel of a soft pillow can be one of the greatest things ever.

We were still in the middle of our mojito fest when we started hearing the sound of helicopters and sirens around Kathmandu. The news gradually filtered through that there had been a big avalanche on Everest that had killed eleven people and injured many others.

We sobered up immediately. The news was utterly devastating: on the one hand we were incredibly grateful to Russell and Ed for having made the decision they did, but on the other hand we were appalled that people had had to die in order to prove them right. I wondered if anyone I had met on the mountain had died, if they had families they would never be going back to. It brought home the fact that we had made the right call, but I was heartbroken for the people who had lost their lives up there.

Despite the fact that our expedition had ended in disappointment, I had taken Harry Taylor's words to heart. I might not have conquered Everest, but I had a newfound love for mountaineering and had proved to be a very strong climber who was able to handle altitude. There was no doubt in my mind that I would come back to Nepal one day to attempt Everest again, but in the meantime there were plenty of other mountains in the world. Our failed attempt to summit Everest wasn't the end.

Instead, it was just the start.

XII

AMONG THE MOUNTAINS

By the time I came back from Nepal in May 2012, I had all but transitioned into civilian life. Although I was still officially a soldier, I was sharing a flat in Woolwich with Kingsley Ward, a triple amputee from 1 Para who was also going through the resettlement process. No longer living in a military environment had definitely helped me to adjust, but I don't think anything could have made me feel fully prepared for 12 August 2012. I had the right people around me to make it bearable – including Sian, my girlfriend at the time, who came over to the flat in the morning with a bottle of South African brandy – but when the resettlement officer knocked at the door I didn't want to open it.

In the end, all it took was my signature on a few forms, and then I was asked for my army ID. Handing it over was really tough – it truly felt like giving up part of my identity. The officer walked out and closed the door on a significant chapter of my life. My heart was broken, but I clearly remember thinking how a new one was about to start.

*****

I hadn't known what I would go on to do when I left the army, but my experience of Manaslu and Everest had ignited a new passion. Mountaineering is hard. Extremely hard. But it was also something I hugely enjoyed and, as I found out when we got back from Everest, it didn't take long to forget all the bad bits. After a few days in the comfortable environment of home, I was already asking myself which other mountains I could tackle. There are a number of challenges within the climbing community, like the Seven Summits (the highest mountain on each continent) or the world's fourteen 8,000-metre peaks, and I was desperate to start ticking some of them off.

I had made good friends on the Everest expedition, including a few experienced mountaineers. We hadn't even left Kathmandu before I was discussing potential expeditions with two of our guides, Harry Taylor and Henry Chaplin – conversations that Martin Hewitt also picked up on. Alec Turner, a member of the Everest team who wasn't affiliated with Walking With The Wounded, had invited us to stay with him in Alaska if we ever felt like climbing Denali and when Harry and Henry both said they'd recommend it, it seemed like too good an opportunity to pass up. By late summer 2012, preparations were well under way.

At 6,190 metres, Denali (which used to be known as Mount McKinley) is the highest peak in North America. Unlike Everest, it involves only a few days of classic mountain climbing with crampons and ropes; instead, the vast majority of the route is covered by ski touring. Our small team of five – Harry, Henry, Martin, Alec and myself – was experienced in pulling sledges on skis, but Martin was keen to add a sixth person to the group. Craig was a fellow ex-Forces member who had been blinded in a bomb blast, and Martin wanted to take the opportunity to show him and other visually impaired servicemen and -women that it was still possible to go off and do extreme challenges.

Although this wasn't a Walking With The Wounded expedition

– we just arranged it as a group of friends – we were still hoping it might have a wider impact on the disabled community.

Craig had never climbed a mountain or used alpine skis, so the first thing to do was assess his abilities. Harry invited us to his house in Chamonix for a week to introduce Craig to mountaineering and allow the rest of us to brush up on skiing and safety drills. We also had to learn how to guide a visually impaired team member up and down the mountain safely. One of us was always attached to him by a rope around the waist, and there were various methods of keeping the tension correct and making sure he was walking the right way.

Losing his sight had made Craig extremely organised and his memory was phenomenal: he knew where everything was and could instantly remember the exact sequence needed to tie a knot. He did struggle with the long, thin skis, but then we tried snowshoes which proved to be the best method for him. I loved how independent he was, and by the end of the week I think it's safe to say that he had blown us all away.

We set out for Denali in May 2013 in a positive frame of mind. It felt different to going to Manaslu and Everest, which were highly organised trips with large support teams and lots of equipment. This time, we flew to Alaska and were met by Alec in a giant Ford pickup truck with a massive tank on the back. 'I just need to collect some water for the house,' he explained as we pulled into what looked like a petrol station.

In fact, it was a water station – Alec and his family lived completely off-grid in the middle of a forest, which meant regular trips to fill the water tank for all their daily needs. It was incredible to see his home and stay there for a couple of days while we made our final preparations.

Just like when we'd gone to the North Pole, travelling light was hugely important. We bought food and supplies in the nearby town and stripped it all down to the bare minimum. As we would be dragging everything we needed for three to four weeks on sledges, we didn't want to be carrying more than we absolutely had to. All excess packaging was left behind – it might not have added much to the weight, but we would need to carry all our rubbish off the mountain – and we made new ration and snack packs to see us through to the summit and back.

Denali is in the middle of a huge area of protected forest, the Denali National Park and Reserve. Visitor numbers are strictly controlled and there are regulations in place right across the mountain to manage waste and keep the park clean. (Even going to the toilet had its own set of rules – human waste was collected in special bags and would be carried with us until we reached the next designated dumping site, which was usually a deep crevasse.) Alec had arranged our permits and transport in advance, so we drove to the park entrance, signed ourselves in and waited around for a lift to Base Camp.

It was a beautiful day to be hanging around in a forest, but the view from the air was even better. Transport to Base Camp was a little Twin Otter plane, which flew in to collect us late in the afternoon. It was a tight squeeze with all our kit and I could feel how heavy the plane was even before the engines started roaring – it was another moment, like flying out of Lukla, when I thought we just weren't going to take off.

The pilot dragged the plane into the air and the forest spread out below us in an endless expanse of trees dotted with shining lakes and rivers. The scale of the landscape was phenomenal, and as we headed straight for the mountains we could see the scenery beginning to change, from green and brown to snowy white. It looked so untouched; an utterly beautiful place.

UNEQUIVOCAL

Our plane came in to land on a runway that was basically just a stretch of snow on a small plateau. We jumped out, unloaded our kit and found a spot on the edge of Base Camp to pitch our tents for the night. I say 'night' – we were so far north that we were experiencing almost-twenty-four-hour daylight – but we knew we needed to get some sleep before making our first steps towards the summit. There was one more important thing to do before getting our heads down, though.

Back in town, Alec had insisted on buying a crate of beer along with our other supplies. Now we dug a big hole in the snow just behind our tents, buried the beer and covered it over, marking the spot with a spare skiing pole. With any luck it would still be there when we returned.

The next morning we set off... downhill. Base Camp's location on a plateau meant we first had to drop on to the valley floor before climbing the lower slopes of Denali on the other side. We lost quite a lot of ground before we started gaining it, which was an unusual start to an expedition, but then nothing about this mountain experience was like anything I'd encountered before. For a start, our acclimatisation phase wasn't just about slowly building up fitness and getting used to the altitude. We would also be using it to cache.

Denali lacks the infrastructure that a mountain like Everest has, meaning that caching is the only way to climb it. Rather than dragging all our kit with us every day, we would drop loads of it at various points along the route, burying it in marked caches and returning the next day to collect them.

On a typical cache day we would ski a certain distance up the mountain, dig a hole to bury a stash of food and equipment we'd only need later on, then ski back down to make camp and sleep at a lower altitude. We would repeat this process a few times, eventually adding in collection trips in the morning to pick up whatever had been left further down the mountain and bring it up to our new camping site. It involved a lot of logistics, which Alec, Harry and Henry were fortunately experienced in, and it was a fantastic way to acclimatise and improve our fitness. The loads were very heavy, but I did every single caching run – often with Martin, but sometimes with Harry or Henry. I really enjoyed the skiing and felt it was something I could do well for the team; as I'd learned in the Arctic, only having one arm meant it was harder for me to contribute as much when it came to putting up tents or cooking our meals.

Pretty quickly we got into a nice rhythm and developed a good team dynamic. Every evening we would set up camp with our sleeping tents arranged around a communal kitchen area which we dug out of the snow and covered with a tarpaulin. It looked like a cross between an igloo and a tent: depending on the weather and how much time we had, we often cut blocks of solid snow to make walls and seating areas.

We were following a pretty well established route set by the National Park authorities, which included designated areas for camping and waste disposal, so we were often lucky enough to come across a little igloo built by a team that had been there earlier in the season. It was great to walk into camp after a hard day's work caching and find a ready-made structure that only needed a bit of a clean and a canvas roof.

As much as I enjoyed skiing up and down between caches, there were some scary moments. We spent a couple of days stuck at Camp 2 when we were caught in a blizzard, and in the days that followed visibility was very poor. To make matters worse, that area of the mountain was renowned for its crevasses, and the helpful orange and pink marker posts laid out along the recommended route between them were almost impossible to see. Harry and I were returning to camp from dropping a cache higher up the mountain when we realised we had veered a long way off the track. Luckily, Harry managed to spot the next marker and we found our way back, but I spent the whole trip terrified of falling into a crevasse.

The weather cleared up over the next two days, but by this time we had another issue on our hands. Craig had really started to struggle and was finding it more and more difficult to maintain the pace. We were actually walking pretty slowly because of the kit we were dragging, but even when we tried taking as much weight off him as possible he was unable to keep up.

Finding it hard to follow the rope, he regularly stumbled off the track and into the soft snow, dragging down whoever was attached to him for guidance. Martin, who was often leading him, was getting very frustrated, so I tried to take over whenever I could. Craig was clearly determined, but he seemed like a different person to the guy who had impressed us all in Chamonix.

As we climbed, the days were getting progressively harder, and at Camp 3 – just over 4,300 metres high – we found ourselves snowed in once again. While we were there, Alec, who made a brief call to his family every evening to say goodnight to his kids, turned on the satellite phone one night to find a flood of messages. His wife had been trying to contact him all day to tell him the unthinkable: his brother had just died in tragic circumstances. Alec was in absolute bits. He went off for a walk by himself saying he didn't know what to do, while the rest of us sat there terrified that he would end up in a crevasse.

When he eventually came back, we told him he had to go home straight away. His family needed him, whereas we would be OK. Of course we were relying on him for much of the expedition – he was our transport in and out of the park, and most of the pots, pans and other equipment was his – but we knew we could find an alternative solution. It had been wonderful having Alec there: he was our chef and guide, a super-strong, helpful and all-round brilliant guy. I was very sad to see him go, especially in such painful circumstances.

Shocked by the news, we waited for the storm to clear before continuing up to Camp 4. At 5,200 metres, it's the last camp before the summit and only accessible by a proper climbing route. We had lots of advice from Alec, Henry and Harry, who had climbed Denali before, and also spoke to several other groups who were coming down from the summit, so we had a pretty good idea of what to expect. There were a few technical sections coming up, a very narrow ridge, a couple of bits of scrambling and a sheer climb similar to the Hourglass on Manaslu. Craig, who was struggling with the altitude as well as the pace, was our main concern – we no longer felt confident that we could get him safely to the summit.

After a lot of discussion, we decided that he was sadly going to have to stay behind. Craig was understandably disappointed but felt it was for the best too, and we left him at Camp 3 in the care of a Special Forces team who happened to be there on a mountain exercise.

In the space of two days, our little team of six had been cut down to four. And it wasn't going to stop there. The next day we set out early, roped together in pairs for safety, only for Henry to start suffering from the altitude almost immediately. I was his climbing partner and found it incredibly frustrating – he was still able to move, but very slowly, whereas when I'm attempting a mountain I really need to keep going.

For most of the day I had to concertina my way along, climbing up close to Henry, waiting there while he went on and the rope stretched out between us, and then quickly closing the gap again.

The first part of the day involved a steep climb and a scramble, but after that we found ourselves walking along a ridgeline with unbelievable views of the mountains and forests around us. The ground was rocky in places but conditions were good, and apart from the slow pace I loved every minute of the route. When we reached Camp 4 in the late afternoon I was still feeling really strong. That was more than could be said of Martin, who had also started to suffer very badly with altitude sickness: he had slowed the pace right down and was complaining of a terrible headache.

Despite his struggle in the morning, Henry had started feeling better in the afternoon, so when I suggested pushing for the summit he was keen to go. To me it made perfect sense – it was an unbelievably beautiful day, with clear blue skies and very low winds, and because of the twenty-four-hour daylight we would always be able to see our way. I was feeling very good and thought I might never have such a perfect summit opportunity again, but I needed either Harry or Henry to guide me.

Harry was always feeling strong, but he agreed to stay behind and look after Martin while Henry and I headed to the top. Martin wasn't happy about it – he wanted us all to stick together – but Harry assured him they'd have another chance in the morning.

To help Henry I carried all the climbing equipment we would need, while he just had food, warm kit and water in his backpack. It was about six o'clock by the time we set out, and pretty soon we started passing lots of people coming back down. 'Are you crazy?' they kept asking us. 'It's far too late for a summit!' Even though we pointed out that it was still daylight, several of them tried very hard to convince us to turn around. We just ignored them and carried on, which did eventually prove to be entirely the right decision.

There was no way I would have been able to climb Denali on

my own. Henry used all his experience and did a fantastic job of getting us to the summit in good time, not to mention keeping us both safe. As we got closer to the top, things got pretty gnarly – we had to walk along a knife-edge in a strong wind that threatened to blow us off the edge of a sheer drop.

The temperature was much lower than it had been earlier in the day and after a while I had every single one of my layers on. It was so cold it felt like being back on Everest again, and I wrapped my head and neck in several balaclavas, trying desperately not to expose any skin. There was no communication between Henry and me at this point – we were focusing all our efforts on not sliding off the ridge – but then he stopped and started reeling me in on the rope. We took the last couple of steps together and were suddenly on the summit. It was eleven o'clock on the dot.

The view from the top of Denali was simply stunning. Henry and I were the only people up there, and we could have been alone in the entire world. Around and below us was nothing but a phenomenal expanse of snow, mountaintops and forest, and the sun cast the shadow of Denali out across the landscape. I was blown away by that silhouette – I just couldn't believe how far it stretched.

It put the height of the mountain I had just climbed into perspective and added to the sense of extraordinary achievement. Six thousand, one hundred and ninety metres might not be high in Himalayan terms, but standing there I really did feel on top of the world.

*****

We came back to earth with a bump. Arriving in Camp 4 at around three o'clock in the morning, we were met by other climbers just getting up for their summit attempts. One guy came over to us to say that he and his teammates had loads of pasta left from dinner and would we like it? Henry and I were starving, so I asked the guy to tip it into my mess tin and put it straight on the stove. It didn't take long for a terrible smell to fill the tent – in my hurry I had forgotten to put any water in the tin and the pasta had stuck to the bottom. It was completely burnt, but we ate it anyway. At five thousand metres you don't have a lot of choice.

Martin had managed to get some sleep and was feeling much better, so he and Harry set off for the summit while Henry and I recovered. By that time the wind had really picked up and the temperature had plummeted; visibility was poor and the traverse of the narrow ridge below the peak was very dangerous. We were expecting them back at around two o'clock in the afternoon, but it was gone six before they finally arrived, exhausted. Of course they were elated to have reached the summit as well, but conditions had been far from perfect and we all wanted nothing more than a warm shower and a night in a bed.

The hard work doesn't end when you reach the top of a mountain. Coming back down can be just as tiring – especially on Denali, where our loads got heavier as we picked up more kit and the sledges became almost impossible to control. Instead of dragging them along they were running free in front of us, pulling us down the mountain in all kinds of directions so we were constantly falling over.

Trying to guide Craig safely and control several sledges – at one stage Harry and I had three between us – was incredibly difficult, and that day tempers got very frayed. By the time we got to the valley floor we were all completely spent, but the worst bit was still to come. Heartbreak Hill.

Heartbreak Hill is the nickname of the long, steep slope we had walked down out of Base Camp on the very first day of the expedition. We knew that a plane would be waiting for us at the top, but that only seemed to make the walk harder. It was steep and slippery, my sledge was heavy, and I felt like it was never going to end. Each of us walked at our own pace, with Harry leading Craig right at the back, and Henry was the first to go over the crest of the hill.

When I finally got to the top and the ground flattened out, I saw him waiting for me with a beer in his hand. Beside him was a hole in the snow and the crate Alec had insisted we bury. I'm not much of a beer guy, but that drink was bliss – I drained the bottle in one go and it barely touched the sides. Sadly Alec wasn't there to share the moment with us, but we couldn't have been more grateful.

I came back from Denali looking like a twelve-year-old boy. I had lost so much weight that my jeans no longer fitted and I barely recognised myself in the mirror. There was no doubt that it had been a hard expedition – the days were long with all the toing and froing, digging holes and dragging sledges, but we still always had to leave a little bit of energy in the tank to build a cooking igloo, put the tents up and feed ourselves in the evening.

On Everest and Manaslu we'd had a team of Sherpas to do all that for us; we'd just carried a bit of kit and done the day's climbing. It might sound strange, but the fact that we had absolutely no luxuries was what I loved most about Denali. The sense of achievement was much greater because we'd done it unsupported – much like the North Pole, it was a pure expedition. Because of that and its unbelievable beauty, to this day Denali remains my favourite mountain in the world.

*****

Several years later I would find myself in the Andes climbing Aconcagua – the highest peak in South America and a mountain of a very different sort. I was part of the Adaptive Grand Slam team, which had been set up by Martin off the back of our early ideas about doing some kind of mountaineering challenge. In Nepal, after our failed attempt at Everest, I had started getting keen on doing the Seven Summits, but Martin had expanded this by adding unsupported expeditions to the North and South Poles to make it a challenge usually known as the Explorers' Grand Slam. The Adaptive Grand Slam group aims to be the first disabled team to complete the challenge, and I had unwittingly become a part of it through the North Pole and Denali expeditions.

In November 2015 the team attempted Aconcagua, but bad weather had forced them to abandon the climb just short of the summit. Due to my cycling commitments – a new career that began shortly after our ascent of Denali – I had been unable to join them, but in January 2017 I was part of the team that flew to Argentina for a second attempt at the 6,962-metre peak.

This would be quite a different kind of mountaineering, with rocky rather than snowy terrain and a lot less technical climbing. As I found out, though, Aconcagua is not to be underestimated.

It all started out easily enough. I had just got back from a long cycling expedition through Chile, and despite having had to spend a few days in hospital because of a cyst – a story I'll go into in a later chapter – I felt at the top of my physical game. I was fit, lean and still quite well acclimatised to living at altitude, and I knew that this would be a simpler mountain than almost anything else I had experienced. The straightforward, sunny trek in to Base Camp along a track filled with donkeys and horses did nothing to prove me wrong.

The team was one of the biggest I'd ever climbed with, so there were always people to hang out with during the few days we spent at Base Camp. Although I ended up disliking my experience of Aconcagua, it was for reasons entirely to do with the mountain itself; the people I was there with were really great.

Aside from Martin and Harry Taylor, with whom I had climbed Denali, the team included Terry Byrne, Matt Nyman and Jake Gardner, who had all been injured in Afghanistan or Iraq, and non-military team members like Kelda Wood, who had had her career as a professional horse rider cut short by a severe leg injury. She was the only girl on the team and still walking on crutches, but she was incredibly tough and never once complained – her attitude was just amazing.

A few members of the public who supported the Adaptive Grand Slam had also joined us, adding a bit of variety to the group. A couple of people were suffering from altitude, but our main guide, Andy, announced that we would be taking things slowly to allow everyone to acclimatise.

From Base Camp we climbed up to Camp 1 before coming back down to sleep; a few days later we went up to Camp 2 and descended to sleep for a couple of nights at Camp 1, and so on all the way up to Camp 4. It was similar to the way we'd tackled Manaslu and is the best method for dealing with high altitude. Climbing during the day helps your body get used to the lack of oxygen, but it's very important always to sleep at a lower level in order to recover.

Aside from the dust, which I could constantly feel sitting in the back of my nose and which made my throat incredibly dry, everything was going well. The weather was brilliant – the days were warm, nights were cold and we only had a few windy spells – and I still felt in great shape. I was coping fine with the altitude and even as high as Camp 4 I felt that the mountain was easy. We barely even needed a pair of crampons – it was walking or rock-scrambling almost all the way. Coming back down to camp in the afternoons was particularly fun: the mountain was full of big scree fields that we would run up and skid through. There were lots of hilarious moments as someone took a bad slide and fell over.

It might have been fun for skidding, but I didn't particularly enjoy the landscape we were walking through. The Himalayas had been majestic and I loved the untouched purity of Denali, but Aconcagua was just rock and gravel.

On the way from Base Camp to Camp 1 we had passed a small glacier sandwiched between two layers of rock, and occasionally we'd come across a little river or some scruffy patches of snow. Mostly, though, the scenery was barren and brown, nothing but slate and scree and constant dust.

We reached Camp 4 in good time and planned an early start the next morning to reach the summit. That night the temperature dropped a lot, and when we started walking we found ourselves facing an icy headwind in the shadow of the mountain. The path we had to traverse was extremely narrow, and looking down I could see all the way to Base Camp. If I fell off the edge, I thought, I would probably roll straight into a tent.

It wasn't long before I started to shiver. Andy had insisted that we all stick together so the pace was very slow, the wind was freezing, and no matter how many layers I put on I just couldn't get warm. I kept having to move my neckwarmer around – after a few minutes of breathing into it the part covering my mouth would have turned to ice, so to prevent frostbite I would rotate it to have a drier bit on my face. That meant there was always a lump of ice melting at the back of my neck. As well as worrying about my face getting frostbitten I was paranoid about my stump, and the fingers of my right hand had already gone numb.

AMONG THE MOUNTAINS

By the time we stopped for our next break, I was so cold my brain had stopped functioning. Sitting on the ground with my backpack next to me, I knew I needed to open it and get out something to eat. My hand was hovering over the bag and I was looking at the zip, but my brain couldn't tell my fingers to pull it. I couldn't even speak to ask for help; the words just didn't come out. Eventually Dave, one of our civilian supporters, noticed I was struggling and came over to help. I was physically shaking, but the only thing I could do was to sit in the sun and hope to warm up.

When Andy and Martin started calling for everyone to get ready to go again, all I wanted was to sit there for a little bit longer. I'd read about people just sitting down in the snow on a mountain like Everest and dying, and that was the first and only time I've ever come close to that feeling. It wasn't that I *wanted* to die – I just didn't know how to carry on.

It was also the only time I've ever seriously thought that I wouldn't make it to the top of a mountain. Somehow I managed to get myself up and moving, and taking big steps in the sunshine gave me a tiny bit of warmth. I wasn't shivering as badly any more, but the cold had sapped all the energy out of my body and I was utterly exhausted. Just putting one foot in front of the other took a superhuman effort, and I could only take four or five steps before having to stop for a five-minute break. I never once thought about the summit; all I did was focus on a big rock or a bend in the path and promise myself that if I made it that far I could stop for a rest. Then I would start looking for the next target.

I continued doing that and went on and on and on, all the way to the summit. It was ironic, really: in the space of a few hours I had gone from feeling untouchable to battling my way through the hardest climb of my life.

Aconcagua had been a strange experience – even the summit

was weird. We came out on to a small plateau where there was a pile of rocks marked with a cross, but not far away we could see another point that actually looked higher. It wasn't really – we were at the real summit – but it did slightly take away from the sense of achievement. Still, when I touched the cross I was flooded with relief like nothing I'd ever felt before. Usually I'd be in high spirits to have reached the top of a mountain, but that day I had been drained of every ounce of energy.

To me, Aconcagua was not a pretty mountain. It was a harsh environment, and a place that gave me a sense of the human body's limits in quite a frightening way. I've been very lucky never to have struggled badly with altitude, but what the cold did to me that day, both physically and mentally, is something I won't forget in a hurry.

I've now climbed the two highest peaks in the Americas and am glad to have had the experience, but while I'd go back to Denali tomorrow and would love to try Everest again, I feel relieved that there's no need to return to Aconcagua. Not all mountains are created equal, and I'm perfectly happy to keep it that way.

XIII

TEAM GB

Although I loved mountaineering from the word go, it wouldn't end up becoming my career. Throughout my rehab at Headley Court and the time I spent training to climb mountains like Manaslu, Everest and Denali, there was another sport I turned to for fitness, fun and a feeling of confidence in what my altered body was able to achieve.

Growing up in South Africa, I had always loved cycling. As a kid I spent lots of time on my BMX bike and in my teens I would cycle to school – at least until I learned to drive and using a bike as transport suddenly became uncool. When I came to the UK and joined the army I had basically given it up, but in the months of rehab following my injury I was struck by a sudden feeling that it might be nice to get back on a bike. I mentioned this to George, my occupational health therapist at Headley Court, who told me about Jon-Allan Butterworth, a former RAF serviceman who had also lost his left arm.

Jon-Allan had gone on to take up cycling and become a member of the British team, and as we shared similar injuries George thought it might be a good physical activity for me to try. I didn't think much more about Jon-Allan at that stage; I could have had no idea that a few years later we would end up being teammates.

Cycling was a great idea, but there was one problem: I didn't own a bike. As my left leg grew stronger I spent more and more time on the exercise bike in the gym, but it wasn't quite the same as being out on the open road. The rehab instructor at my regimental base in St Athan, Phil Dodds, finally came to the rescue by finding out about a grant scheme open to wounded veterans. He helped me apply for funding to buy a bike and took me down to Forza Cycles in Llantwit Major, our local town. I knew almost nothing about bikes at that stage, but as soon as I walked through the door I saw a beautiful frame in the Team GB colours, part of a special series that had just been brought out by Pinarello. The bike was within budget and the shop owner, Neal Craig, knew all about the adaptations I would need thanks to a friend with one arm with whom he sometimes raced. A few weeks later, I was cycling slowly around the perimeter of the base.

I fell in love immediately. Once I'd got used to cycling with one arm, which meant having the brakes and gears on just one side, I began to push myself further, exploring the narrow lanes of the Welsh countryside. It could be quite difficult steering, especially when there were potholes, puddles or lorries to avoid, so after a while I decided to wear a prosthetic for cycling.

I usually didn't need one in daily life, but on the bike it enabled me to bear a bit more weight across my shoulders and offered a great deal more control and stability. My rides started becoming longer and faster and my confidence was given an enormous boost.

Looking back on it now, I can't believe the way I cycled. For one thing, my position on the bike was absolutely horrendous, and I had a very basic set-up in terms of brakes and gears. The prosthetic arm I wore was actually designed for sitting on a motorbike, but I made it work because it was all I had – and, at the time, it was perfect.

Being able to ride my bike independently reminded me of all

the late afternoons I had spent touring around the South African countryside and really rekindled my love for the sport. Over the next few years my life would change a lot: I would leave Wales for London, walk to the North Pole, climb mountains, be discharged from the army and even start a new job working for an insurance company in Henley. Throughout it all I just kept pedalling away.

*****

In many ways I felt that cycling had given me a new lease of life, but in the years following my injury it was only ever about fun. In 2012, though, just before attempting Everest, I signed up for an Ironman event along with a team from Help for Heroes. Training didn't begin in earnest until I got back from Nepal, and with the weeks at high altitude having boosted my lung power I found myself really able to push it on the bike. Riding ten miles was suddenly nothing; almost every week I was setting a new personal-best distance.

The Ironman (a long-distance triathlon involving a 2.4-mile swim, a 112-mile bike ride and a marathon, completed in one day) was pretty much what I expected it to be. I just got through the swim – I was the last member of the Help for Heroes team to emerge from the water – but once I got on the bike I overtook everyone and put quite a bit of distance between us.

With that gap, I had enough leeway to plod my way through the run and still be one of the first on the team to finish. It was a tough competition and I didn't instantly sign up for another one, but something about the triathlon format had got me interested.

That summer, while I was training for the Ironman, the Olympic Games had come to London. Like many people in the UK, I found them hugely inspiring. The atmosphere surrounding the events was amazing and for me the timing was perfect. Having left the army in August 2012, I was looking for something to do with my life – working in risk mitigation for an insurance company wasn't terribly fulfilling, but competing in the next Paralympic Games seemed like it might be. I was especially pleased when I heard that the first ever para-triathlon would be hosted at Rio 2016, so I looked online and signed up for a Team GB Triathlon open weekend.

As luck would have it, it was the one weekend on which I absolutely couldn't get time off. Being officially discharged from the army had meant that I had needed to find a new job, and in November 2012 I had started working for an insurance company, based first in London and then in Henley-on-Thames.

Risk mitigation and global security – two big factors in insurance – seemed to attract quite a high number of army veterans, so I had been drawn to the job by the potential of finding like-minded colleagues and a sense of camaraderie. I felt I had been lucky to get the position after a tough round of interviews that involved giving a presentation on topics I was unfamiliar with, so I had accepted the offer without hesitation.

After working in London for a couple of months, I had begun 2013 by moving to the new offices in Henley, which were in a beautiful barn conversion beside the river. Victoria Nicholson, a fundraising manager who worked for Walking With The Wounded, had very kindly put me in touch with Adrian and Sophie, friends of hers who lived in the nearby village of Nettlebed.

We'd never even met before, but they had a spare room above the garage which they suggested I could stay in while I searched for a place to live. Their house was beautiful, right on the edge of the village cricket pitch, and luckily we got on very well. What started out as a couple of weeks soon turned into a few months... and in the end I would stay with them for almost two years.

The company I worked for did twenty-four-hour surveillance for their clients, monitoring conflict and security situations all over the world, so my job involved shifts at night-time and weekends. During the Team GB Triathlon open weekend I was due to be on nights, and as we were short on manpower anyway there was no one I could swap with.

There was simply no way to get out of working, but nor did I want to give the triathlon opportunity up. It left me with only one option: I would have to do both.

At six o'clock on Saturday morning, Sian, my then-girlfriend, arrived at the office to pick me up. We folded down the seats in my car and I crawled into the back to try to get some sleep as she drove the two and a half hours to Loughborough. The first day involved an introduction to para-triathlon, followed by a running trial and an afternoon swim. In terms of running I've always had a bit of a traction engine on me – I can cover fairly long distances at a decent pace – but I'm not terribly fast so my results were only OK.

Swimming, on the other hand, has never been my strong point, and losing an arm had only made it worse. As a kid I had never had official swimming lessons; my sister, Lizanne, had come back from hers and repeated what the teacher had told her to do. I had taught myself to swim then and re-learned when I lost an arm, and although I could complete the required number of lengths it wasn't at a great speed.

Sian drove me back from Loughborough and I went to work, where my colleague kindly kept an eye on things as I grabbed a couple of hours' sleep in the office kitchen on a camping cot.

The next day was a repeat of the one before, only this time it was the cycling trial. We were given a few minutes to warm up before getting on to an exercise bike for a power test, in which we had to cycle as hard as we possibly could for three minutes flat. They turned out to be some of the most important minutes of my life. The figures I pulled in were impressive – I even did better than some of the guys already on the team – and at the end of the day the triathlon coach took me aside. Based on the entire weekend, he said, it might be worth focusing on cycling alone.

I was disappointed to have my triathlon dreams crushed, especially after such a gruelling weekend, but in the back of my mind I still had the name of Jon-Allan Butterworth, the RAF veteran-turned-cyclist. As it happened, he and another wounded serviceman, Terry Byrne (with whom I later climbed Aconcagua as part of the Adaptive Grand Slam) were some of the best para-cyclists on the British team and actively looking for new talent in the ex-Forces community. They recognised that servicemen and -women usually had the right mindset and willingness to work hard, which is absolutely essential when you're training to become a professional athlete. Jon Paul Nevin, or 'JP', a rehab instructor with Help for Heroes, had heard about this and mentioned it to me. He agreed to set me up with Chris Furber, who was in charge of the national para-cycling team at the time, and a few weeks later I went to the Help for Heroes facility at Tedworth House in Wiltshire to undergo another power test.

After taking into account my injuries and the fact that I was working in an office job, Chris said that the figures from my power trial looked promising. I was invited to Newport in South Wales for a weekend of further testing and introductions to British Cycling, and after getting through with good results I was formally accepted on to the Development Team.

It all seemed relatively casual – we would be asked to attend a team weekend occasionally; otherwise the only requirement was to ride our bikes for at least two hours a week – but at the same time I was very aware that this could be the start of a new career.

The British Cycling Development Team was a relatively new programme, inspired by the fantastic results seen a few years before with young riders like Mark Cavendish, Geraint Thomas and Luke Rowe. As sixteen- and seventeen-year-olds, they had been put together in a house and given strict rules for looking after themselves and their bikes. Discipline was key, but more than anything it was about understanding what went into racing: you didn't just get to be a professional athlete with a cool bike and a whole team of people to do every little thing for you. Cyclists like Mark Cavendish who became top of their class had started out fixing and oiling and washing their own bikes, and the British Cycling Development Team worked on exactly the same principles.

Whenever we had a training camp we were expected to turn up on time with a pristine bike – if yours was dirty you were given a punishment like washing the minibus or cleaning everyone else's bikes after a long ride. It was all about respecting our kit and equipment and never getting too above ourselves. If we wanted to achieve something, we had to be the ones to earn it.

Relatively early on I realised that if I wanted to take cycling seriously it would require total commitment. I had started to think a little bit about my diet, but beyond that my lifestyle just didn't fit with training. Even though the Development Team aimed to build us up slowly – for the first year and a half we trained mainly on our own – I knew that things would soon be getting tougher and that the coaches would require me to truly prove myself.

I was still doing shift work, which meant that I often needed daylight hours to sleep or run errands, and on my days off I felt so tired that the last thing I wanted to do was get on a bike. It was very difficult to find the right balance, and about nine months in I knew that something had to change. I had had to leave the army – a job I had loved – and now here I was being offered the chance of a new career in something I also had a huge passion for. If I really wanted to be a cyclist, I had to give it my all.

The decision to quit my job in summer 2014 wasn't taken lightly. Although I was fortunate enough to be in the position of receiving a pension from the army, it was far from ideal to be drawing on that money rather than investing it in a pension plan or savings. Still, I knew that I had to follow my passion, and as soon as I stopped working I could be a cyclist full-time. It was a big gamble to take – British Cycling had promised me nothing – but I still maintain that it's hugely important to listen to your heart. Sometimes it really isn't practical, but if there's something you really want to do I think you can almost always find a way of making it work.

I say that I became a full-time cyclist, but it isn't like I was on my bike from nine till five. People often have a misperception of what it takes to be a top-level athlete, because actually your rest is just as important as what you do on the bike. Every day you need to be as strong as you were the day before – if not a little bit better – and that means sufficient rest and recovery as soon as you get in from training. Stretching is very important, as is having your feet up and not walking around too much. Even with all that, as a bike rider you're constantly tired. It's something I've got used to over the years, but back then it was a shock.

For someone like me, who had always been a fan of the gym, my body had to change dramatically. As time progressed it was amazing to see my physical transformation: for the first time I had a bit of top-to-bottom symmetry. Whereas previously I had always focused on my arms, trying to make my biceps and chest bigger and stronger, now everything was about my legs. From never really having thought about them, suddenly I was obsessed. My legs were driving my entire life and nothing else mattered but how they felt. If they were tired, I'd have a bad day on the bike – it was as simple as that. If they were strong and I looked after them, they'd be able to take me miles.

My training plan was variable, but it revolved around my local race calendar. I had started taking part in competitions at Hillingdon Cycling Circuit on the outskirts of West London, which hosted time trials on Tuesday and Thursday nights, plus races at the weekend. I took to racing quickly and really enjoyed it, and by late 2013 I had become very active on the domestic racing circuit. The road-racing season lasts from the end of April to roughly early October, with a road event taking place almost every Saturday. Then, from October to April, it's track season, which involves high-speed cycling in a velodrome rather than longer distances on the road. I did both kinds of competition – there was never a week off – and slowly started pulling in my first few wins.

By early 2015 I was seeing consistently good results and had graduated from the Development to the Academy Team. I had new kit, a brilliant bike, and a funding package that was largely dependent on my race results. At the lower end of the scale I received a small athlete grant, plus occasional sessions with a nutritionist and a supply of products like energy bars, gels and whey protein. As I progressed through the ranks, I'd start earning more money, receive better kit and also be able to book a weekly sports massage.

It was good to feel like a serious athlete, but my new life required a lot of changes. I had to move from Henley-on-Thames to Manchester, where British Cycling is based, which meant that my relationship with Sian would become long-distance. As the clock started ticking on the countdown to the Paralympics in Rio, the carrots dangled in front of me were getting bigger – but so was the stick.

*****

The world of cycling is a complicated one, full of jargon and classification systems that probably seem very confusing to an outsider. When I first started para-cycling I was classified as a C3 rider, which meant I was right in the middle of the scale when it came to physical impairments. The C categories, which are for riders of standard bicycles, range from C1 to C5, with C1 riders having the most severe impairments (maybe a serious neurological condition) and C5 riders having the least severe (like only one hand). As well as trying to keep riders of a similar level competing with one another, the classifications determine the distances athletes race over. C3 track cyclists, for example, race as individuals over a maximum distance of three kilometres – or twelve laps of the velodrome track – while C4 and C5 riders have to race over four kilometres, or sixteen laps of the track. In road racing there are fewer differences: C1 and C2 riders race seventy-five kilometres, while C3 to C5 riders cover a hundred kilometres.

My initial classification was made by British Cycling based on the injuries I had sustained in Afghanistan, which affected both my upper and lower body. I began training to ride three kilometres in a certain time, only to get to my first international event in December 2013 – a track race held in Newport – to find that the race authorities were reclassifying me as a C4 rider.

The next day I would have to race an entire extra kilometre on the track. It was a shock suddenly to be tipped over from the high end of one category into the lower end of another, and of course my results didn't reflect all the hard work I'd been putting in. With British Cycling's backing I protested against the new classification, but the UCI (Union Cycliste Internationale) stood firm.

There were two options open to me: throw my toys out of the pram and walk away from cycling, or take it on the chin and carry on. I've actually seen plenty of riders turn their back on the sport in a situation like that, opting for the easy way out. But if that's the attitude you take to life, what are you ever going to achieve? I knew it wasn't going to be easy, but I thought I might as well give it a go and try to become the best C4 rider I possibly could be.

Because I had gained such strength in my injured leg I was now in a category where I would compete against riders with below-knee amputations and two functioning arms – they were, to all intents and purposes, as good as able-bodied. They could certainly handle a bike much better than I could at that stage, had brakes on both sides and could steer a left-hand corner as well as they could a right. I felt so far behind them but I had to dive right in, starting with that race in Newport and then chipping away slowly until I worked my way up.

One of my first top-level cycling events as an official C4 rider was the 2015 UCI Track World Championships at Apeldoorn in the Netherlands. My expectations were incredibly high – I had been selected for the Road World Cup the previous year but had broken my scapula just a few days before and been unable to race – but the experience was, honestly, disappointing.

I rode the 4k individual pursuit (where two riders start at opposite ends of the velodrome and have to try to catch each other over a specified distance), the men's team sprint with Jody Cundy and Louis Rolfe (in which two teams go head to head with all their riders on the track; each team member has to take it in turns to lead for a lap), and the scratch race (a classic race in which everyone starts at the same time and the first rider over the finish line wins). I placed lower than I had wanted to each time. The men's team sprint was particularly frustrating – we had practised in a certain order where I always led the second lap. On the day of the race, however, the team coach suddenly changed the plan so that I would be third to lead. I wasn't rested from the day before and this last-minute adjustment completely threw me off course. We ended up coming fifth when I really think we should have been in with a good shot at the medals.

This kind of thing was always happening at competitions, especially the major ones that counted for more points. In order for a country to take part in a top-level event like the Paralympic Games, the national team has to collect points at UCI events. Although it's individual riders who score the points – anyone placing from first to tenth will receive some – they all go towards the country as a whole, and the total number of points is then converted into quota spaces on the Paralympic team. The number of points available at an event also depends on the level of competition: for example, first place at a World Cup event might give you fifty points, whereas first place at a World Championship equates to one hundred and fifty points. The higher the level of competition, the more is at stake, and because we were competing not just for ourselves as individual athletes but for the future chances of Great Britain, the pressure we were under was absolutely immense.

Over the months I had seen many of the Development Team members fall by the wayside, as they were unable to juggle work and training or keep up cycling alongside family commitments. Some just weren't strong or fast enough to make the regular cuts; others decided to give it up because they simply weren't enjoying it any more. By the time we got round to professional racing we were a long way from the days of rocking up at training camp in Newport and washing each other's bikes as punishment for sloppy behaviour. Instead, on race day we were treated like the athletes you see on TV, with a team of mechanics to check the bikes over for us, cars to take us from the hotel to the velodrome, and *soigneurs* who were in charge of things like nutrition, clothing and massages. That kind of support did make it a lot easier to manage the nerves, but I've never lined up for a race without feeling under a lot of pressure to prove myself. As a cyclist, you are only ever as good as your last race, and whatever position you achieved can be very quickly taken away from you.

At the start of 2016, nine months away from the Paralympic Games in Rio, the cracks started to show. The group of riders I was part of had been consistently getting smaller, but until that point we had always felt like a team. We always raced for each other, with each other, and we were happy for one another's results. If a friend of mine like Louis Rolfe or Jon Gildea went away with a medal, I would be just as happy as he was. But suddenly there came a point where we started to understand how the British Cycling selection process for the Paralympic Games worked. That year, in men's para-cycling, Britain had been awarded five out of a possible thirteen places across track and road to share among a much larger group of extremely talented riders. We had to recognise that not all of us would be going to the Games and, worst of all, we were fighting our friends for spaces.

It was all an enormous, terrible mind game. At the time I had my own issues with the way British Cycling had handled the points system for getting quota spaces – they had a tendency to flood the lower-level competitions, which exhausted our riders and brought in fewer points, leaving other countries with fresher riders to clear up at the top-level events where more UCI points were up for grabs – but aside from that I hated how we were played off against one another. Some riders were clearly outstanding and were guaranteed a place at the Games unless something terrible happened, but others were on the same level as me and suddenly nothing mattered beyond what they – and I – were doing. Where previously I had felt happy to see a good friend winning a race or getting a new personal best, now I saw his results as a threat to the one remaining space that could potentially be mine. It sounds awful, but sometimes I felt comforted to see someone else – one of my *teammates* – having a bad race day. I think we all saw the shift in our friendships, and the entire meaning of sport began to change.

It was a time in which I learned who my friends really were. Despite the fact that we were very evenly matched and it could easily come down to a toss-up between us, I was lucky to maintain my friendship with Jon Gildea. Jon and I had joined the programme at the same time and I had seen him struggle to juggle cycling with running his own business and being the sole provider for his wife and two young children. Like most athletes, Jon has made a lot of sacrifices in his life. Even aside from the financial pressure, there were times when cycling had a big impact on his family life – I remember occasions when he had to stay at my flat because one of his kids had flu and he was terrified of getting ill. Any setback like that could damage beyond repair our chances of winning an event or getting to the Games.

I didn't have a family to provide for, but I did make my own sacrifices when it came to relationships. Conducting a long-distance relationship with an athlete isn't easy, but Sian and I did our best to keep things going even after I moved to Manchester. Because I spent most weekends racing, our time together was extremely limited and usually involved a number of hours in the car or at one track or another. I couldn't do late nights, had to watch what I ate and didn't drink, and most of the time I was in a state of exhaustion.

Even when we managed to go on holiday I'd need to combine it with training, so although that took us to some beautiful parts of the world – Mallorca is a favourite for cyclists because of the hills – I'd be getting up at five o'clock to fit in a few hours of cycling and couldn't do much for the rest of the day. There were no late-night parties or cocktails on the beach; after dinner in the evening I'd be ready for bed.

It didn't only apply to holidays either – Christmases, birthdays and anniversaries were just the same. I wasn't able to take time off: I felt incredibly guilty if I ever skipped part of my training plan and often had to be away at a team camp or competition. In the end, I just didn't have the time or mental energy, and Sian was able to see it. She was very patient, but as the months progressed we started fighting more and more – something that I'd then blame for my performance on the bike. It was a big ask for me to make, but my mindset at the time was that I just needed to get to Rio and then everything would be OK. But before that could even happen, the constant strain had taken its toll and we broke up. Having gone through all that – having sacrificed a relationship to it – the effect that the pressure of being a professional athlete can have on your personal life is still one of my biggest fears.

As I say, all of us made sacrifices, big or small, to be in with a chance of competing at Rio. Since 2013 – and in some cases longer – it was all we had worked for, and I think it was frustrating for all of us to see that Great Britain had fewer spaces than we deserved. As one of the best-funded and most talented nations in terms of cycling, we had been granted just five men's spaces in total, which was fewer than other well-known cycling countries like France and Italy. Even when Russia was banned from competing and we were given an extra space, it still wasn't enough. People were always going to be left disappointed, but until the early summer we didn't know who.

*****

The announcements came in June and August. Even right up to

the very end – the extra place that came from Russia's exclusion wasn't revealed until the end of the summer – I kept hoping I would have made it.

My results at the 2016 UCI Track World Championship hadn't been as good as they ought to have been, but I had at least taken bronze in the men's C4 scratch race. In May, at the UCI Road World Cup in Ostend in Belgium, I had crashed out of the road race before the end but then had ridden a great time trial that saw me come in ninth.

I can't say that I was completely confident I would be granted a place – I knew too many brilliant cyclists like Jon-Allan Butterworth, David Stone and Jody Cundy who would definitely be going – but I believed in my abilities to bring in a medal. What's more, I could prove myself on both the road and the track, and with the team already quite track-heavy it would be useful to have someone who could race in both disciplines.

It wasn't to be. In the end, neither my friend Jon nor I made the team, not even when that extra space opened up. A day or two before the final line-up was made public, a message landed in my inbox. *British Cycling would like to thank me for all my hard work, but they were sorry to tell me...* I almost couldn't read it. More than the disappointment of not having been selected, I think it was the way in which they told me that hurt the most. After all the sacrifices we'd made, the time, the effort, the sweat and the tears, the crashes and victories and everything we'd put into it, I'd assumed they'd have the decency to pick up the phone and tell those of us who hadn't made it that we weren't on the team.

Instead, they had sent me a standardised email. For three years, British Cycling had been everything to me, but now I felt that I meant nothing to them.

I had just received the biggest disappointment of my life and I had no idea which way to turn next.

XIV

ON THE ROAD

Two days after receiving that email I finally met with John, my coach.

As soon as I walked into the room I could feel that the atmosphere was different. There was no 'I'm so sorry', no 'How are you feeling?' – just a business-like discussion about the way things were going to work. Of course British Cycling's focus had switched entirely to the team of riders going to Rio, but people like Jon Gildea and I were still expected to train just as hard as we had done previously. I was given a schedule of power tests and training sessions in the velodrome, and told that my targets for the coming months involved riding my bike for a minimum of seventeen hours a week. It was only a little bit less than I had been doing in preparation for the world's biggest sporting event.

I understood that I was still part of the programme and needed to ride my bike to justify my monthly athlete grant, but it wasn't the right time for my coaches to set me new targets. What I really needed was a break – I was exhausted from the physical build-up to Rio and utterly crushed by the disappointment of not getting a place on the team.

To be honest, I didn't even want to see my bike, let alone ride it for a set number of hours per day. I felt that the situation had been handled in completely the wrong way – we were treated like machines, not humans – but at the same time I had the old sense of obligation and pressure to fulfil what was required of me. But for what? I wasn't even going to Rio – surely I could take a few days out. My mind was a whirl of unanswered questions and I could feel the anger slowly building inside me.

Jon and I were in exactly the same situation, and in a way it was lucky that we had each other for support. That summer was also the Euro 2016 competition and, although I'm not usually a fan of football, we spent a lot of time in the park or a pub garden watching the matches to keep our minds off our emotions.

It was hard, but I struggled on through my training plan, doing as little as I could get away with. But then, in August, when the extra space on the team was announced and I found out I hadn't made the second cut either, I found myself at breaking point. Desperate to escape, I booked myself on a plane to South Africa.

Of course I still took a bike with me – I was too institutionalised not to do that. This, though, was a new bike, the first one I had ever bought for myself.

My childhood BMX had been given to me by my parents and as an adult I had been lucky enough to receive my first bike through a grant scheme. All the ones that followed had come from British Cycling. But scrolling through Instagram one day that summer, my eye had been caught by a bright orange frame. At first I couldn't understand what I was looking at – the wheels were bigger and fatter than any I'd ever seen – but I soon learned that it was a bike for gravel riding, something that was then very popular in the USA.

The main advantage to a bike like that was that you could change the wheels to use it for both on- and off-road cycling, and perhaps because I'd spent the past three years being so confined to thin track and racing wheels, I found myself loving the idea. I'd never had a bike like it before, but I splashed out and bought it straight away.

Despite my new wheels, for that first week in South Africa I was still quite committed to my training plan. Friends would ring up to ask if I wanted to come for a beer and I'd turn them down because I hadn't yet got my cycling hours in. But the more I rode my bike, the more my mindset changed.

The Garmin computer affixed to my handlebars recorded all my data – heart rate, distance covered, power output, pedal speed – and logged it in the British Cycling system. For months I had been absolutely addicted to data (we had a saying that if something wasn't on Strava, the recording software, it couldn't have happened), but now I found myself switching the computer display to a simple map screen that blocked out all the numbers. For the first time in a very long time I could just sit up and watch where I was going.

In the second week of my stay, I thought *sod this*, and started riding my bike whenever and for however long I wanted to. Some mornings I did two hours and spent the rest of the day with my friends; on others I'd see a single-track road leading off somewhere and decide to take it, ending up exploring the countryside for hours. That bike opened up a whole new world for me. It reintroduced me to the idea of having fun while cycling and brought back the essence of the sport I had once fallen in love with. Now, instead of constantly chasing the numbers, I was out on my bike simply because I wanted to be. And every time I got on it, it asked me only one question: where do you want to go?

*****

In a broader sense, there was no easy answer. I returned to the UK around the same time as the Paralympic team got back from Rio, but while they were all given an extended break, Jon and I were straight back into the normal swing of things. A couple of weeks in South Africa hadn't been enough for me; I was still tired from the last three years of training and in need of a longer period to wind down. I also really wanted a debrief: for someone to explain to me why I hadn't been selected, where I had fallen short, so that I could take that on board and start to address it. I'm just one of those people – if something goes wrong, I need to know why in order to work out how I'm going to fix it. There was nothing like that, though. Our coaches acted like nothing had happened and told us we would start preparing for Tokyo 2020.

The Paralympic Games that were four years off seemed like an almost impossible dream. I had come back from South Africa with something new within me – a different attitude towards British Cycling and my entire career. Yes, I had managed to maintain my love for the bike, but my heart just wasn't in the training.

At least not right then. The riders who had been to Rio were facing a relatively relaxed year, with some planning to go off and get married, travel or study. Short of a couple of months I had done almost exactly the same training programme as they had, so I had also started planning a year that didn't revolve entirely around cycling. In twelve months' time, towards the end of 2017, I would be able to focus properly on the bike again.

I did also have another motive for spending a bit less time cycling. In 2016 I had become a brand ambassador for Roseville, and when I had gone to the Essex office to meet the sponsorship team I had got to know Kathryn.

I clearly remember standing in front of this beautiful, friendly girl as she took my photo for the website and feeling absolutely star-struck. There was no way I could approach a girl like her. But then she was assigned to be my in-house contact and we started to be in touch regularly about what I was planning or whether I could take part in a company event. Emails led to drinks and by the autumn we were officially dating. After what had happened with Sian I was nervous about embarking on a long-distance relationship, but I had fallen hard for Kathryn and we were both determined to make it work. And at a time when everything else in my life seemed so uncertain, finding her had given me hope.

In the early autumn I sat down with my coach to discuss the plans I had made for the coming year. In actual fact, two of my major goals were bike-based: in November and December I would be cycling through Chile with some friends from the British team, and in June 2017 I would be part of a Help for Heroes team competing in the Race Across America, a long-distance cycling event.

In between those challenges I wanted to climb Aconcagua with the Adaptive Grand Slam, which I described in an earlier chapter of this book. But despite the fact that all my plans were sports-related – they would only help to increase my fitness and rack up quite a lot of hours in the saddle – my coaches weren't keen. Chile was acceptable, they said; the other things weren't. I felt strongly that they took that attitude because those challenges lay beyond their control and would take me to places where British Cycling would struggle to keep an eye on me. I seemed to be under observation and it was beginning to feel stifling.

In the weeks leading up to Chile I felt very confused. There were pros and cons to staying with British Cycling, but I didn't know which side held more weight. The pros were mainly the people I knew and friendships I had made; I also enjoyed the lifestyle that came with being a member of the team and obviously wanted the chance to compete at the Tokyo Games. At the same time, though, I had started to hate the system. I felt that the programme was incredibly badly managed, that individual people weren't worth much and that there was an inherent bullying culture within the organisation. I felt like I had been abandoned when – for reasons still unclear to me – I failed to make the grade; and because I had dared to voice my opinion, my career was probably in danger anyway. Too often I had seen a rider question a coach's decision only to be mysteriously asked to leave the team a couple of weeks later.

The trip to Chile came at a good time – I desperately needed to get out of Manchester. Travelling along with me were Steve Bate, a visually impaired tandem cyclist who had joined the programme at the same time as me and gone on to win two golds and a bronze at Rio; his wife, Caroline, who isn't a professional athlete but a serious cyclist and climber; and Karen Darke, a hand cyclist who had won a silver medal at London 2012 and taken a gold at Rio. As well as being a para-cyclist, Karen is an extreme adventurer – since becoming paralysed from the chest down in a climbing accident, she has skied across Greenland, climbed Mont Blanc and El Capitan, and cycled, skied and swum the length of Japan. They seemed like the perfect group of people to embark on a new challenge with.

Our goal was to cycle the length of the Carretera Austral, a 1,240-kilometre route that runs through Chilean Patagonia, from Puerto Montt in the north to Villa O'Higgins in the south. From the outset we were clear that this was to be an adventure – aside from having booked our flights, we had no plans, which meant that we could stop where and when we felt like it. We would be undertaking the trip entirely unsupported – my favourite kind of expedition – carrying all our camping equipment and stocking up on supplies as we travelled. It was the kind of cycling known as bikepacking.

With all the excitement and then disappointment of Rio, I had all but forgotten about Chile until it was nearly time to set out. But as we flew out of Heathrow towards the end of November, I suddenly couldn't wait to get started on a new adventure.

*****

We flew to Puerto Montt via Santiago, arriving in the late-afternoon heat. Travelling from winter to summer felt amazing and for the first part of the trip we had beautiful weather. Cycling a fully laden bike while pulling a trailer that was equally loaded with kit was a bit hair-raising at first – at the end of the first day I remember thinking it was going to be a *very* long month – but if there's one thing I've learned from expeditions, it's that people can get used to almost anything.

I found myself adjusting amazingly quickly, and as the first week drew to a close we had established a good rhythm to our days. Every morning we would set ourselves a rough target, often picking a recommended campsite or local tourist attraction from the guidebook. Some nights we wild-camped, and every so often we would book ourselves into a simple guesthouse or cottage to have the chance to wash clothes and dry our kit.

Whenever we passed through a small town we stocked up on food. Fuelling sufficiently was something I started struggling with at a fairly early stage – my metabolism is fast at the best of times, but as the terrain got more mountainous it started running away with me. My energy levels started dipping dangerously low and I sometimes found myself running out of steam in the worst possible places.

But if there were days on which I was absolutely exhausted, I had no idea how Karen must have felt. She cycled incredible distances and over enormous hills using only the power of her arms, and every morning she was up and ready to go again. I never once heard her complain or say that things were too much for her, something for which I had an enormous amount of respect.

She never willingly gave in, but there were times when the gradient did prove too much for Karen. Cycling through Patagonia is not for the faint-hearted and sometimes the hills filled me with dread.

Beyond a certain level of steepness, the front wheel on Karen's hand bike would simply spin out and we would have to take it in turns to push her up in a kind of relay system. Ongoing roadworks meant that the route was often dotted with lorries and heavy machinery, and it could take three hours or more to work our way up to the top of one hill.

The mountains were a pain to cycle over, but they provided some of the most stunning scenery I've ever encountered. To me, Patagonia remains one of the most beautiful places in the world – remote, unspoiled and constantly changing. One day we would be cycling through lush green valleys that looked just like Wales, the next day the terrain would become more rocky and mountainous, reminding me of the Pyrenees.

We cycled alongside huge rivers and passed thundering waterfalls, staying on the outskirts of tiny, isolated villages or picking a wild-camping spot in a flower-filled meadow. Despite all the physical hardship, it was never less than utterly beautiful.

As we moved away from the coast, however, things began noticeably to change. Two weeks in we were high up in the mountains bordering Argentina, and the warm summer sunshine had given way to what felt like permanent rain. One night we were almost washed away in our tents when we pitched them what we thought was a safe distance from a riverbank, and on many days we found ourselves cycling into a headwind. In Patagonia the winds are incredibly strong and they started playing a big role in determining the mood of our group.

About two-thirds of the way to Villa O'Higgins, we stopped on the shores of General Carrera Lake. It's a huge lake – the second largest in South America – and it crosses the border between Chile and Argentina.

One of the reasons it's so popular is the network of nearby caves, which are the most incredible shades of blue and white. The town beside the lake is small but quite buzzy, and as we were making good progress we decided to stay for a couple of nights, do a boat tour of the caves, and give ourselves the chance to rest and enjoy some good food. It was a much-needed break, but as we were packing up to leave I began to worry about a pain in my left side that had been lingering for a couple of days.

Our journey continued through brutal weather: non-stop rain and extremely high winds. Only occasionally did the clouds clear and allow us to enjoy a night of dry camping. On one of those evenings we stopped at a beautiful campsite on a farm, with a wide area of grass to pitch the tents on and a small lake where Steve, who had been optimistically carrying a fishing rod ever since Puerto Montt, managed to catch his first and only fish of the trip. He was so proud to take it back to the girls and it made a welcome change to our carb-heavy diet.

Five days after I had first noticed it, the pain in my side not only hadn't gone away, it had become almost unbearable. It wasn't just pain any more either – my left abdomen was becoming swollen and I noticed that it felt more tender after I'd eaten.

I was also having breathing problems – every time I took a deep breath my ribs ached and I couldn't fill my lungs all the way. It was starting to impact on everything I did, from cycling up a steep hill to getting comfortable on a camping mattress, and I found myself less and less able to help the team. I had no idea what was wrong with me but I knew it wasn't good, and because of the location of the pain and its apparent effect on my digestive system, I had started to worry that it might have something to do with my colostomy procedure.

It got to a stage where I simply had to switch off from the pain mentally. Once on the bike, I had to stay there – if I stopped to rest or eat, the pain was so excruciating that I thought I might never get back on again.

The final day in particular was absolutely awful. The weather was horrendous, I was in agony, and even my bike was starting to fall apart. When we finally reached Villa O'Higgins in the pouring rain, I didn't really take in the fact that I had made it to the end; I was just so relieved to be somewhere I could get into bed. But what I really needed was a hospital, and soon.

The nearest medical facility was all the way back in Coyhaique, the biggest town we had passed through on the entire trip and a two-day bus journey away. It was an agonising trip back up the road we had just cycled down, involving not just a bus but also a lift on the local vegetable truck, and by the time we reached the hospital I was in terrible shape.

I was given a scan that produced immediate results: I had a cyst growing in my abdominal wall. As the swelling got bigger it had started pushing on my spleen, which in turn was pressing against my lungs and causing me difficulty breathing. The doctor was incredibly concerned by what he saw and said he would like to operate immediately.

I was aghast. An operation would mean two to four weeks recovering in hospital, but I had a flight home booked in a couple of days. It was my first Christmas with Kathryn and I hadn't seen her in over a month. I was exhausted and ill but completely adamant: I wasn't going to be operated on abroad. It took a lot of conversations with the doctor, a prescription for antibiotics and promises to monitor myself closely before I was given the all-clear to fly. The doctor didn't hold back from warning me that if the cyst burst mid-air then I was going to die.

I was terrified about the transatlantic flight, but I was so determined to get home that I tried not to let myself think about it. Fortunately, the antibiotics started to kick in and I made it back to the UK without incident. Kathryn was there at Heathrow to pick me up and we drove straight to Royal Berks Hospital, where I was taken in for a procedure to drain the fluid off the cyst. I did have to stay in hospital for a few days, which is how Kathryn and I ended up celebrating Christmas in the Royal Berks. It's definitely not what I would have chosen for our first Christmas together, but the fact that she's still around today means it can't have been *that* bad.

It was a strange ending to what should have been the trip of a lifetime. Before I got ill – and even occasionally after – I had absolutely loved cycling the Carretera Austral. It was just the kind of challenge I relished, an unsupported trip in incredibly harsh conditions that also showed me the unspoiled beauty of one of the remotest regions in the world. I felt lucky to have gone there with the people I did, but for me the end of the trip did feel quite sad. Instead of celebrating an incredible achievement, I found myself simply wishing it over.

At the same time, Patagonia had helped me. Before we left I had felt like I was in quite a deep rut when it came to cycling. I knew that I had to decide whether to stay with British Cycling or leave the team, but I didn't know what would be best for me.

When we went to Chile I forgot my Garmin, and this actually proved to be a blessing in disguise – four weeks of cycling without recording any data made me step back from the need to constantly monitor my progress. Instead, I was able to focus on cycling in its purest form and, just like in South Africa when I had ridden my gravel bike along countryside trails, I felt myself falling back in love with the sport. By the time I was on the plane home I had made my decision. It was incredibly difficult and I had no idea what the future would hold, but I knew that listening to my heart was the right thing to do.

*****

When I was released from hospital in early January 2017 I drove straight up to Manchester to resign from British Cycling. My coaches were disappointed, but probably not surprised. We had a conversation in which I was very honest about my reasons for leaving, and agreed that we would review my situation towards the end of the year – if I wanted back in and was still performing at a high level, we could consider my re-joining the team. A couple of days later I went to the velodrome and handed in my bikes and most of the kit. I had grappled with the decision for many months, but that day I walked away feeling free. I knew that I would miss training with my friends, but also that I would stay in touch with people like Jon, Karen and Steve. We were bound by more than just being on the same cycling team.

I scrambled around putting my old bikes back together – now that I'd handed in my British Cycling gear I barely had anything of my own to ride – but before long I had my sights set on other things. The Adaptive Grand Slam attempt at Aconcagua took place at the end of January, though even as I boarded the plane I could feel the cyst starting to swell up again.

A course of antibiotics kept it stable all through that long, arduous climb, but as soon as I got back to the UK I had to be admitted to hospital. This time I was given an operation to remove it completely and the doctors discovered that my colon was still full of grit and shrapnel from the night I had been injured in Afghanistan. A tiny piece of shrapnel had been rubbing against my abdominal wall all this time, eventually causing the cyst that had given me so much trouble. As well as having the swelling removed I was thoroughly cleaned out, and I came round from surgery feeling that life could continue as normal.

And continue it did, but perhaps not in a normal way. Besides trying to adjust to life as an independent athlete, Kathryn and I were searching for a place down south to move in together – we felt ready to take our relationship to the next stage and were looking forward to spending quality time together in a day-to-day way.

I was also busy training for my next challenge: the Race Across America. I'd signed up and been selected by Help for Heroes back in 2016, but what with Chile and Aconcagua I'd barely had time to focus on training. Given that it's commonly called 'the world's toughest bicycle race', it seemed I would be wise to start. Two days after being discharged from hospital, I found myself slowly pedalling an exercise bike.

*****

The Race Across America (RAAM) is an annual cycling challenge held towards the end of June, in which solo riders and teams of cyclists have to cross the United States from Oceanside, California, to Annapolis, Maryland. The route changes a little bit every year but is around 4,800 kilometres long and, unlike the Tour de France or the Giro d'Italia, isn't broken down into stages. Instead, cyclists push right through, only stopping for breaks when they feel they need them – it's effectively a giant time trial.

The RAAM was something I had wanted to do for a while, so when Help for Heroes announced that they would be putting together an eight-man team, I jumped at the chance to be involved.

The final line-up was a real mixture: Ryan Grey, Craig Preece, Andrew Perrin and I were all upright cyclists, while Michael Swain, Josh Boggi and Joe Townsend were in hand bikes and Rob Cromey-Hawke in a recumbent bike (which you cycle with your feet from a sitting or lying position).

The selection process had been tough and because of everyone's other commitments our team training was quite simple – we had done a couple of SAS-style cycling camps in France, on which we would be woken up in the middle of the night to ride a time trial up a mountain – so to a large extent we had all been responsible for our own fitness.

As a team, we had mainly needed to practise the logistical side of things; there were lots of rules about handovers between cyclists and what our support vehicles could and couldn't do for us. To be able to cycle constantly, we divided ourselves into two teams: Ryan, Josh, Joe and I would cycle in the day and the others by night. There was usually only one cyclist on the road at a time, with the others in the support van that drove immediately behind the rider.

We would switch regularly throughout the day, and when we handed over to the other team at night we would get some rest in an RV as it drove us to the next morning's changeover point. Teams have a maximum of nine days to complete the race, but we were hoping to do it in six.

As soon as we arrived in Oceanside in the middle of June 2017, I could feel the buzz in the air. As one of the last teams to set off, we had plenty of time to enjoy the hype, and when our turn came to cross the start line I was raring to go. Knowing that Josh and

ON THE ROAD

Joe would be slower on the uphill sections but were extremely fast on the flat or downhill, we had decided that Ryan and I would be responsible for climbing. The first couple of days, which took us through California, Arizona, Utah and Colorado, featured two mountain ranges – the Sierra Nevada and the Rocky Mountains – so the two of us were going to be doing a lot of the work.

It soon became apparent that the heat was a factor we hadn't reckoned with enough when we had been working out this team strategy. We had decided to spend anything from thirty minutes to an hour on the bike before changing over, but the brutal heat of the desert soon made us re-evaluate. As the temperature climbed to forty-eight degrees I found myself going through water at an impossible rate.

I would have drunk a litre in fifteen minutes and my mouth would still feel dry, while my energy levels were through the floor. We quickly adjusted the handovers so that each of us would spend a maximum of twenty-five minutes on the bike, and even cycled with ice in our pockets and cold towels on our necks to try to keep our body temperature under control.

By the third day it felt as though we'd been racing for a lifetime. Sleep deprivation had well and truly kicked in – getting good-quality sleep in the back of a moving RV is nearly impossible – and the hours were beginning to pass in a blur. Sometimes I would find myself on the bike without even knowing how I had got there; the last thing I could remember was dozing off in the van.

The landscape had changed from rocky and mountainous to the flat, endless plains of the American Midwest, where the road would stretch out straight for miles in front of us. We passed the ends of tracks leading to enormous farms that reminded me of South Africa, but no matter how many miles we covered we never seemed to progress.

UNEQUIVOCAL

The sat-nav screen in the van showed us as a tiny dot in the middle of a vast continent, moving east at a snail's pace.

The heat was now less intense than it had been in the desert, but as we moved east it started to get more humid. I was dehydrated and suffering from a stomach upset after an encounter with a bad burrito, so I kept having to sit out a rotation, and when I was on the bike I felt dazed and had difficulty breathing. The race was stunning – there was no doubt about it; we were passing through some of the most varied and beautiful landscapes – but for a lot of the time I had my head down and was gritting my teeth to try to get through it.

After riding through Kansas, Missouri, Illinois, Indiana and Ohio, the final two days took us through West Virginia, Pennsylvania and Maryland to the finish line in Annapolis. We still had to cross one last mountain range – the Appalachians – but the end was finally in sight. We started to feel focused and excited, and occasionally passing two-person teams or solo riders gave us an enormous confidence boost.

A confidence boost was doubly necessary, because the final day started with yet another horrendous hill. To make matters worse, it was pouring with rain – the complete opposite of the scorching heat we had experienced at the beginning of the race. All of us were feeling quite cold so we did longer stints on the bike, especially when evening fell and we knew we were close to the finish line.

Ryan was the last rider and shortly after one o'clock in the morning we pulled into a service station on the outskirts of Annapolis, where all eight of us got on our bikes to cycle the final leg together. The streets were rainy and eerily silent as we passed through.

When we got to the finish line there were no screaming crowds or speakers blasting out music – to be honest, like the end of the

Carretera Austral, it was a bit of an anti-climax. The race organiser had been woken up to come and greet us, there were a couple of camera crews, and of course our support crew was waiting with Kathryn and the other guys' families who had flown out to be there. They all gave us a big cheer and we were invited on to the podium to receive our medals, but almost before I knew it we were off to the hotel. I was so exhausted that it was hard to focus on the sense of relief or achievement at having finished.

In six days and a matter of hours we had cycled from one coast of America to the other – it had been a true test not just of physical fitness, but also mental endurance and team spirit. Afterwards, Kathryn and I celebrated with a few days exploring Washington, DC and other parts of the East Coast – in between my long naps beside hotel swimming pools.

I'd ticked another adventure off my list, but I was already thinking of ways we could have improved on our time and raced more efficiently. Having experienced the RAAM as a member of an eight-man team, I'd love to try it as a four-man team and eventually as a solo cyclist. It takes a lot of physical and mental preparation to be ready for such a challenge, but I'm sure that one day I'll tackle it on my own.

In early July 2017, almost a year after the disappointment of Rio, I returned to the UK in a stronger frame of mind. The past year had taught me that I could overcome any challenge with optimism, hard work and determination.

I would be faced with plenty more tests, especially as I continued to develop my career as an independent athlete, but I felt more ready than ever to see what life would throw at me next.

XV

TO RIO

When I returned from the Race Across America, I knew deep down that I wasn't going to get back in touch with British Cycling to review the situation as we had agreed. Nor did anyone from the programme try to contact me. More than eight months had passed since I had left and I found that I simply didn't miss it. I was still in touch with my friends from the team – Steve and Jon in particular – and also kept up with one of my old coaches, John Hewitt, with whom I had a good relationship. Shortly after I got back from the States we all went on a ride together and John did ask me for my thoughts on coming back to the team. I told him openly that I didn't feel quite ready yet. To be honest, I wasn't sure if I ever would.

The one thing I did know was that I wanted to carry on cycling – but I wanted to do it on my own terms. To be honest, I'd never heard of anyone becoming an independent athlete before, training and competing at international level without the backing of a national team, but I couldn't see any reason why such a thing wouldn't be possible. I knew how the system worked, I had experience of competitions and, most importantly, I knew what worked for me and what didn't. It was going to be a learning curve – there was no instruction manual – but I was determined and passionate enough about cycling to at least want to give it a try.

TO RIO

Becoming an independent athlete did require a lot of adjustment and at the beginning it felt like a scarily big leap to be taking. Yet at the same time it was an eye-opening and incredibly rewarding experience, which gave me the feeling that British Cycling had been a chain holding me back. I suddenly found myself with the freedom to manage my own life and the ability to say yes to interesting opportunities that came my way. It was tough, of course, but throughout my life I have tended to do things the hard way. Now I had made my decision, I knew I would see it through. It was just about taking ownership of what I was going to do next.

The first step was getting myself set up with a coach. Even after leaving British Cycling I had never abandoned my bike, but I had spent the first part of 2017 recovering from an operation and doing a different kind of training in preparation for the Race Across America. Now I needed to start focusing on the track again. The new racing season would be starting in the autumn and I was determined to bring in some good results.

I started working with Adam Duggleby, whom I knew from British Cycling where he was the tandem pilot for Steve. As well as cycling with the British team he worked as a private coach for independent athletes. Adam and I get on very well, but at the beginning it was a learning curve for him as much as me.

Both of us were used to working with a British Cycling training plan, in which daily targets were provided at the start of each week and had to be stuck to with absolute rigidity. But I soon realised that this kind of system wouldn't work for me.

Being an independent athlete is exactly what it says on the tin: you have to rely on yourself for absolutely everything. Gone were the days when I just needed to book an appointment to access a high-class physiotherapist or gym, or could hand my bike over to someone who would fix a broken chain. As well as being responsible for my own training, I was in charge of my nutrition, bikes, kit and equipment, general physical wellbeing and, last but certainly not least, my own income.

Dealing with all of it – from ordering nutritional products to finding a good masseur or taking bikes to the shop for repairs – required a lot of research and therefore time.

Instead of arranging my day around a training schedule, I started adapting my training to fit my day. Adam and I began to work out a good system, in which he suggested a weekly training plan and I made adjustments depending on what I had in the diary. It felt unusual at first, but I soon learned to adapt to my new situation, making sure that whenever I did get out on the road it was for a good-quality ride.

Over time, and with Adam's help, I figured out that as long as I did the right form of training, I didn't necessarily have to do a great deal of it. I started training smarter, not harder.

One of the trickiest aspects of all this was the mental adjustment. If at any time during my career with British Cycling I had failed to complete my training plan, even for a single day, I had been overwhelmed by guilt for not sticking with the programme. As an independent athlete, I had to learn to see a day that hadn't gone according to plan as simply a recovery day, and to believe that my fitness wouldn't suffer because of it.

It was hard at first to get out from under that crushing sense of guilt, but after seeing it happen for myself often enough, I could feel my mindset beginning to shift. I know now that my fitness never suffers because of a couple of days off. In fact, I can get back on the bike with fresher legs.

So much of cycling – and sport in general – is mental. Take food and drink, another element of an athlete's lifestyle to which I found my attitude changing when I started riding independently.

Kathryn and I love good food, but we do try to eat very healthily: I know it's important for my body and I prefer eating lots of protein and fresh salads anyway. At the same time, we do go out for a burger now and again, and I do eat dessert and have a drink when I feel like it. I never take the piss by going out for a big night two days before an event, but I have most definitely had a beer in the same week as an important race.

In the end, I think I'm probably better off drinking that beer than not. I've won medals eating pretty much exactly what I want, and I think that having a less extreme lifestyle – certainly with less guilt involved – has been one of things that has helped me achieve them.

The other major thing I had to get to grips with was learning to manage my time effectively. Training and recovery are hugely important, but everyone – even an athlete – needs to be able to eat and when I left British Cycling I had lost a small but very steady income. In the early days I did worry a lot about how I was going to support myself, but somehow I knew that staying on for purely monetary reasons wouldn't help me achieve anything. To be a top cyclist you really need to love riding your bike, not just be doing it to pay the bills.

Whereas before I had devoted my days to training, now I had to use them productively to go out and find ways of making money. I've been lucky enough to gain several ambassador roles with companies including Asset Academy, the Wigley Group, Nuzest, Core Health and Wellness, and thinAir Sports, and I also began exploring the world of public speaking, which I'd been interested in for quite a while.

Several times during my career with British Cycling I had been approached to give a talk on my expeditions and adventures, only to have to turn down the invitation due to my training commitments.

Now that I was able to adapt my cycling to suit myself, I was thrilled to be able to take up more of these opportunities.

I started working closely with a friend of mine, Matthew Quinn, who runs a speakers' agency based in Edinburgh. Together we hosted some free events at which I gave a brief talk, and I always found myself with a few new bookings afterwards. I loved being able to take a creative approach to finding new business and especially enjoyed the opportunity to talk to other people about my experiences.

Despite all the hard work involved, I also found myself with more time for other people: Kathryn, of course, but also family and friends, and organisations I had been asked to support over the years and now wanted to give more to. One of them was the Endeavour Fund, which was set up by Prince Harry in 2012, off the back of the Walking With The Wounded expeditions to the North Pole and Everest, and whose board I sit on along with Ed Parker.

The Fund supports various organisations and charities that help wounded servicemen and -women take part in physical challenges as part of their recovery, and is a truly inspiring project. It was this that had led me to become involved in the Invictus Games – the only cycling events I had taken part in independently while still a member of British Cycling, and by far the ones I had enjoyed the most.

*****

In many ways, the Invictus Games were my first taste of what it is to compete as an independent athlete. The competition was another initiative of Prince Harry's and, thanks to my link to the Endeavour Fund, I had been lucky enough to know about it before it became reality. Inspired by walking partway to the North Pole with us, but also by watching the Warrior Games, a sporting competition for wounded service personnel in the USA, Harry had realised the power sport can have in helping people – especially military men and women – to recover from serious injury.

He had been impressed by the attitude of all the competitors, who were driven to give their best no matter what and didn't seem to mind whether they came first or last – competing was what was important to them, and that's what sport should be about. The only thing missing from the Warrior Games were the crowds, and it was Harry's vision to show the world the belief and determination he had found so inspiring.

The inaugural Invictus Games were hosted by London at the Olympic Park in Stratford, two years after the 2012 Olympic and Paralympic Games. I had only joined British Cycling the previous year, but there was some doubt as to whether I could take part in the competition – as an event for Forces personnel and veterans, it has nothing to do with British Cycling and my coaches were worried that it might have a negative impact on my training. This became even more of an issue two years later, ahead of the 2016 event, but in 2014 it almost didn't happen anyway.

At the beginning of the year I had broken my shoulder blade in a bad crash during a training ride, which stopped me competing at the Road World Cup and saw me spend a few months in recovery.

By September 2014 I had built my fitness back up and the Invictus Games were my first big event back on the bike. I had joined the British team as something of an outsider, never actually training with them and only showing up on the night before my races.

By that time the opening ceremony had already taken place and everyone was well and truly settled into the competition. I didn't even receive a full set of kit: all the non-essential items like tracksuit top and trousers – basically everything apart from my cycling skinsuit – had been divvied up among other people who wanted spares or different sizes. At first it was a strange feeling to be competing for Britain without properly being part of the team, but it turned out to be an amazing experience.

I barely slept the night before the race, I was so nervous. I didn't know how my form was, but the hardest thing for me was not knowing any of the competitors. Thirteen countries were taking part in the Games and, as many of the competitors weren't professional athletes, I didn't know them from previous competitions or have any idea where their strengths lay. It was something I would just have to find out.

Both cycling events were held on the same day, with a time trial in the morning and a road race in the afternoon. The time trial was one lap of the Lee Valley VeloPark circuit – a single lap that you have to ride as hard and as fast as possible. It was the first real effort (hard ride) I'd done in a long time and it hurt enormously; I crossed the finish line with my legs in bits and my lungs burning. Looking up at the scoreboard, I saw that I'd posted the fastest time of the day so far, but there were still eleven riders to go. I had no expectations, so when the end of the race came and my time was unbeaten, I was absolutely elated.

In my first race back after a serious injury, I had taken a gold medal for Great Britain.

Once I had that medal I was so relaxed and happy that it almost didn't matter what happened in the road race. We would be riding fourteen laps of the time-trial circuit and at first the pace was fairly relaxed. I decided the best thing to do would be to try to stay out of trouble, but winning a gold medal that morning had made me a marked man. Every time I tried to attack, moving ahead of the pack even very slightly, the other riders instantly reacted to bring me back. Sitting in the middle of the group, I started to feel pushed around and slightly intimidated, almost as if people were trying to make me crash.

With my memories of a crash injury so fresh in my mind, I didn't feel entirely comfortable. I knew that I had to make a choice between sitting right back and really pushing the pace.

Almost as soon as I made my decision and broke away, I found a couple of riders with me: my fellow teammate Terry Byrne and two French cyclists. Helping each other to maintain a good speed, we managed to put quite a bit of distance between our little group and the main pack. Turning to the others, I suggested that we work together to maintain our advantage and then battle it out in a sprint finish on the final lap. That's the way road cycling usually works – breakaway riders take turns to ride at the front of their little group, which reduces resistance for the others and helps maintain their position. Then, when it comes to the last stretch of the race, they have fewer competitors left to beat.

Terry and one of the Frenchmen were willing to work with me, but the fourth guy absolutely refused. I found myself spending most of my time at the front, which is the most tiring position to be in, and got very frustrated that I was effectively dragging this guy along.

At some point I found myself aggravated enough that I really started to push the pace, taking a few corners extremely fast. I actually thought I was going to come off on one of them, but I just made it round and on to a straight section, only to hear an all-too-familiar sound behind me. The French rider's pedal had clipped the road as he cornered, sending him spinning into a crash that Terry and the other Frenchman only narrowly avoided. They quickly dropped back to sit with the rest of the pack and I was left riding on my own. The peloton never caught up with me and I ended up winning the road race by more than a minute, with Terry coming in second.

I rode a victory lap of the circuit and when I came to a stop I found Prince Harry waiting. He gave me a huge hug and laughed about my win. 'I was hoping you'd do it,' he said, 'but I didn't expect you to obliterate the field. You need to make it look a bit harder than you did!' Later on, he handed me my medals on the podium, which was the most amazing experience for me. Harry had seen me at my worst and best – he had visited Selly Oak Hospital during the time I was there on a ward and had been part of the team that had walked to the North Pole when I was still adapting to my new post-injury life. Now I was facing him as a professional athlete, standing on a podium to receive not one but two gold medals for my adopted country. It was a very special moment for both of us.

The other person I was glad to share the Invictus Games with was my sister. Lizanne and her family had been cheering me on during the road race, standing on a corner with a homemade banner that read 'Go, Jaco, go!' next to a big South African flag. We spent some rare time together after the race, which made it into an even more memorable day.

With both my events completed on the Saturday, I was able to enjoy being a spectator on the Sunday. I was particularly impressed by the power lifting, in which double amputee Micky Yule put in an amazing performance, and in the evening we attended the closing ceremony along with all the other competitors. The atmosphere that night was incredible. The Foo Fighters and Bon Jovi played, and every single athlete received a participation medal, no matter what his or her results had been. What was most phenomenal was walking into the stadium to see thousands of people cheering from the stands: other veterans and their families, army husbands and wives, but also a huge number of people from the general public who wanted to show their support. It was an unforgettable moment for all of us, and one I was thrilled to recreate two years later.

The second instalment of the Invictus Games was held in Orlando, Florida, in May 2016. In the two intervening years Lizanne and her family had moved from London to Florida, so once again my sister was able to stand on the sidelines and cheer me on. I shared some wonderful moments with her and came away with both a gold and a silver medal, but what I loved most about this event was that I was a proper part of the British team. I flew in with them and took part in the opening ceremony, and over the three days before the cycling races we were spectators at many of the other sports, from swimming to wheelchair rugby. I could see the bigger picture of the event, which felt very different to my experience in London, and I absolutely loved the time I spent there. The Invictus Games really do have a different spirit to any other event in the world.

*****

As well as being moments of personal triumph, the Invictus Games had helped prepare me for competing at large-scale events without the backing of British Cycling. I had still been part of a team in London and Orlando, but the experience had been different and showed me that not all races had to involve sticking to a British Cycling game plan. Strangely enough, I had also had some of my best-ever results at the Invictus Games. I don't know how much of that can be put down to the competition experience – London and Orlando did have unique atmospheres – but I'd certainly say that I felt more relaxed before those races than most others I had competed in.

When I first started working independently with my coach, Adam, we established some goals to aim for throughout the year – it always helps to have an event in mind to train towards. One of the ones we chose was the forthcoming National Track Championships. Organised by British Cycling, in January 2018 it was held in the Manchester velodrome, where until just over a year ago I'd done my daily training.

I had never lost my passion for racing, but this time it felt different. Better. One thing I've always been incredibly grateful for is Kathryn's support – she tries her hardest to be there at all my competitions, and went above and beyond by acting as my *soigneur*. With British Cycling we had had team *soigneurs* to support us on race day, but as an independent rider I was on my own. Right from the very beginning, Kathryn has always wanted to do as much as she can, and having her there at my races – in whatever capacity – has made a world of difference.

The National Track Championships were also the first time I really saw a difference in the way I was training – or, rather, in the results it got me. Having taken the approach of eating and drinking pretty much what I wanted, training when and how it suited me, and managing my time so that I could say yes to other opportunities too, I succeeded in riding a time (4:39.997) that would have won me a bronze medal in the 4k pursuit if I had done that at the 2016 Paralympics in Rio. Normally, any rider who comes within a certain margin of the bronze-medal time from the most recent big competition (whether that's the Paralympics or the UCI World Championships) will qualify to take part in the next World Championships – and having just smashed that time, I was overqualified. There was no way I was going to turn down the opportunity of competing in one of the cycling world's most important competitions, but to get there I needed to go through British Cycling.

Making as strong a case for myself as I could – although my

results spoke volumes, I wanted to be sure – I applied to my old coaches to be taken to the UCI Track World Championships in Rio as part of the British team. Including me as an independent athlete did involve some expense, but otherwise it was a win-win for the organisation: they didn't have to pay me anything, and if I did well I would be gaining qualifying points for them towards Tokyo 2020. As I'd learned from the run-up to Rio, more points meant more riders on the team, and with British Cycling under new management it seemed to make sense that they would approach my situation with open minds.

When they agreed to take me, I was extremely excited. I felt as if I had finally been given a chance to show them what I could do. We were now two years down the line, but I would be going to the same city to ride in the same velodrome that the 2016 Paralympics had been held in. Part of me wanted to prove to British Cycling that they should have taken me then, and part of me wanted to demonstrate how it is possible to succeed outside the confines of a strict training programme. All I needed to do was to put in a good performance, but I knew I had something in me that would make competing worthwhile. I didn't know what colour it would be, but I had absolutely no doubt that this time I would go to Rio and return with a medal.

One of the weapons in my arsenal was a guy called Dale Hancock, a mind coach I had recently started working with. My sessions with him proved hugely beneficial in terms of my self-belief: you can put in all the hard physical work you like, but if you're stressed out and doubtful about your abilities, all that effort can go to waste very quickly. By March 2018 I had been working with him for a number of months and confidence was one of the key elements of my riding. I boarded the plane to Rio believing in myself and not feeling pressured by anyone else – whether it was a sense of creeping doubt because I could see other athletes doing things differently, or the feeling that I had to take every single one of the British Cycling coaches' suggestions. I had the confidence to say no to things I felt weren't right for me, whether it was a warm-up effort the day before the race or spending less time with Kathryn.

Kathryn came to Rio with me, and although she wasn't acting as my *soigneur* this time, she was incredibly supportive. Being with her in the lead-up to the race really helped to take me out of that competitive environment. Rather than constantly talking about training, bikes, other riders' performances and what they were or weren't doing to achieve that, we talked about anything and everything that didn't have to do with cycling. It completely took my mind off what was coming up in a couple of days, providing a much-needed distraction in the best possible way. What with her support and Dale's coaching, by the time I found myself lining up at the start I knew I had never entered a race feeling more relaxed. Of course there were still nerves – I think it would be impossible not to feel any – but I knew how to use them in a positive way.

Most World Championship races are divided into qualifying heats followed by the medal ride-offs, in which the four fastest riders from the qualifying rounds compete in pairs for the medals. The fastest two qualifiers ride for gold and silver; the second-fastest pair races for bronze and... nothing. The bronze ride-off is without doubt the most horrible race to be in, because despite putting in an extreme amount of effort, if you lose you walk away with nothing to show for it. In actual fact, the qualifying race is the most important of the lot, because only that will determine whether you end up in a ride-off.

I hadn't raced at international level for a while, but I still knew how much the qualifying heat counted. I was competing in the 4k pursuit, and I rode as hard and fast as I possibly could, going well over my planned pacing. Usually it's very important to pace yourself in a race like the individual pursuit, because you need to be able to sustain your speed over four kilometres, but the nerves and adrenaline made me throw all my tactics out of the window and instead give it everything I had. Somehow I managed to maintain my speed and came out of the qualifiers with the third-fastest time overall. I had won myself a place in the bronze medal ride-off.

Despite the fact that I was in the worst ride-off, I was extremely happy with where I was. I was thrilled with my performance and still riding high on just being in Rio. During the hours that followed the qualifiers, as I had something to eat and began to warm up for the evening race, something in me knew that I was going to win that medal.

I felt pretty good as I walked to my bike, which was set up on the start line. I was calm and quietly confident. I planned to do exactly what I'd done earlier in the day, only this time I would stick to the pacing Adam and I had agreed on a little bit better. I knew that kind of speed would work for me over the duration of the race, so I'd set off like that and do my best to maintain the pace. Tom, a coach for the British team, stood at a corner of the track, holding out an iPad on which I could read the time I'd taken to complete that lap – I used the numbers to know whether I was on track and at what point I needed to increase my speed.

My opponent was a very young American rider named Jacob Waters. I built up quite a comfortable lead over him in the early stages of the race, but again I had over-paced myself slightly and found my legs starting to tire. I had no idea what was happening, but Jacob had begun to pick up the pace, gaining three-hundredths of a second on me with every lap we completed. Five laps to go... four... three... by the second-last lap he was ahead of me.

UNEQUIVOCAL

With my mind focused entirely on my bike and hardly any time to pay attention to what was going on, I had absolutely no idea that I had just lost my lead and was in danger of losing the race. All I could hear was the crowd going crazy, people screaming words that I couldn't make out. The rest of the British team were yelling from the spectators' area, and Tom had thrown his iPad on the floor and was shouting at me to go harder and faster. I was giving it absolutely everything I had, but there was still another lap to go.

From somewhere far away I heard a bell ring. Because the riders are on different sides of the track, each has their own bell, which rings when they begin their final lap. A fraction of a second before mine was rung, I heard the sound of Jacob's from across the velodrome, and to this day I have the bell assistant to thank for making me aware of the fact that I was behind. *This cannot happen*, I thought, as a surge of pure energy shot through me. *No*, I said to myself, *I can't lose this race. I can't. I can't.* It was almost impossible, but I pedalled harder and faster.

With half a lap to go, I had nothing left. I sat up, breaking the aerodynamic position track riders crouch in, and instead went into a sprint position, leaning forward over the handlebars and standing up on the pedals. It was an unheard-of move and made absolutely no sense whatsoever, but it allowed me to throw myself and the bike forward towards the finish line. Jacob and I crossed it at almost exactly the same moment.

We kept circling the track, gradually slowing down, but the scoreboard above our heads remained blank. It had been such a tight finish that the race officials were still trying to work out who had been ahead. I kept riding past Kathryn and looking at her to see if she could tell me what was going on, but she only shook her head and mouthed, 'I don't know.' Finally, after what felt like an eternity, the screen changed from black to white.

My name was at the top, followed by my time: 4:43.461. I had won the race by three-hundredths of a second, setting a new British record in the process.

It didn't matter how big – or small – the margin was. I'd won that race, and the emotion I felt as it dawned on me was simply unbelievable. It was pure joy.

I came off the bike absolutely exhausted. My legs were so tired I could barely walk, so instead I was wheeled on my bike to a stationary turbo trainer where I could warm down. I sat there cycling away, trying to drink a protein shake, and all of a sudden the full realisation that I'd just won a World Championship bronze medal sank in. Part of me still couldn't really believe it, but there was so much emotion in me ready to come out that I burst into tears. Sitting there, I cried for about ten minutes. I couldn't stop – I was just so happy.

Words can't really describe just how joyous that moment was, or what my win in Rio did to me. I had proved to myself, my competitors and British Cycling something that deep down I had always known, and it kick-started my desire to go on and achieve even more. Only after Rio did I seriously start to wonder if it would be possible for me to compete at the Tokyo Games in 2020 – perhaps my Paralympic dreams weren't over after all. For me, cycling isn't all about winning – it never has been – but that medal helped reinforce the passion I had always felt for my sport. Finally, after many long years of hard training, doubts and difficult decisions, I felt that my efforts had paid off.

Standing on the podium in Rio with a bronze medal round my neck, a long-held dream came true. Yet the feeling I had there went deeper than joy, pride or satisfaction. For me, it wasn't even a happy ending.

It was something far better: a beginning.

XVI

RAINBOWS

Rio might have marked the beginning of a new chapter for me as a cyclist, but there was one circle that still needed to be closed. I'd been living in the UK for more than twelve years now, but South Africa would always be a home for me and was where my cycling journey had begun. In March 2019 I would return to complete one of the hardest bike-based challenges I'd ever done.

After I fell in love with bikes as a kid with a BMX, riding along dusty tracks through the stunning South African landscape had saved me more than once: when I was recovering from a knee injury at school, and when I'd felt I might even be finished with cycling after not being selected for the British Paralympic team in 2016.

That summer, riding my new orange gravel bike, was when I'd first developed an interest in off-road cycling. It was completely different to the road and track cycling I'd mainly done up until then, and an area I knew I wanted to explore further.

I can't say exactly when I started seriously considering competing in the Absa Cape Epic. In a way, the idea had always been at the back of my mind. I was still at school when the event was first held in 2004 and I was instantly intrigued by the idea of a multi-day mountain bike race. Life got in the way of me ever doing anything about it, but over the years that followed I noticed the race growing in popularity and status, particularly when it became a UCI event that allowed pro mountain bikers from all over the world to compete and gain points towards their international ranking. By the time I left British Cycling, the Cape Epic was known as the hardest mountain bike race in the world.

It was that status, combined with my new interest in off-road cycling, which made it stand out as a possible next challenge. But what really made me feel I *had* to compete in it was when I realised no all-amputee team had ever completed the race before. Attempts had been made, but here was a world-first that was still wide open, and I knew straight away I needed to go for it.

In terms of technical skills and experience, I was anything but a mountain biker, but that was something I could worry about later. First and most importantly, I needed to find someone to do it with me. Several close friends sprang to mind, but there was one who stood out head and shoulders above the rest.

Stu Croxford and I first got to know one another during the build-up to the Race Across America. He's a below-knee amputee who was a candidate for one of the four upright cycling spaces available, but sadly didn't get selected for the final team. Instead he joined the support crew, driving one of the vehicles, but it was during the training and selection phases that I really saw what he was made of.

Stu is exceptionally committed and hard-headed in just the right way; his drive and ability to push through a lot of pain and suffering is incredible. And, like me, he loves a challenge. When I asked if he would be interested in being my partner for the Cape Epic, there was absolutely no hesitancy. Despite never even having heard of it before, he said yes immediately.

It was a huge relief to have Stu on board, and we both had fantastic networks that were as enthusiastic about the challenge as we were. The Wigley Group gave a very generous donation and became a headline sponsor, and we also received amazing support from Asset Academy, Blesma, Presca and One Pro Nutrition, who gave us some of their newest nutritional products to trial.

My local Wokingham bike shop, Mountain Trax, put us in touch with SCOTT Sports, who couldn't have been more helpful or supportive – not only did they agree to loan us bikes, which we could use to ride the Epic and return afterwards, but they also sponsored us with matching helmets, sunglasses and shoes so we really looked the part.

Training was a lot of fun. For both Stu and me it was a big learning curve – the set-up on a mountain bike was completely different to what we were used to on road bikes; there was only one gear on the front and loads on the back, the bike was heavier and we rode more upright. At first, we both looked like Bambi on ice, but after many training rides in the UK and an entire week spent in the mountains north of Granada learning from Simon, a friend of Stu's who runs the adventure cycling company Freeride Spain, we felt fit, confident and in control. Stu's ability to perfect new skills quickly was very impressive, and again I thought how glad I was to be entering the race with him.

A couple of weeks later we were on a plane to Cape Town. For me, it was the most amazing feeling to be home. I hadn't been back to South Africa in a very long time and it made it even better to be able to show Stu around, as well as taking part in practice rides and team social events put on by the race organisers.

The practice rides were very helpful in showing us some of the terrain we could expect to encounter, but they also made us quite concerned about the heat. Even though South Africa was nearing the end of its summer, temperatures were soaring, and we knew riding long days would be a challenge – particularly for our stumps, which would swell even more inside their prosthetics.

In fact, that did turn out to be one of our biggest problems. Although the first day of the race was cool and overcast, three or four days later the heat had become intense and all the sweat from my upper body was pouring into the liner covering my stump. The pressure it created was unbearable, so every fifteen or twenty minutes I'd have to stop, clip out of my prosthetic, remove the liner and pour out the liquid. It was disgusting and painful, especially when we were riding sections that were too steep to stop on – then I just had to grin and bear it.

The race involved some very long days and tough climbs, as well as some extremely challenging technical sections, but thanks to Simon's hard work in Spain, Stu and I made it safely through them all.

We even managed to enjoy ourselves most of the time – the scenery we passed through was absolutely stunning. Much of the Epic is routed through private land opened especially for the race, so we were riding tracks that most people never get to go on. On those remote trails we saw the true beauty of the Western Cape, and as tough as I was finding the race, I felt so happy to be home in such a beautiful country.

At the end of each day we rode into a massive tented village that had been put up especially – we had two or three nights in each location along the route. Each rider had a tent to themselves, and there was a big scoff tent, shower stalls and all kinds of bike facilities. We could get massages or laundry done, and there was a team of mechanics who did a fantastic job on my bike after the front suspension collapsed completely midway through Day Five.

If evenings were about recovery and getting as much sleep as we could, mornings involved a pretty rude awakening: at five o'clock on the dot, a guy in a kilt would walk the length of each and every row of the tent village, loudly playing bagpipes. Stiff and exhausted as I might be feeling, it certainly always got me out of bed.

The final day of the Epic contained some very difficult climbs, but it was also one of the most beautiful and memorable. We rode through rivers and green vineyards, seventy kilometres from Stellenbosch to Paarl, where the finish was set up on the Val de Vie estate. Despite having ridden hard for days, my legs felt amazingly strong, and at the points where Stu was really struggling he'd grab the back pocket of my jersey and I'd pull him along. Other times we made great progress, overtaking rider after rider.

As we rode to the finish I could see huge crowds there to cheer us all on, with Kathryn and Stu's wife, Lizzie, who had flown out to meet us, waiting for us as soon as we crossed the line. The atmosphere was electric, the feeling amazing. We'd just completed the Cape Epic, becoming the first all-amputee team to do so, and on top of that I was in South Africa, sharing a beautiful moment with Stu, to whom I'd grown very close, and with Kathryn, who has been there for me for so long. Right from the moment we met she understood and supported my dreams, and achieving this meant all the more because she was there to share it with me.

No sooner were we off the bikes than Stu and I started talking about our next challenge. For the Cape Epic we'd named ourselves Team KT18, in homage to Headley Court, where we'd met – the postcode of the centre began with KT18. It's thanks to Headley Court, to its wonderful staff and facilities, that we are where we are now, and that we'd just made history. It was a tick in the box for the Cape Epic, but by no means the end for Team KT18.

*****

The high the race left me on was about to get even higher when, a

few days later, on a rock overlooking Cape Town, Kathryn agreed
to marry me. Following the Cape Epic we'd spent a few days on
a beautiful wine estate in Paarl and then travelled to Pretoria to
visit my mum, before coming back for a final week in Cape Town.
I'd spent a lot of the time worrying about how to propose – I'd
been trying to do it for months now, but never found the right
moment. I'd brought the ring out to South Africa – leaving it with
my brother-in-law's parents during the Cape Epic – and when we
got up before sunrise one morning to hike up Lion's Head, a peak
right next to Table Mountain, I put it in my backpack just in case.
Up there, no one else around, beneath a beautiful clear-blue sky
and with a panoramic view of Cape Town, the moment suddenly
felt right. I got down on one knee and Kathryn said yes, turning
that trip to South Africa into some of the most special weeks of
my life.

Coming back to the UK didn't feel easy for either of us, but spring
had arrived and we had a future to plan. I was also pleased to get
back on my bike – two solid weeks off had done me a lot of good.
I was keen to represent my sponsors on the international stage, so
my coach, Adam, and I had set our sights on the Road World Cup,
held that year in Ostend, Belgium.

It wasn't a particularly major event for me, but it was something
to train for and, at the back of my mind, I was still holding out
hope that it would help set me on the path towards Tokyo.

I would be going to the Road World Cup as an independent rider,
but I knew British Cycling was keeping a close eye on me, having
come back into my life the previous year. Before race day arrived,
though, there was another hurdle to jump: in the years since I'd left,
the UCI regulations had changed and I needed to be reclassified.
I saw this as a good opportunity to put forward my case for being
switched from the C4 category to C3. Because I'm missing an

arm but also sustained serious injuries to my leg, I tend to fall into a bit of a grey area when it comes to classification, and when I'd previously been classed as a C4 rider I'd found myself racing against athletes who maybe had a leg missing, but who didn't need the adaptations I require for my prosthetic. It didn't feel like an equal playing field, particularly when it came to technical sections which are harder to handle with only one arm, and I jumped at the chance to present my medical files and have my case re-examined.

Eventually the commission agreed to let me race the World Cup time trial as a C3 rider and see how I did – if my time was too fast compared to the others, I'd be moved back to C4. A few people told me I was in a great position, as all I needed to do in the time trial was not race my heart out. But I've always believed in fairness and honesty, and to do that would have gone against all my morals, everything I stand for – even what I learned in the army.

That kind of thing stays with you and I knew that even if no one else was aware of it, if I didn't give it my best effort, *I* would always know I'd cheated. That was all that mattered. And so I went out the next day, rode the time trial as hard as I possibly could and came in sixth. Later, the decision was confirmed: I was now officially classified as a C3.

It was good news, but the reclassification process was also a horrible one. I was so used to being a C4 rider that suddenly being a C3 didn't feel right. All kinds of odd thoughts started popping into my head: was my injury actually worsening? If they'd previously thought I was a C4 but were now willing to accept me as a C3, did that mean they could see my body had deteriorated?

It took a few weeks for me to accept it fully, to realise I was still racing among top athletes, just that we were now on a level playing field determined by our bodies.

At the road race itself, held two days after the time trial, I came in second behind another British rider, Ben Watson. Even before I left Ostend, British Cycling had approached me again, and that September I rode for them at the Road World Championships held in Emmen, in the Netherlands.

It turned out to be one of the most dramatic races of my life up to that point – just a couple of laps in I was involved in a crash with three other riders. Somehow, I managed to get back on my bike, and with a bent brake lever and a gash in my knee pouring blood, I dragged myself back up to the pack. With four laps to go I finally caught them, made an attack at exactly the right moment and ended up in a photo finish with the German rider Steffen Warias, who edged his bike over the line just ahead of me. To this day, I don't know how I did it, but I couldn't have been more delighted with my silver medal. I was exhausted but elated as I stood on the podium. Somewhere deep down, I knew I still had so much more to give.

*****

Once again I was in talks with British Cycling, and this time I said yes. I had to think about it carefully – there were many benefits to being back on the team, but there were negatives too and I was reluctant to give up my freedom – but a lot had changed in the years since I'd left. I spoke with John Hewitt, my coach, and Jon Pett, head of para-cycling, and together we agreed I would return with a bit more flexibility.

It's a decision I have never regretted: this time around, my relationship with British Cycling has been extremely happy and positive.

I understood I had to fall in with their guidelines, but I wanted to avoid some of the politics involved and, most importantly, feel that they trusted me in my training. By that time I knew what worked for me and what didn't, and I had the results to prove it. In the end we reached a compromise and I was welcomed back on to the team to train for what would be the most important race of my life so far: the UCI Track World Championships in Canada – in Milton, Ontario – in January 2020.

The staff at British Cycling instantly made me feel part of things, but I was surprised to find some of the riders doing exactly the opposite. Many whom I'd had good relationships with before made me feel uncomfortable. I could see why – we were less than a year away from the Paralympics in Tokyo, which were then still scheduled for September 2020 – and I'd arrived as an outsider to potentially take one of the spaces on the team. I'd seen it before in the run-up to Rio, when we'd felt in competition for a small number of places, but this time I was in a different position. It was difficult, and the emotional stress was compounded by the impact of having to travel up to Manchester from my home in Wokingham at least once a week.

Kathryn and I had decided not to move to Manchester – she had a job and we had our life in Berkshire. As far as I was concerned, I would aim for Tokyo 2020 and afterwards my cycling career would be over, at least as far as British Cycling was concerned. I'd have ticked that box and be able to move on. But then our landlady threw us a curveball in the form of three months' notice.

Forced to find a new place to live, we decided it might as well be in Manchester, where we would even be able to afford to buy. Suddenly, my days were full: with Kathryn still working in Wokingham, I'd view properties in the morning, train in the velodrome in the afternoons, and spend hours each evening discussing the houses I'd seen that day and arranging new viewings.

It was hectic and draining, but eventually we managed to find a place. We moved just a few days before it was time for me to board the plane to Canada.

All this time I'd been doing great work with Dale, my mind coach, visualising myself on the track and learning to believe in myself. I'd seen it so many times before and been a victim of it myself – even the greatest athletes in the world, the fittest and best-trained people, can have it all blown apart on race day when their mind lets them down.

A strong mentality was my secret weapon going to Canada: I knew I was in good shape and mentally I was in a great place as well. I knew how important this event would be, but mainly it was something I was doing for myself. I wanted to go out there and have fun, not just focus on proving something to others.

Kathryn flew in just before the race days began, which helped my mindset even more – just the same as at other events, I was able to switch off completely from racing whenever we spent time together. It's something I've found works really well for me, having the chance to think about topics other than cycling, and this time we had plenty to discuss as a friend of mine, Anthony, was busy decorating our new house. Did we want that dimmer switch to the right or left of the door? What colour were we planning to paint the hall? It was the biggest week of racing of my life and I was there in a hotel room worrying about furniture. For me, the situation couldn't have been better.

For the Track World Championships I'd entered the omnium, which meant I had to ride every race within my category. At the end of the event all the points would be added together, with medals awarded for each race, then additional ones for the omnium.

It was a tough programme, but the race I'd mainly been focusing on was the very first one: the men's 3k individual pursuit. As I'd recently been newly classified, I was starting afresh with no UCI ranking points, meaning I was the first rider out on the track in the qualifying round. I rode the twelve laps as hard as I could and came away with a personal best of 3:29.266. For the majority of the race it stood as the fastest time, beaten only by David Nicholas, the defending world champion. We found ourselves going head to head in the ride-off race for gold and silver, which was a dead heat until the very end. It was another situation where I finished a race not knowing if I'd won or not, but David's wheel had crossed the line just before mine.

For a moment I was disappointed, until I realised I ought to be very proud. I'd just won a World Championship silver medal, almost beating the best guy in the world.

And with that first race over, I felt able to relax. Of course the other events were important to me, but British Cycling had seen I was at the level they needed and now I really was just there to have fun. It would start the next day with the 1k time trial – four laps of the track as fast as you can. Unlike the 3k pursuit, there weren't separate qualifying and medal rounds. We each had one shot and at the end of the event the best time would stand.

As on the previous day, I was the first rider on to the track. I'd never cracked the 1:08 mark in a time trial before, but that day I pulled in another personal best: 1:07.867. Feeling pleased with my performance, I settled on to a turbo trainer for a half-hour warm-down.

From where I sat I could see most of the track, including the finish line, with the final corner and scoreboard behind me. As I cycled away on the stationary bike, I kept checking over my shoulder to see that my time still stood. I was ahead even when we got down to the final two riders, both of whom I knew were specialists in this event. Aleksei Obydennov, a Russian athlete, was next, but his time was slower than 1:08. The final rider was Joseph

Berenyi, a US rider I knew had taken gold medals before.

Joe set off and rode the first lap faster than me. The second lap, too. His time for the third lap was roughly the same as mine had been. It all hung on the fourth and final circuit. I felt I could see his legs seizing as he hurled himself towards the finish line, but his time for the first two laps had been fast and the scoreboard behind me had gone black. I looked away again, towards the track, but then I heard a massive cheer go up and saw a huge smile appear on my coach's face – he was standing facing me and the scoreboard behind.

I couldn't believe it. I glanced over to see my name still at the very top of the board. My time was still the fastest – I was number one. As the realisation sank in that I was now a world champion, as John Hewitt, my coach, and Jon Pett came over to hug me, a huge rush of emotions flooded me and I covered my face and started to sob. The feeling was just unbelievable. It was relief and pride and happiness, but at that moment I also knew how true it was that if you do something because you love it, if you do something because you're having fun, the results will come of their own accord.

And that was exactly what I'd done. For seven years I'd looked at other riders standing on the top step of the podium, having a rainbow jersey pulled over their head and being presented with a gold medal, and suddenly I was the one standing there. In the cycling world, earning a rainbow jersey is the pinnacle of our sport, no matter what age or level you are.

The significance of that jersey is the same for everyone, and I knew I'd just joined a very unique club. Standing on the podium in Canada was a moment that meant everything.

*****

UNEQUIVOCAL

Nothing could beat the feeling of that first gold medal, but two days later I was amazed to find myself standing on the podium for a second time, having not one but two rainbow jerseys presented to me. After coming fourth in the Flying 200 – a short, sharp race in which your time is only measured over the last two hundred metres – and riding in the qualifying round of the mixed team sprint, I had somehow managed to come first in the scratch race, which meant I'd gained the most points in the omnium event. I would be leaving Canada a three-time world champion, almost certain that come the summer I would be sitting on a plane to Tokyo.

What I felt perhaps more than anything at that moment was an overwhelming sense of relief. I'd worked so hard and for so long, but in the end I'd done what I'd set out to do – I'd proved myself and had fun doing it. The road had been long and winding, but the past year in particular, from the Cape Epic to Canada, had shown me what I could do if I put my mind to it and had so many amazing people there in support.

As I stood on that podium, I knew there would be more storms ahead, but also that I would weather them and there would always be a rainbow – whether it came as a jersey or not. It's who I am; it's what life has made me. I try to do what I love and I put my heart and soul into it. Every time, unequivocally.

And that, quite simply, is what I felt in that moment.

This is me, I thought. *This is what I'm here to do.*

Epilogue

TOKYO GOLD

Little did I know it, but the clouds of that next storm were gathering as Kathryn and I flew back from Canada. In early February 2020, coronavirus was already in the news, but just what it would mean on both an individual and a global level couldn't have been further from my mind at that point.

Arriving back in Manchester, things felt different. Previously, after competing in a big event, I would feel an enormous sense of relief at having achieved what I'd set out to do – when I won bronze at the World Championships in Rio, it was like a pressure valve had suddenly opened. I would be hit by a sense of enormous pride and justification, but there was exhaustion too. Afterwards, it could be a bit of a struggle to find my motivation again. I needed to have time off from racing.

Following Canada, though, I didn't have that feeling. I was absolutely exhausted – I'd raced in every event, given it my all and desperately needed some time away from the bike – but ten days were sufficient. Suddenly, competing at that summer's Paralympic Games in Tokyo was a real possibility, and what I felt more than anything else was excitement. With that goal in sight, it was now all about finding the right balance between maintaining my upward trajectory and not overdoing it. I needed to keep myself on top form and avoid any kind of slump.

UNEQUIVOCAL

My confidence was high on the track side of things, but I wanted to be able to compete in the road racing too, as an added extra. In the gym and the velodrome I started looking at the smaller areas I needed to improve in – position has always been a sticking point with me, as there's a very fine line to tread between aerodynamics and power, and I'm naturally constrained by wearing a fixed prosthetic. For a while I had been toying with the idea of getting a new arm made for use on the bike, but with the Games just over six months away, there simply wasn't enough time.

I soon established that there wasn't enough time for lots of things – and that included training for everything I wanted to do. Looking at it realistically, I had to pick the races I wanted to concentrate on in order not to spread myself too thin. The 3k individual pursuit – the race David Nicholas had just beaten me in in Canada – had always stood out, so I sat down with my coach, John Hewitt, and together we created what we called Project 325.

The aim was simple: to ride the 3k individual pursuit in a time of three minutes and twenty-five seconds or less. It was a clear goal that I could work towards with the rest of the British Cycling team, and I walked away from that meeting feeling confident. I had a new plan to ramp up my training as we went into spring, and I knew I was going to do everything I could to ensure I was on that plane to Tokyo.

Even though the final team hadn't been confirmed yet, I started to notice a natural separation within British Cycling between those who would almost certainly be going and the athletes who were still very much maybes. It was a situation I recognised from the build-up to Rio in 2016 and I did my best to ignore the stresses it brought with it.

Despite the fact that none of us was 100 per cent guaranteed a place on the team, we all started training for the heat and humidity we would encounter in Japan. One way of doing this was using a heat chamber at the Manchester Institute of Health & Performance – a little room in which we could crank up the temperature to around thirty-five degrees Celsius and train in above-80-per-cent humidity. It was important, but horrible. I soon learned to get in quality training earlier in the day if a heat-chamber session was on the cards, because afterwards my body would be totally drained.

In March, as the world slowly started shutting down, I still had absolutely no concerns whatsoever. In the worst case, I thought, this new thing called lockdown might last about three months; a postponement of the Games never even crossed my mind. Only when we went into full-on lockdown and I found myself riding through eerily deserted streets did I begin to realise that we were entering new territory.

Through all the confusion of that initial lockdown, British Cycling did an absolutely fantastic job of ensuring that we could still train. In fact, one of the only positives of that period was that it was an amazing time to be a cyclist – the normally extremely busy roads near our home were suddenly almost empty. I could ride for miles and see no cars or pedestrians; it was like I was completely alone.

Being able to enjoy cycling that much was a blessing, as it was around then that rumours about the Olympic and Paralympic Games started circulating on TV and in the press. One day, I received an email from the British Paralympic Association (BPA) telling me to avoid listening to the news, followed shortly by lots of texts and emails from friends and family telling me how sorry they were – the media were reporting that the Games that year were off.

Actually, there hadn't been an official announcement at that stage, so I had to ignore them for several days. Only after another week or so had passed did we get a follow-up email from the BPA:

the decision had been made to postpone the entire Games by a year.

I read the email, but the words didn't sink in. I watched the news on television, but just stared blankly at the screen. For around eight days afterwards, I carried on training – going out on hard rides that left me so exhausted I had to lie in the back garden to recover. One day, out there on the lawn, I had a sudden realisation: *Why am I doing this to myself if the goalposts have been moved?* At that point, it suddenly sank in. There was no chance of me going to Tokyo in 2020. I was devastated.

With the need to train suddenly gone, I took time off from my bike. Instead, while Kathryn worked I did stuff around the house, and we enjoyed spending the rest of our time together. I wasn't too strict about my diet and gave myself the chance to relax and find some headspace.

John and I had a good chat about the situation – from a training point of view, it was obviously far from ideal, but we needed to work out how to utilise it. Working backwards, we made a new plan for the next eighteen months, and decided we would turn things to our advantage by using the time we'd gained to investigate a new prosthetic arm.

In the meantime, British Cycling had turned the Manchester velodrome into a very safe environment, so I was eventually able to get back in the gym and on to the track. As restrictions slowly started easing across the country, I met up with Jody Cundy, Jon Gildea and John Hewitt for an off-road ride in Snowdonia, eager to try out the new SCOTT mountain bike I'd purchased in lockdown.

It felt great to be with them and out on a trail... until, not long into the ride, I landed badly on a bumpy section of path and totally lost control of the bike. As I fell heavily on to my left side, I felt a familiar pain in my shoulder and knew instantly that my scapula was broken – an injury I'd already sustained back in 2014. Luckily, Jody was behind me and could stop to assist, but there was no way out of the situation except to ride back down the trail and drive myself to Manchester. At home, I was finally able to hand over to Kathryn, who immediately took me to A&E.

Although I needed a period of recovery, I was fortunate that I wasn't under any pressure. As travel became possible again, Kathryn and I spent a few days at Lake Como, but in December we faced a bigger, more complicated journey. Over the past few months, my mum's health had been declining and, if I could, I needed to go to South Africa to see her and arrange for her care. As news of another UK lockdown began to mount, we took the decision to fly to Pretoria with three bikes and lots of kit, unsure when we would be able to return to Manchester.

It was a shock to see just how much my mum had deteriorated over the course of that year. Her doctors had struggled to get to the bottom of what was wrong, but eventually diagnosed her with multiple sclerosis – a condition that can be especially difficult to treat at her age. As the days and weeks ticked by, I tried to make the most of the time I had with her and also took the opportunity to go on plenty of training rides.

The sunny South African weather was completely at odds with how I felt inside. After a long day out on the bike, I would be physically drained, but I was also emotionally shattered from dealing with Mum's care and worrying about her future amid all the global uncertainty. After several visits to care homes in her area, some of which I found quite upsetting, Kathryn and I were lucky enough to find two sisters who would care for Mum at home. Linah and Elizabeth have looked after her with such grace, and I am infinitely grateful to them.

At this point, hard as it may be to believe now, Kathryn and I were still planning to get married in South Africa in April 2021.

Towards the end of our stay we took a beautiful road trip to Cape Town, where we'd got engaged almost two years before, to see some more of the country and pack in a final few days of summer. Returning to a locked-down UK in early February was quite the culture shock, but my shoulder was now fully healed and the Paralympics were once more coming into focus.

We got back to Manchester just in time for me to take part in an in-house race organised by British Cycling, as all other competitions were cancelled for the foreseeable future. It was a good five or six months since I'd last been on the track and I felt incredibly excited to be back. There was also a bit of apprehension in there – I had no idea which riders might have improved since I'd last encountered them, or by how much. In the final, I found myself up against Fin Graham, a young Scottish lad whom I mainly knew as a promising road cyclist. Whereas before the pandemic I wouldn't have put him down as a definite contender for Tokyo, Fin had taken lockdown as an opportunity to push himself and really excel. His talent was something he would prove again and again over the coming months, showing that no matter what we all thought of our own performance, no one's place on the team was ever guaranteed.

Racing against Fin in the final, I shocked myself and everybody else by riding the 3k pursuit in 3:25 – the very goal John and I had set when we'd created Project 325 the year before. Despite my injury and all the time off the bike, I knew I was in a very good place. Now, I needed to reset my goals – if I could ride a 3:25, someone else easily could as well. I began to push the target to 3:23 or even 3:22.

Around this time, my coaches and I also started working hard on my new prosthetic. With the help of a fantastic team from

Dorset Orthopaedic, we tested a few radical ideas in the form of 3D-printed prototypes that would fit over my current prosthetic. The aim was to improve my position on the bike and make me more aerodynamic, which, if done right, could gain me as much as five seconds. That might not sound like much, but in the split-second world of cycling, the difference between gold and silver can come down to a hundredth of a second. After several trial sessions in a wind tunnel, yet more testing and even more prototypes, we finally had a useable arm to put forward for approval by the UCI.

At the very start of May 2021, I took part in two road races in Belgium – my first international cycling competitions since the Track World Championships in Canada at the end of January 2020. The first was the one-day Classics Ronde, held in Flanders, at which all three medals went to Great Britain: gold for Fin Graham, silver for Ben Watson, and bronze for me.

Quite aside from the pride I took in our success, it felt amazing to be racing again. But the following weekend in Ostend, where we were racing in the Road World Cup, couldn't have felt more different. This time we were focusing on gaining the precious UCI points that would give us spaces for athletes at the Paralympic Games. We had to calculate which of us needed to end up on the podium and ride accordingly, so it felt quite different to a normal race, in which you would simply ride for yourself and give it your all. Everyone had a heightened awareness that while we were definitely teammates, Tokyo was the priority, and there wouldn't be enough spaces for everyone.

The stress of racing like this was compounded by the quarantine rules we faced in Belgium – we didn't leave our hotel rooms except to race – and on returning to the UK. There were also nasty rumours going around again about the Paralympic Games being further postponed or even cancelled. While the BPA was extremely good at providing regular reassurance, I had to work hard to ignore the media reports and push aside my negative thoughts: a small part of me really did believe the Games would be called off. If they were, I knew that was my Paralympic dream over. I'd narrowly missed out on Rio in 2016, and this would be the final straw. I knew that if I couldn't ride in Tokyo, I wouldn't have the appetite to go for Paris 2024.

At the same time, I was becoming increasingly worried about my training and the claustrophobia I'd felt doing back-to-back quarantines. At the start of June, British Cycling was planning to send a team to the Road World Championships in Cascais, Portugal, but I wasn't in the right frame of mind. I knew that all the points counted and every race was important – and I was terrified that dropping out would negatively impact my chances of selection for Tokyo – but I also knew I needed to look at the bigger picture. The knock-on effects the travel would have on my training were simply too big to ignore. It was a bold decision, but eventually I asked my coaches not to take me to Portugal. The relief when they agreed was enormous.

Shortly after the World Championships, the Paralympics selection panel sat. Although the official team announcement wouldn't be made until later in the summer – an appeals process had to be held first – we were told to expect a decision on 22 June. It was a Tuesday and I sat nervously at home, constantly refreshing my inbox. No new emails. The waiting was awful. Eventually, at around six o'clock, Kathryn told me she'd booked a table in a fancy restaurant to celebrate – she'd been so sure I would be selected and would have heard by that point. We decided to make the most of the reservation and go anyway, but it wasn't until we were seated that I finally received the email. Remembering a similar moment in the summer of 2016, I opened the message apprehensively to see that this time I had been selected – and I would be competing in all the C3 events for which I had trained. 3k individual pursuit. 1k time trial. Mixed team sprint. Road race and time trial. It was dizzying.

The sense of relief and happiness that washed over me then is hard to describe. I had been working towards this opportunity for eight long years, and all the delays, uncertainties and personal challenges thrown up by the past eighteen months had made the wait even more difficult to bear. Part of me felt that it was just my luck for obstacles to appear in my path at the very last minute. But I had persevered and now, finally, the moment I'd longed for was here. In less than two months' time, I'd be touching down in Tokyo.

*****

It took a few days for the news to sink in, but it wasn't until later in the summer when the line-up was officially announced that I really started to feel the pressure of competing. Kind messages of congratulations came flooding in, but strangely enough, it was the off-hand, perhaps even jokey comments that I really took to heart. Whenever anyone said something like, 'You'll smash it,' or 'Don't come back with anything less than a gold,' I felt the nerves rising.

As an athlete, you're on an emotional roller coaster, never knowing how it will be from one day to the next. Just because you pull off a great performance at one event doesn't mean that the next day it won't all go horribly wrong. There are so many factors to contend with, especially in cycling. I found that I was constantly having to remind myself just to enjoy the journey – that was what really mattered here.

Of course, being professional and prepared was also very important, but I found myself in uncharted waters. I've been lucky enough to experience a lot of different things in my life, but the final build-up to a Paralympic Games was like nothing I'd ever done before.

It felt strange not having any prior experience to fall back on, but the one thing I could do was look at my past results and trust the processes that had led me this far. If I'd won those gold medals in Canada, if I'd now been selected for Tokyo, then I must have been doing something right. It was hard not to get caught up in what everyone else was doing – the shift in mindset was noticeable as the entire team stepped their training up a gear – but I continued to stick to what I knew. There was no need to alter my routine drastically; for me, training has always been about quality rather than quantity.

And even if I didn't have any similar scenarios from my own life to refer back to, I was surrounded by a team of phenomenal athletes whose experience I could tap into. Looking around the velodrome on the day of the official press release as Penny Briscoe, Chef de Mission for Tokyo 2020, gave a wonderful speech, it finally became real to me. I was in this now, along with incredible Paralympics veterans like Dame Sarah Storey and Jody Cundy; good friends of mine, including Steve Bate and Adam Duggleby; and other newbies like Fin Graham and Sophie Unwin, who, like me, were taking it all in for the very first time. It was going to be a steep learning curve, but I felt ready.

The difference between summer 2021 and summer 2016 was astonishing. Back then, when I hadn't been selected for Rio, I'd felt as though the umbilical cord between British Cycling and me had been abruptly severed. Now, I was being supplied with everything I could possibly need – and more. All the little adaptations I'd spent months fighting for, whether it was how I clipped in and out of my pedals or which shape of helmet integrated best with my riding position, were suddenly given the green light. The mechanics even finished a check on my bike by offering to give me a newer-looking frame, though to be honest, that was going a step too far for me. I deal with change on a daily basis, but I actually hate it unless it has real purpose. So what if my frame looked a little bit scratched? It was my bike and I knew exactly where I was when I was riding it.

There was always going to be plenty of new kit, though, and the day we went to pick it up was a real highlight. Usually all the Paralympic athletes would meet at the National Exhibition Centre in Birmingham for a big event, but this was an exceptional year and so we just collected our stuff from the velodrome.

As we walked in, we were handed two massive bags and sent off in small groups to the changing rooms to try it all on. The staff at the velodrome tried really hard to make it a memorable day, and we had a lot of fun.

For all the excitement of the build-up, there was also an element of anxiety. As our departure date grew closer, simply staying healthy became increasingly important. I started almost isolating, turning down event invitations and even work, like speaking engagements or filming, knowing that if I did get ill, my training or even participation in the Games would be at risk.

It wasn't just Covid that was on my mind – even going out for a bike ride, I felt far more nervous than I usually would. The confidence I normally had around cars was gone. I felt I needed a layer of bubble-wrap.

Finally, on 3 August 2021, it was time to leave for holding camp. We would be spending the last two weeks before flying to Tokyo at the Celtic Manor Resort in the Usk Valley near Newport, making our final preparations and ensuring we were on top form. There was a real buzz as we gathered outside the velodrome, but leaving Kathryn was tough. We were fortunate that we didn't find being in lockdown particularly hard – we're one of those couples who can spend every second of the day together – and all the months we'd had in each other's company were only making this separation more challenging. When I'd first found out that no spectators would be allowed at the Games, I'd been really sad and disappointed. So many people had helped me get to where I was, many had already booked tickets to attend, and I was gutted that none of them would be there to cheer me on. But the Games were still going ahead, and in the end that was all that counted. As we said an emotional goodbye, I knew Kathryn would be supporting me from home, just as she always has.

We arrived at Celtic Manor on a beautiful summer's day and checked into our accommodation in little lodges dotted around the grounds. I was sharing with Crystal Lane-Wright, Steve and Adam, and another tandem pair, James Ball and Lewis Stewart, but was lucky enough to have a room of my own. Each lodge had a hot tub and beautiful views across the South Wales countryside. Less happily, we found a greenhouse tent set up on our veranda. While going in the hot tub was an official form of training for the warm conditions we'd be facing, there was nothing like a greenhouse tent for getting us acclimatised to extreme humidity.

Overall, the set-up was great, and the training we did was very successful. On one memorable day we all completed a time trial just outside Bath – the weather was gorgeous, spirits were high and we all rode very fast.

Towards the end of the first week, Fin and I did a rehearsal of the 3k individual pursuit, our main event. Both of us set a new personal best, but I came off the bike feeling very unhappy with my performance. John Hewitt was grinning from ear to ear, but I knew I hadn't executed the ride as well as I could have. Yet that was what a rehearsal was there for – now was the time to make mistakes, not later. When we staged a second one in the final week of holding camp, this time with me wearing full Games kit, I crossed the finish line feeling so much better. A great cheer went up from the sidelines and John came over, smiling even more broadly. 'That was phenomenal – a three twenty-one!' he said. It was the best confidence booster I could have hoped for.

Almost before we knew it, we were packing up again and getting on the coach to Heathrow. There were loads of British flags at the airport and a fantastic atmosphere as we lined up to check in. We were then escorted to a dedicated lounge – partly to give us some special treatment, but mainly as a Covid precaution. Throughout the entire Paralympics, health was never very far from our minds.

Arriving in Tokyo on a beautiful day, we encountered an army of smiling volunteers and the famous heat and humidity we'd spent all those months preparing for. It took quite a long time to get through the airport – we were each given a massive stack of paperwork to complete and had to wait around for the results of Covid tests – but by early evening we were on a bus and heading for our accommodation near Izu Velodrome.

What should be a roughly two-hour drive took five hours thanks to the Tokyo rush hour, so it was completely dark by the time we arrived. Once again, we were staying in lodges – this time I was sharing with Neil Fachie and Matt Rotherham – but unlike those at Celtic Manor, these featured sliding doors and traditional Japanese flooring. It was a lovely touch, and the legendary cardboard beds proved absolutely fine to sleep on.

The next morning, we were finally able to take in our new surroundings. The accommodation was on a hilltop surrounded by greenery, with spectacular views across to Mount Fuji in the distance. Each nation had its own little area of the hotel decorated with flags and banners, and we all came together in the dining room for meals. It didn't take long to realise that the menu was rather select – for three weeks I ate rice for every meal, mixed with ketchup and scrambled eggs for breakfast, and topped with meat and vegetables for lunch and dinner. Some other elements of our new life also took a bit of getting used to, like the Covid tests that involved spitting into a tube the minute we woke up each morning, and wearing sunglasses until around midday to help our bodies slowly adjust to being in a different time zone.

Over the next few days, we gradually acclimatised and got in some training sessions in the velodrome. As soon as I got on the track, I felt happy. Each velodrome is different, but this one was beautiful – it was very fast to ride and felt quite similar to the Sir Chris Hoy Velodrome, part of the Emirates Arena in Glasgow, a venue I've always liked. In fact, the track was so fast that I ended up with a dilemma. Riding in the way I was used to, my leg speed was actually too high – unless I went up to a higher gear, I was in danger of spinning out. John and I studied the data and decided that even though it was a risk to go up, sticking to what I knew simply wasn't an option if I wanted to be able to control my speed and reach the new target I had set myself – 3:21.

I always take the day off before a race – by that stage, I don't feel that anything I can do is going to change the outcome – so my final training session was on 24 August. I came off the track feeling good and went back to my room to rest. Later that afternoon, I was in for a nasty shock, when John Hewitt knocked on the door to tell me that, in a surprise decision, the UCI had banned my new prosthetic arm.

It was a devastating blow. The new prosthetic had already been approved by the UCI in Belgium at the beginning of May, and I had been training with it ever since. But the reason for the decision soon became clear: in order for the prosthetic to be used in a Paralympic competition, it had to have been raced before. This was something I hadn't done – back in Belgium, because this new arm wasn't quite finished, I'd still been racing in my old prosthetic, and then I'd decided not to attend the Road World Championships in June.

There was no point in 'if only'. The decision was final; I would not be wearing my new prosthetic. I knew I could still race happily in the old one, but in my mind the new arm had enormous significance for how fast I could go. I called Kathryn and also spoke to Dale, my mind coach, who always finds exactly the right words. By the end of the day, I felt much calmer and more accepting. There was nothing I or anyone else could do about it now.

The night before race day, I slept really well. The C3 men's 3k individual pursuit was the final event to be held in the velodrome that day, but somehow I got through the wait and was soon doing my warm-up for the qualifying round. As times began to be posted I didn't feel particularly worried, but in the heat before mine, things started to get interesting.

My teammate Fin Graham was up against the American rider Joseph Berenyi – they were my two main concerns, along with Australia's David Nicholas and the Spanish athlete Eduardo Santas Asensio. By the time Fin got to his last lap I was already in my helmet and visor, switched off a bit from the rest of the world and giving myself a pep talk, but I was still more than capable of registering the fact that Fin had just ridden a time of 3:19.780, smashing the world record in the process.

It was an unbelievably fast time, but right then, I didn't panic. Walking up the stairs towards the starting gate, I couldn't really hear anything but the song I was singing inside my head: 'Are You Gonna Go My Way' by Lenny Kravitz. I had visualised myself in this moment so often – walking around my bike, clipping into my pedals, getting settled into position – and each time I had sung those words to myself. I took a deep breath, filling myself with air, and I knew somewhere deep inside me that this was my time. The timer started beeping, counting down from ten, and when the gate sprang open I felt a strange sense of relief. This was what I had trained for. All that time on the road, all that time in the gym, all that time on the track, all the sacrifices I'd made – it had all been leading to this.

Now, all I had to do was ride.

I started well, my legs feeling good, and on the second lap I could sense myself relaxing into the race. My third lap is always the fastest, but after that I found the right rhythm and stuck to it, all the way through the next few laps. I felt as though I was barely touching the pedals; the bike beneath me was flying. By lap ten, I knew I needed to push on – my legs were starting to hurt. I kept my head down and stared at the black line on the floor in front of me. *Keep a good line, keep your head down*, I told myself, over and over again. I wanted to be a train and for that black line to be my rail. The eleventh lap came and went, the bell for the final lap sounded and I knew it was time to empty the tank. I pushed as hard as I possibly could and shot over the finish line, looking up immediately to see the number on the scoreboard.

3:17.593. A new world record.

A bundle of emotion surged through me, all the way from my belly up into my chest. I opened my mouth and released it in the loudest cheer I could manage: 'YES!' I was so happy – with my line, my speed, the way I'd executed the ride. The moment Fin had posted that amazing time, I'd wanted to beat him, wanted my own world record. I'd got that, and I felt this enormous sense of relief and achievement and pride in myself.

The final qualifying heat was between David Nicholas and Eduardo Santas Asensio, but from the stationary bike where I was cooling down, I could see they weren't going to ride faster than Fin or me. When they finished, a big cheer erupted from the British Cycling support staff and riders in the pit – it was going to be an all-British final.

By the time I'd finished my cool-down, I felt horrendous. I'd pushed so deep that all these horrible emotions came rising to the surface, along with nausea and fatigue and a cough I always get after cycling that hard. There was a considerable gap between the qualifiers and the medal ride-offs – around two hours – so I would need to eat as soon as I could to make sure I had enough fuel. I forced down a protein recovery shake and then tried to eat a sandwich, which proved extremely challenging.

Putting on my tracksuit and the heated pants we wore to keep our muscles warm, I decided to step away from the race environment and cool down in the air-conditioned unit each nation had been allocated outside the velodrome.

Stepping into the open air, even just for a moment, the heat and humidity were unbearable – a serious contrast to the air-conditioned track. Fin joined me for a few minutes and we spoke a bit about the race, but he soon went off to do his own thing and left me alone with my thoughts. I had an emotional moment when it all suddenly sank in: I was in a final at the Paralympic Games.

I knew Fin was on incredibly good form, but I told myself I was just going to do the same as I'd done before. *You've got this*, I kept thinking, all through that wait and my next warm-up.

As the fastest qualifier, I was starting on the home straight, and John – who also coached Fin – was standing by with an iPad that he could hold out to show me my split times for each lap. Everything was set up and I found myself in that moment again, singing my Lenny Kravitz song and filling my lungs with air. Weirdly, although I was tired and my legs no longer fresh, I had the profound sense that I was OK. The timer started beeping... and we were off.

As expected, I was slightly slower than Fin on the first lap – I start from a seated rather than a standing position, which gives me a slight disadvantage in pushing the bike over the line. By the second lap, our times were similar, and from the third lap onwards I started gaining a hundredth of a second or so each time we went round. Everything felt good; I wasn't riding quite as hard as I had in the qualifying heat, but was a lot more measured and in control of my pacing.

This was up until laps eight and nine, when suddenly my legs went. From that point on, the race began to feel really, really difficult. *Don't worry, you've still got this*, I told myself, but the hurt had come a lap or two earlier than I'd anticipated and the effort of turning the pedals was becoming harder with each rotation. Looking back on the video of that race now, I don't appear to have slowed down in the slightest, but to me at the time it felt like I was going backwards. I was really suffering and even started reassuring myself that it would be OK to get second place – something I've never had to do before. By lap eleven, I was fighting against myself.

And then the bell went for lap twelve, and I knew it was now or never. Grimacing, clenching my teeth, feeling as though my legs were going to come off, I gave it everything I had left. I can only remember shouting as I crossed the line; I heard my finishing bell go and then, a second later, Fin's sounded from the other side of the velodrome, but even at that point I wasn't sure what had happened.

My lungs were screaming and I could taste blood in my mouth. I sank my head into my hands as I continued going round the velodrome, utterly exhausted. It took around a lap and a half before I was able to look up at the scoreboard – and there was my name with a number one beside it. It was the most amazing feeling. I had ridden a time of 3:20.987, beating Fin by 1.013 seconds.

It wasn't faster than my previous ride, it wasn't a new world record, but it was fast enough to win a gold medal and that was all that mattered. It's hard to put into words just how happy I was in that moment. Pride, joy, relief, accomplishment – this was everything I'd worked for, the very thing I'd come here for, and it had all paid off.

As I continued rolling around the track, gradually slowing down, I grabbed a British flag from someone in the small crowd of spectators and held it up. An instant later, I regretted that move – I couldn't steer properly with just my prosthetic, and as I brought my hand back to the handlebars, the flag almost got tangled up with my wheel. Now was really not the time to fall off, I decided, ending my victory lap sooner rather than later and gratefully allowing the support staff to help me off the bike. The atmosphere in the pit was electric. I waved to the crowd and wished with all my heart that I could search the smiling faces and lock eyes with Kathryn. As elated as I was, at that moment I desperately missed her.

All too soon, any thoughts were pulled from my head as I was taken through to the press area for interviews and photos. It was unbelievable – so many voices and questions after the quiet intensity of the track – and I felt utterly drained. There was no time to cool down or even have anything to eat or drink before we were getting dressed in our podium tracksuits and lining up to receive our medals.

The Covid regulations meant we wouldn't be presented with the medals as usual – instead, we were offered them on a tray and had to hang them around our necks ourselves. Yet when my turn came, Fin, who was standing next to me, called the official over and said he wanted to present me with my medal. It was a beautiful touch, such a kind thing for him to do, and as we stood there listening to the national anthem I felt a huge rush of emotion all over again.

UNEQUIVOCAL

Still unable to believe it, I allowed the tears to come.

From the podium all the way back to the hotel I could hardly stop staring at my medal. Even my phone, which was exploding with messages, could barely distract me from it. Back in my room, I dumped all my bags and only then took it off, laying it softly down on the bed along with the little mascot we'd also been given. I stared at it some more, an enormous grin on my face. And finally, after a minute in which it all sank in, I pulled my gaze away. Out on the balcony, the turbo trainer was waiting. I still had a job to do.

*****

The next morning, after somehow managing to sleep, I woke up to a very similar procedure. The day before I had managed to break one of the longest-standing world records, but now I had my sights set on another. That day's event was the men's 1k time trial, and I was determined to set a new record in the C3 classification. A factoring system meant that all C1 to C3 riders would be racing against each other, which made getting a medal harder, so my sole aims were to enjoy partaking and set a new record for my classification.

The previous C3 world record had been set by Russia's Aleksei Obydennov back in 2014, so my goal was to come in just under his time of 1:06.131. A C1 rider, Li Zhangyu from China, rode an amazing factored time of 1:03.877, and I knew there was absolutely no chance of me beating that. Based on my ride the day before, I was in two minds about whether to go up another gear or not – it was the same question again about sticking with what I knew or taking a risk to try to gain better control of my speed. Looking back on it now, I think I could have gone up a bit, but in the end I decided to stick with the same gear I'd ridden the day before. My legs were still tired from the pursuit and it felt like a very hard effort, but when I crossed the line I looked up at the scoreboard to see a time of 1:05.569. It was far beyond my expectations – not only had I broken the men's C3 world record, I'd also won the bronze medal. It was another surreal, amazing day.

As on the previous afternoon, I came back to the hotel feeling slightly dazed, put my bronze medal down on the bed next to the gold and then headed out to do a long cool-down on the turbo trainer. The next day was the mixed team sprint, one of the events British Cycling had targeted and one in which I wanted to excel.

I knew my recovery had to be spot-on – this was a team event, so my performance would impact not just me, but two other riders. Kadeena Cox and Jody Cundy are phenomenal athletes for whom I have a lot of respect, and I was especially aware that Jody – who had been pipped to the post in an unbelievable race the day before – would settle for nothing but gold.

When the event came round, I tried not to let my nerves show. I kept my heated pants on until the last possible moment, making sure my muscles were really warm and ready to go. We were the second-last team to ride in the qualifiers, during which we would have the track to ourselves; only in the final do two teams take to the track at once.

Having watched her previous race, I knew that Kadeena was on her very fastest form at these Paralympics – she was in position one, with me second and Jody third, and I was aware that I would have to make use of every single nanosecond in order to keep the gap between us as small as possible.

The order in which we rode had been the subject of much discussion in Manchester, but I had always felt very strongly that I should be in the middle, rather than third. That said, I was concerned about keeping up with Kadeena, and my eagerness to ride hard from the moment the starting gun went meant that in training I had had one or two false starts. Lining up for the Paralympic qualifying heat, I was suddenly extremely conscious of those false starts, knowing that now was absolutely not the time for something like that.

Ironically, this pushed me almost too far the other way – the gun went and Kadeena was out of the gate like a bullet, closely followed by Jody, leaving me almost at a standstill. It was a horrible start, and though every ounce of me worked as hard as possible to catch her, the gap between us never closed as much as I would have liked. I kept my head down and did what I could, then Jody rode a phenomenal final lap. Amazingly, when we crossed the line we had broken the Paralympic record and set a new personal best.

At the time, all I felt was disappointment in myself. We had ridden a fantastic time, but I knew that my race had not been up to the standard that was required. I was really down about it, and even more so when the Chinese team went up on to the track. They were so well drilled that it was impressive to watch them going round, and no one was terribly surprised when they set a new world record. Although we would be in the gold medal ride-off against them, they'd just executed a perfect team sprint and were clearly the favourites to win. It was a fact that was hammered home to me by an off-hand comment made in the pit: 'You'll get a full set of medals,' someone told me. 'That's really cool!' It wasn't meant nastily, but still I felt upset that the chances of us winning anything other than silver had effectively been written off.

While we were waiting for the final, Jody couldn't have been kinder. He knew I was feeling gutted about the slow start I'd had, and he told me that he'd made a mistake too in misjudging the gap between him and me. All of us could improve, he said, and so the three of us sat down with our coaches to discuss what we needed to do to win. It sounded counter-intuitive, but we decided that Kadeena needed to ride a little bit slower in order for me to close that gap between us and deliver Jody to ride the final lap as fast as possible. Both Kadeena and Jody put their bikes up a gear, while I stuck to where I was and promised myself no false or too-slow starts. As we lined up at the starting gate, I told myself over and over just to do the basics right.

This time, I hit the pedal almost in the same instant the starting gun fired. The three of us were seamless. Kadeena, once again, was incredibly strong, but the gap between us was significantly smaller and I knew I had it right. As we came around the final corner on the lap for which I led, I could see the black line ahead of me and Jody was there the second we crossed it.

'Come on, Jody!' I shouted with the last bit of breath I had left, craning my neck to look at the scoreboard for an indication of where we were. I couldn't work it out – it was neck-and-neck – but then, just as soon as it had started, it was over. A number one popped up beside Great Britain, along with a new world record: 47.579. It was absolutely unbelievable, the best moment of my life.

Against all the odds, defying all expectations, we had beaten the Chinese team by one hundredth of a second. I had never experienced joy like it. Winning the individual pursuit had been amazing, but it's quite different when you're riding by yourself.

This time I was part of a team with two incredible individuals, compared to whom I had always felt myself to be the weakest link. I was so proud of what we had achieved as a collective, so honoured to be a part of that team. It was my final day on the track at the Paralympic Games and I felt it would be impossible to go any higher.

*****

275

UNEQUIVOCAL

As it turned out, I was right about that. In the evening, a handful of us were picked up from the hotel to drive to the foothills of Mount Fuji, where the road racing was going to be held.

The rest of the team, who were track riders only, would be flying back to Heathrow in a couple of days' time. I would be lying if I said that there wasn't a very small part of me that wished I was going with them. I was extremely tired, I missed Kathryn, and I suppose in some ways I did want to end on an unbeatable high.

The atmosphere over at the Fuji Speedway was quite different to Izu. We were put up in a grand, Western-style hotel that lacked all the flags and celebratory vibe of the lodges we'd been in for the last couple of weeks.

One thing that was very impressive was the view – we arrived again at night, and when Fin and I opened the curtains of our shared room in the morning, we were met by the sight of a giant lump of rock. Mount Fuji, which we'd only seen from a distance, was now practically sitting on top of us. It would have been hard to get any closer to one of the world's most iconic mountains.

That day, the road race circuit was briefly open for riders to get familiar with it, but I was in desperate need of time off – after three straight days of racing, my legs were very fatigued. John Hewitt and I took a quick tour of the circuit in the car, and the rest of the time I sat around on the Speedway and snoozed in the sunshine. Several people took photos of me doing that; it was one of those surreal Paralympic moments. The entire world was going mad around me, with riders whizzing past every which way, and there I was with my legs up on a railing, having a little sleep.

In actual fact, I was taking the road race very seriously – it was one of the events I had come to Tokyo hoping to win. From the get-go, though, I faced a series of setbacks. A new regulation about rider positioning and distance from the handlebars meant that my bike had to be adjusted the day before the road events started, and in the course of that, my gears developed problems and the carefully calculated seat height got accidentally adjusted. Seat height is one of the things I really care about – it takes me ages to find that fine balance between too high and too low – so I was very upset. It was a bad preparation day, but I knew that days like that can happen. All that counts is working hard to make sure they don't affect you.

The day of the time trial dawned warm and beautiful, and I woke up feeling surprisingly relaxed. While I love time trialling as an event – I like what it stands for, just you against the clock, and the really sleek kit is an added bonus – it's not something I'm especially good at, so I had absolutely no expectations that day. All I wanted was to enjoy it, and that's exactly what I did. By the time I finished the steep course, my legs were in bits, but for a brief moment I was actually leading the field.

Gradually, other riders started coming through, several of them seconds faster than me. In the end, I came sixth, with Ben Watson taking gold by a margin of almost a minute. I was thrilled for him – and for Fin, who came fourth – and extremely happy that I had come well inside the top ten.

That afternoon we followed the usual procedure: recovery, massage, dinner. The next day we took a team ride to prepare for the road race, which followed a very confined route but still allowed us to see some more of Japan. There were some beautiful lakes and wooded areas near the hotel and I was pleased to be able to see even a tiny bit of the country.

Road race day came as a massive shock. When we opened the curtains to get our daily dose of Fuji, the mountain was gone. In its place was a massive wall of cloud. The temperature had plummeted overnight from twenty-eight degrees Celsius to just fourteen and it was raining torrentially. The mood switched instantly. We had trained for this event for months in heat chambers and greenhouse tents, and now that the day had finally arrived, we were facing Manchester weather. It could have played to our strengths as a British team, but everyone was fairly depressed.

Road racing in the rain is not fun at all. As soon as we set off, I could tell it was going to be a long haul. The tyres I had been advised to use didn't seem to be giving me any grip on the wet surface; it felt unnervingly as though I had a puncture. I could see that other riders in the bunch around me were feeling far from confident, and things only became harder as we went along.

At the first corner I got a huge fright when my bike skidded and jumped beneath me, I felt we were taking the downhill stretches far too fast, and things were only made worse by a series of large metal ditch covers that made our bikes slither all over the place. Several times the pack split up and then came back together again, and I could tell that lots of people were dreading the corners as much as I was.

As the race proceeded, I found myself in a small bunch that had managed to break away from the peloton. Normally, it's a good thing to be part of a smaller group – it's safer, for a start, and you can work together to control the speed and share the load. But as a rider with three medals to my name, I seemed to be a marked man.

Every time I even appeared to be making a move – even if it was just to lead from the front – I was swiftly brought back. I couldn't understand it, especially when road-specific riders like Ben Watson were also there and clearly in amazing form. But even when he managed to break away from our little group, no one made an attempt to chase him down.

As his teammate, I certainly wasn't going to be doing that, and soon he was far ahead. In that moment, I knew the race was his. By the end of the fifth lap, Fin was in a similar position and I watched him ride off, certain he would be taking silver. The rest of the race became really negative and slow at that point as the other riders realised what would happen, and soon our little group had been swallowed up by the bunch.

By then, I knew that my only chance of reaching the podium would be to give it my all in a sprint finish, but I was absolutely exhausted and the tyres just weren't giving me the grip I needed to stand up on the pedals. I crossed the finish line in fifth place and my instant reaction was total disappointment. Of course I was happy for Ben and Fin, both of whom had ridden an amazing race, but I was gutted that I hadn't managed to get even the bronze medal.

I was well into my cool-down before I rationalised. When all was said and done, I'd had an incredible Paralympic Games. Yes, the conditions for the road race had been against me, but I was walking away with three medals – two of them gold – and three world records to my name. I had competed with and against the very best cyclists on the biggest stage in the world.

For me, the Paralympics really do stand out as the most significant event in an athlete's career – it's the one time that we, the disabled community, get the opportunity to show the world who we are, what we can do and what we can achieve. Taking part had been a dream come true, the pinnacle of my sporting career.

Yet, as is always the case in sport – and life – you never know what's going to happen. The road race had been a good reminder of that fact. But if there's one thing I've learned, it's to take life as it comes, to adapt to change as best I can, and to never give up. And slowly, faintly, at the very back of my mind, an idea I had never considered before was starting to form.

Paris was already lining up to take the baton from Tokyo.

And maybe, just maybe, I was only getting started.

ACKNOWLEDGEMENTS

It would take an entire book to thank the many people who have taken part in my journey and helped me get to where I am now. To the individuals named here or elsewhere within these pages, and the many more who remain behind the scenes – thank you, for your unfailing belief, support and generosity. I am grateful to each and every one of you.

To Eleanor Updegraff, without whom this book would not have been written, my sincerest thanks.

To Tim Thackrah, for introducing us, and for encouraging the idea from the outset. To Matthew Quinn, for opening the door to public speaking, and to the many brilliant audiences who have listened to me over the years and shown such interest in my story.

To Alex Rayner at Chase Communications and Paul Dove at Reach Sport, who championed this book all the way to publication – thank you. To editor Chris Brereton, for his sharp eyes, immense patience and sensitive reading. Thanks also to Michael McGuinness and Claire Brown for their hard work and dedication.

To Ed and Cas, who so generously gave their time and memories to help with the writing of this book.

To Phil Dodds, Neal Craig and Andy McKenzie, for getting me on the bike in the first place, and to the many more people who have helped me to stay there – in particular Adam Duggleby, John

ACKNOWLEDGEMENTS

Hewitt, Jon Pett and the incredible team at British Cycling. Thanks also to Matthew Hughes at Dorset Orthopaedic, for understanding my vision and making it real.

To my British Cycling teammates and the legion of inspiring athletes who make up the squad – I am proud to be your teammate.

To Stu Croxford, for true grit and determination, and a friendship that extends far beyond cycling. To his wife, Lizzie, for being willing to share him.

To Dale Hancock, for always having the right words. And to Stefaan Vossen, for keeping me aligned so I can always perform at my best.

To the wonderful individuals at Asset Academy, Core Health and Wellness, Lifejacket Skin, Roseville, SCOTT Sports, thinAir Sports, the Wigley Group and 32Gi, for your generous support in so many ways.

To Ed, Simon, Inge, Guy, Martin, Steve, Alexis, Rob, Petter, Rune and Harry ('H') – the greatest team I could ever have imagined. I could not be prouder of what we achieved together, or that it was you I got to walk with.

To Francis Atkinson, Adrian Ballinger, Henry Chaplin, Chris Gwilt, Andy Hawkins, Karl Hinett, Dan Majid, Manindra Rai, Harry Taylor, Alec Turner, David Wiseman and all the other incredible men and women who have scaled mountains alongside me. Special thanks also to Russell Brice and his brilliant Himalayan Experience team, including the amazing Sherpas without whom we couldn't have taken a single step.

To everyone at Help for Heroes, Walking With The Wounded, The Endeavour Fund and Support Our Paras, and to all those who make the Invictus Games possible.

To Rick, Sally, Scorgie and the entire CSDST team.

To Bobby, Brendan, Cas, Colin, Dan, Gaz, Joel, Koos, Paul, Phil,

Rhys, Stef, Taff, Wayne and all the other boys who were there for me that night, and on so many others before and since. From the bottom of my heart, I thank you all.

To the medical staff at FOB Sharona, and to the wonderful teams at Selly Oak Hospital (especially in the ICU and Ward S5), Queen Elizabeth Hospital Birmingham and Headley Court – without you, I quite simply would not be here today. Words cannot express the gratitude I feel.

To Tom Neathway, for letting me know it was possible, and to the many other individuals I shared wards and rehab admissions with. To the members of the Casevac Club, my fellow unequivocal saves – you are an inspiration.

To the McDonalds – John, Sharon, Darren, Jonathan, Anthony and Christian – for welcoming me into your home without hesitation, and for being a family to me ever since.

To my wonderful friends, old and new, in South Africa, the UK and beyond.

To my beloved Oupa Albert and Ouma Mart, for so many happy days, and for helping to shape the person I've become.

To my family: Elzette, Amelia and Jason.

Finally, to the three women to whom this book is dedicated. Mum – Aloma – Lizanne and Kathryn: you are an endless source of strength, inspiration and love. Thank you, for everything. I couldn't do it without you.